THE MODERN LANGUAGE ASSOCIATION OF AMERICA

GENERAL SERIES

IX

THE STAGING OF ELIZABETHAN PLAYS

Approved for publication in the General Series of the Modern Language Association of America

ERNEST BERNBAUM

JOSEPH E. GILLET

GEORGE L. HAMILTON

HOWARD MUMFORD JONES

WILLIAM KURRELMEYER

KEMP MALONE

*Committee on
Research Activities*

Published under a grant awarded by the American Council of Learned Societies from a fund provided by the Carnegie Corporation of New York

ELIZABETHAN STAGES

I. The interior of the Swan theater, according to a drawing based on the observations of John de Witt, who visited London in 1596.

II. From the title-page of *Roxana*, 1632.

III. From the title-page of *Messallina*, 1640.

THE STAGING
OF
ELIZABETHAN PLAYS

At the Red Bull Theater

1605-1625

BY

GEORGE FULLMER REYNOLDS

NEW YORK: MODERN LANGUAGE ASSOCIATION OF AMERICA

1940

Reprinted with the permission of the original publisher

KRAUS REPRINT CORPORATION

New York

1966

To

MABEL SMITH REYNOLDS

CONTENTS

I. INTRODUCTION 1

II. THE REPERTORY OF THE RED BULL 4

III. THE EVIDENCE AND ITS TREATMENT 30

IV. THE PROPERTIES 52

V. THE STAGE 88

VI. THE STAGE DOORS 109

VII. WAS THERE A REAR STAGE? PRINCIPLES OF STAGE MAN-
AGEMENT 131

VIII. ELIZABETHAN STAGE EFFECTS 164

IX. CONCLUSION 187

ACKNOWLEDGMENTS

ONE of the pleasantest duties in connection with this book is to record the assistance I have received in it. Work has been done on it at the British Museum, the Huntington Library, the Widener Memorial Library at Harvard, and the library of the University of Colorado. To the authorities of these libraries I am obliged for the use of their facilities, and to their attendants for their unfailing courtesy and helpfulness. Professors George Coffin Taylor, Robert Sharpe, Lily B. Campbell, Francis Wolle, and Howard Mumford Jones showed their friendship by reading the manuscript at various stages of its preparation and by their suggestions improved it at numerous points both in clarity and content. To my wife I am grateful for reading the proof, but more for her unfailing encouragement and for her long-suffering endurance of the intrusion of this study into too many of our vacations. To the Modern Language Association for its sponsorship, and to the American Council of Learned Societies I am honored to be indebted. Nor can I close without drawing attention to the labors of those scholars whose results I have freely made use of, as shown by my references, especially Dr. Gerald Bentley, who has been kind enough to tell me some of his findings concerning Jacobean theatrical companies in advance of his publication of them, and Dr. William J. Lawrence, with whom I have been forced in this study to disagree at some points, but of whom my admiration is undiminished, for his enthusiasm, his unfailing fairness and courtesy, and his long and fruitful labors in this field which he has made peculiarly his own.

GEORGE FULLMER REYNOLDS

University of Colorado

CHAPTER I

INTRODUCTION

THIS book is a study of the basic details and principles of Elizabethan staging. Most students are probably of the opinion that we already are pretty well informed about these matters. One book and article after another accepts without question the same general ideas of the stage, and each new model and pictured reconstruction closely resembles its predecessor except perhaps in minor details. This might mean that we had really advanced in knowledge if it were not that this unanimity is in contradiction in some items to probability and in others to the evidence on which we can feel most certain. After all our research, the Swan picture still remains the most complete contemporary representation of an Elizabethan theater; yet the modern reconstructions with their invariably present rear stage and obliquely placed boxes over the doors, not to mention less important features, are far from agreeing with it. And I have seen no real objection to Sir Edmund Chambers' idea that simultaneous settings were used at the private theaters and at court, but never in the seventeenth century at the public theaters. How such a distinction could possibly exist when numerous plays were given interchangeably at these producing centers has not been made clear. Certainly such a divergence of practice seems highly improbable.

Thus present widely held theories are less well founded than they seem to be, and do not warrant the dogmatic assurance of some recent descriptions of the Elizabethan stage, nor even a tentative acceptance of everything as fairly settled and established.

In re-examining the grounds for these opinions, I have, moreover, come upon some evidence, not unknown to students, but apparently not thought of in this connection, which raises further doubts as to our conclusions. This evidence is discussed in detail in chapter III. Here I need only note that it shows the necessity for a different attitude toward the evidence at our disposal, a more careful skepticism, and a stricter discrimination. Specifically, we have accepted the stage directions as literally true and accurate statements of theatrical fact, when they are demonstrably often as imaginative as the dialogue itself; we have, it appears from this evidence, been even more naïve in drawing information from allusions in the dialogue to settings and properties with as much assurance as we might if they were occurring in a modern realistic play. I myself have sometimes erred in this way and am the more anxious to admit it now. There have also been too many generalizations from a few instances; too many uncontrolled suppositions of what might have been, without any ascertained facts of Elizabethan procedure to support them; too many theories advanced by scholars versed only in books and not acquainted with even amateur dramatic production. In short, many of our present conclusions rest on unsound foundations which demand re-examination.

This book offers such a re-examination with stricter methods of procedure and severer checks on conclusions. Instead of studying plays chosen to prove some special point or thesis, it considers all the evidence offered by an objectively selected group of plays. The basis adopted has been the repertory of the Red Bull theater between the time it was opened and its first reconstruction, about twenty years later. In these years we have no reason to believe that it was changed; and the plays given in it, therefore, were planned for the same theatrical conditions. Each of these plays has, in this study, been considered in detail on each point, then as a whole, and then in relation to all the rest. "All the evidence" has necessitated the citation of many passages of little significance and also a good deal of repetition, for no reader can be expected to follow innumerable cross references. But only by all this detail is it possible to make clear why different investigators have cited proof of conflicting conclusions, all partly true, but also partly false. I will confess that when I began this inquiry I hoped to arrive at some definite certainties concerning the Red Bull and its distinctive equipment and methods; the nature of the evidence has not permitted this, but that the results are not what I expected gives them perhaps greater force.

Such a study makes great demands on the patience and the imagination of the reader. To see a play as a consistent whole with only a text in hand requires a careful attention to detail, and when this has to be done from condensed summaries as in a treatment like this, it becomes difficult indeed. The whole of the play must be kept in mind as one studies any individual scene, along with all similar scenes in all the other plays involved in the inquiry. I have tried to make this as easy as possible, but still must implore the reader's patient and actively imaginative coöperation.

Obviously the smaller the number of plays to be considered the less arduous this task will be. That is one reason for choosing the Red Bull plays. Those of the Globe and Blackfriars are more important as literature, and more interesting because of their more

immediate bearing on Shakespeare. But they are much more numerous. Moreover, many of them have been so often edited and studied
that merely to clear away the jungle of suppositions which has grown
up about them would require as much space as the study itself. A
circumstance which has made these suppositions thrive is that many of
the Globe-Blackfriars plays have unusually few directions and thus
permit almost unlimited surmises. Most of the Red Bull plays, on
the other hand, are pretty definitely supplied with directions, and some
of them seem, whatever they did in reality, to have made quite heavy
demands on the theatrical equipment and management. On this subject of staging, therefore, they are of quite unusual interest. Nor have
they been so much worked over as other plays, and therefore offer
fresher material. Most important of all, while it is practically impossible to determine which among the King's men's plays represent a
Globe and which a Blackfriars production, most of these Red Bull
plays were given only in a public theater, and permit more certain
conclusions as to the occurrence there of simultaneous settings.

It is perhaps too much to expect that this book will attract the continued attention of anybody but those students who are interested in
the minutiae of the subject. But should a general reader venture upon
it, it may not be out of place for me to point out the spots in it which
may, perhaps, interest him most: the narrative parts of chapter II,
though containing nothing new, offer some unusual sidelights on
Elizabethan life; sections 6 and 7 of chapter III, the long footnote at
the end of chapter IV, and chapter VIII bring together some curious
details concerning theatrical equipment and management; and chapter
VI on the Stage Doors explores an as yet little traversed part of the
subject. I myself think chapter VII most important in the questions
it considers, but I recognize it has some pretty arid spots and I cannot
expect many to share my interest. Chapter IX summarizes the main
conclusions of the study, but they are purposely stated so conserva-
tively that there is, I am afraid, nothing very arresting about them.

Finally, though this study results in very little that is new or even
precise about the Red Bull theater, its negative results are of considerable importance, and the generalized nature of its conclusions
makes them perhaps even more significant than precise ones about the
Red Bull would have been. The indications surely are that most of
them are as true of the plays of Shakespeare at the Globe as of
Heywood's at the Red Bull.

CHAPTER II

THE REPERTORY OF THE RED BULL
1605-1625

(1)

TO DETERMINE the repertory of a specific Elizabethan theater in a precise term of years is not as easy as one might suppose, and the further attempt to rate the importance of the plays for an inquiry into the stage and staging is even more difficult. Besides general problems concerning any theater, special problems arise from the history of each of them.

Obviously the most authoritative plays for staging are those which were surely acted at the theater in question, and published soon after their first production. If they have prompter's directions or some similar signs of close connection to performance so much the better. The text of the dialogue may be wretchedly printed without much diminishing the authenticity for staging; a pirated edition, *I If You Know Not Me,* for instance, supplied with full stage directions, may be more useful on some points than authorized texts prepared for readers. In the case of plays not published until several years after production, we cannot be sure what date of the performance the stage directions represent. If the play was given at court in the meantime, the text may be for that presentation, or if the play had been revived at its original theater or at some other the text may be that of the revival. As a matter of fact where there exist an early text of a play and another purporting to represent a later form of it ("as now acted" or "as presented at Court") there is seldom any significant difference so far as staging goes. Take, for example, *Edward II:* Chambers, *The Elizabethan Stage* (1923), III, 425, thinks it first given about 1592; it was entered for publication in 1593; the first existing quarto is from 1594; other editions appeared in 1598, 1612, and 1622, the last as acted by the Queen's men at the Red Bull. But the stage directions of the first edition and the last are for all practical purposes identical. To conclude, however, that the stage productions were the same would be hardly warranted; the later editions may have been set up from their predecessors. Still it is clear that *Edward II* was given at the Red Bull, and therefore its problems of staging must be considered in the light of what we know of that theater. Each play offers a special problem.

When a play was not published until long after its first production, the text may be that of any revival in intervening years. Where there may have been several revivals or we have pretty certain evidence of revision, the staging is likely to be that of the latest performance: thus though *Macbeth* was first performed about 1606, the text as we have it is that of a revision, dating probably after 1613. In the case of the two parts of *The Iron Age* the circumstances are different. These plays were, to be sure, not published till 1632, but there is no hint or even any probability of their performance after about 1613, when all the *Ages* were given, and the other *Ages* published. The evidence to be drawn from *The Iron Age* is, therefore, almost, if not quite, as good as theirs.

All these considerations may be only academic. Perhaps there really was little difference in staging between performances in the 1590's and in the 1620's; I myself am of the impression that when plays were given at court their performance was essentially like that they received at the public theaters. But these are points not to be assumed. The evidence of each play must be considered by itself; its value may also vary with the point in question.

We shall, I think, be sufficiently discriminating if we group the plays possibly associated with the Red Bull into three lists. The first, which for ease of reference we may call the *A* list, includes those plays of which the evidence is of unquestionable reliability. Those are the plays which we have good reason to believe were given at the Red Bull in the years we are concerned with, and whose texts may reasonably be taken as representing their performances there. There are from our total list of forty-six extant plays, thirteen which can be thus classified. The *B* list consists of those plays which were probably, but not surely, given at the Red Bull, and also of those plays surely given there but whose texts as we have them may not represent Red Bull performances. Their evidence concerning the construction and equipment of the stage is less important than that of the *A* plays, but their problems of staging must be considered as carefully. Of these plays there are nineteen. The *C* list is made up of plays only possibly connected with the Red Bull in the years in question. They are of little or no authority for the Red Bull. "Possibly connected" is a vague term; it might be extended to take in almost any Elizabethan play which we cannot definitely place in other years or at other theaters. There are, however, fourteen which have seemed to me worth considering. Not all readers will agree with the classification of certain of these plays, but this hardly deserves much discussion since the different ratings of these borderline cases would make little difference in the conclusions.

(2)

Each theater, I have said, sets special problems in the determination of its repertory. This will be clear when we consider the history of the Red Bull.[1] The theater was built by 1605, Dr. Adams conjectures, because Worcester's men, just taken under the patronage of the Queen, needed a better theater than the Curtain in order to compete with the King's company at the Globe and the Prince's at the Fortune. Its builder was Aaron Holland, yeoman, "utterly unlearned and illiterate, not being able to read." A license of 1603 or 1604 to Worcester's men allowing their leader, Thomas Greene, to use any playhouse he might select or build, shows they were thinking of a new theater at that time. His selection was a piece of land and a building called the Red Bull in Clerkenwell, about a mile from the Curtain, their old theater; half a mile from the Fortune, the theater of their nearest rivals; and a mile from the center of the city. The description of the property with its "Gardens Courts Cellars Ways & liberties" suggests to Hotson, p. 83, that the building had been an inn. The new theater seems to have been finished by 1605 or 1606, when Holland sold one share of it to Thomas Swynnerton, one of Queen Anne's company. It seems likely that the company would occupy the theater as soon as it was ready. Chambers, II, 446, cites an allusion in *The Knight of the Burning Pestle*, IV. i. 43, "almost certainly produced in the winter of 1607," to *The Travails of Three English Brothers* as "stale" from performance at the Red Bull. This would mean that the theater was occupied at least by 1607. And the title-page of *The Rape of Lucrece* (1608) describes that play as "acted by Her Maiesties Seruants at the Red Bull." But a license patent of April 15, 1609, authorized them

---

[1] This summary is based mainly on J. Q. Adams, *Shakespearean Playhouses* (1917), pp. 294 ff.; also on H. Maas, *Der Englischen Theater-Truppen* (1907), pp. 99-104, 108-112, 119-121; C. W. Wallace, *Three London Theatres*, University of Nebraska Studies, IX (1909), 287-342; J. T. Murray, *English Dramatic Companies* (1910), I, 185-200, 236-238, 271-276; E. K. Chambers, *The Elizabethan Stage* (1923), II, 445-448; and Leslie Hotson, *The Commonwealth-Restoration Stage* (1928), pp. 82-87.

Since to include all known references to the Red Bull in the period which we are considering requires only a little more space than the details of its history which apply strictly to the repertory, I have attempted to make this as complete an account as possible. The extraneous details at least add to our knowledge of the circumstances in which the plays were presented. For the same reasons the names of lost plays have been included in the repertory list even though the little we know of them offers no information on the staging.

to play "within their now usual houses, called the Red Bull in Clerken-well, and the Curtain in Holywell." As Adams says, they could hardly use two big public playhouses at the same time. He concludes they were perhaps playing intermittently at both. Is it not more probable that with two at their disposal they would use the newer? Perhaps they held control of the Curtain to prevent competition. Their rivalry with the Fortune and the Globe is alluded to in Dekker's *Raven's Almanack*, 1608, and he mentions in his *Work for Armourers*, written 1609, their enforced inactivity because of the plague, while the bear-garden was still open (see Chambers II, 367, 447). The leader of the company was Thomas Greene, alluded to in the comedy named after him, *Greene's Tu Quoque* (1611, p. 1614), as "a good clown" acting at the Red Bull. Their chief playwright was Thomas Heywood.

The bearing of all this on a study of the staging is important but not always clear. The plays given during these years 1605-1609 may have been acted at either or both theaters, though, as I have said, the chances seem rather better for the Red Bull.

(3)

From 1609 to 1617 the Queen's men were certainly at the Red Bull, and intermittently afterwards till 1619. Chambers II, 230-240, gives with considerable detail their history during this period. They were specifically licensed to give "Comedies, Tragedies, histories, En-terludes, Moralles, Pastorelles, Stageplaies" not only in London but throughout the realm. They appeared in most years at court, and toured every year in the country; indeed some of them continued to travel while the others were appearing in London. In 1612 the repre-sentatives of a holder of a half share in the company got £40 at his death, but the widow of Greene was not so fortunate about his share, and after various arrangements which were not carried out—one was for 1s. 8d. a day "for euerye of six dayes in a weeke wherein they should pay" for the joint lives of herself and her new husband—she brought suit in 1623. Sometime between 1609 and 1612, according to Chambers, III, 509, *The White Devil* was presented. Webster in "To the Reader" describes it as "acted in so dull a time of Winter, presented in so open and blacke a Theater, that it wanted . . . a full and understanding Auditory." He adds that "most of the people that come to that Play-house resemble those ignorant asses" who ask not "for good bookes, but new bookes." Other items suggest that the reputation of the Red Bull was scarcely first class. In Dr. Louis Wright's summary, *Middle-Class Culture in Elizabethan England*

(1935), p. 609, it was "from the beginning, frankly a plain man's playhouse, where clownery, clamor, and spectacle vied with subject matter flattering to the vanity of tradesmen." According to C. R. Baskervill, *The Elizabethan Jig* (1929), p. 115, the Curtain, the Fortune, and the Red Bull were the only public theaters mentioned by name in connection with the jigs, those popular and often vulgar song-dramas that closed most performances. Again to quote Dr. Wright, p. 612, "No idle tricks of love but manly plays, full of vigor, were to be seen at the Red Bull," and he cites in support a passage from *Turners dish of Lenten stuffe* (1612), printed in Prof. Hyder E. Rollins' *A Pepysian Garland* (1922), p. 35:

> That's the fat foole of the Curtin,
>   and the leane foole of the Bull:
> Since *Shanke* did leaue to sing his rimes,
>   he is counted but a gull.
> The players of the Banke side
>   The round Globe and the Swan,
> Will teach you idle trickes of loue,
>   But the Bull will play the man.

Another hint as to the standing of the Red Bull in this period is suggested by Dr. Wright, p. 611, on the basis of the remark of a clownish farmer in *Albumazar*, III. i, a play acted in 1614 at Trinity College, Cambridge, before King James:

O 'tis *Armellina:* now if she haue the wit to begin, as I meane she should, then will I confound her with complements drawn from the Plaies I see at the Fortune, and Red Bull, where I learne all the words I speake and vnderstand not.

Wright interprets this as a jibe at the quality of persons who made up the Red Bull audience; does it not also suggest that the later reputation of the Red Bull for big words was already begun?

In 1612 Thomas Greene died, and Christopher Beeston became the leader. Near the end of May, 1610, certain citizens had to answer for "a notable outrage at the playhouse called the Red Bull," and on March 3, 1614, another person was bailed out for picking a pocket there (Chambers, II, 447). Between October, 1616, and October, 1622, the company was several times in trouble with the authorities for not keeping the highways in the vicinity of the theater in proper repair. The Woodford-Holland lawsuits of 1619, 1623, show that the yearly net profits of the theater to its owners were estimated to be £540 (Hotson, p. 84), that seats on the stage were counted among the regular sources of income, and that Woodford claimed and Holland denied that by usual custom the former's eighteenth share carried with it the perquisite of a "gatherer's" place, worth, Woodford said, three pence a day. These gatherers were the persons who collected admission money from the audience; Lawrence, *RES*, VIII (1932), 222, says some of them may also have been used as supers in the later acts of plays. Professor T. W. Baldwin in "Posting Henslowe's Accounts," *JEGP*, XXVI (1927), 62, estimates that there were probably about twenty-one such gatherers at the Red Bull in 1613. That certainly seems a plenty. We also learn that bread, beer, ale, and fruit were sold at the theater. Another allusion to it occurs in Wither's *Abuses Stript and Whipt*, 1613, i. I.:

> His poetry is such as he can cull
> From plays he heard at Curtain or at Bull.

As late as February 23, 1617, the company was receiving silk and other clothes at the Red Bull (Wallace, pp. 318, 332), but by March 4 it was playing at the new Phoenix, often called the Cockpit in Drury Lane, for on that day "a rowt of lewd and loose persons, apprentices and others" "spoiled" the new playhouse, and caused the players to go back to the Red Bull. On June 3, 1617, they again occupied the Phoenix, though not, Adams says, p. 239, entirely abandoning the Red Bull. The death of Queen Anne (1619) caused the company to lose its title.

The plays given by the Queen's company in this period are of the first importance for our inquiry. Among them are Heywood's *Ages*. They demand some of the most spectacular staging ever suggested for the Elizabethan public stage, so spectacular that some scholars have doubted whether they were ever performed, or, provided they were performed, whether the stage directions are really to be taken as actual stage directions or instead as merely literary hopes or descriptions by the too sanguine author.[2] In the latter case, of course, their evidence would not count for much. But I do not think they can be so easily put aside. The *Ages* were performed, if positive statements can be believed at all. The title page of *The Golden Age* describes the text, "As it hath beene sundry times acted at the Red Bull by the Queencs Maiesties Seruants"; and the note "To the Reader" adds, "This is the *Golden Age*, the eldest brother of three Ages, that haue

---

[2] Thus Dr. Joseph Q. Adams, *JEGP*, X (1911), 330: "Not a few of the plays were edited for closet reading, and furnished with stage directions that do not always reflect actual conditions of performance; for example, the *Ages* of Heywood."

aduentured the Stage, but the onely yet, that hath been iudged to the Presse." The Revels records say *The Silver Age* was given at Court, January 12, 1612, but this item has been questioned as forged. In the address "To the Reader" prefixed to *The Iron Age*, Heywood says, "These [the *Ages*] were the Playes often (and not with the least applause) Publickely Acted by two Companies, vppon one Stage at once, and haue at sundry times thronged three seuerall Theaters, with numerous and mighty Auditories." Fleay, *Biographical Chronicle* (1891), I, 285, thought the theaters were the Rose, the Curtain, and the Red Bull; Chambers, III, 345, picks the Curtain, the Red Bull, and the Cockpit. The Red Bull is certainly one of them. In the dedication to the second part of *The Iron Age*, Heywood writes to Mr. Thomas Mannering, "I much deceiue my selfe, if I heard you not once commend it, when you saw it Acted," a remark which must remove any doubt that the *II Iron Age* was performed as surely as the other *Ages*. The Prologue to *The Royal King and Loyal Subject* perhaps alludes to the *Ages* thus: "The gods themselves we have brought downe to the Stage." And finally there is a possible allusion to *The Iron Age* in Edmund Gayton's *Festivous Notes upon Don Quixote* (1654), p. 3:

Our *Don* is not so much transported with *Belianis* his Blowes as a passionate Butcher of our Nation was, who being at the Play, called *the Greeks and Trojans*, and seeing *Hector* over-power'd by *Mirmydons*, got upon the Stage, and with his good Battoone tooke the true *Trojans* part so stoutly, that he routed the *Greeks*, and rayled upon them loudly for a company of cowardly slaves to assault one man with so much odds. He strooke moreover such an especiall acquaintance with *Hector*, that for a long time *Hector* could not obtaine leave of him to be kill'd, that the Play might go on; and the cudgelled *Mirmydons* durst not enter againe, till *Hector*, having pre-vailed upon his unexpected second, return'd him over the Stage againe into the yard from whence he came. (There is also another allusion, p. 271, to the audience joining in the action at these plays, or at least plays on *"Greeks and Trojans."*)

All this contemporary assertion cannot be minimized nor dismissed; these plays were surely presented on the public stages. And the late date of publication of *I, II Iron Age*, does not much invalidate their evidence, since there is no suggestion of their later revision or revival.

The directions must also be taken as real stage directions and not merely as literary descriptions. The directions definitely report the usages of the practical theater and reflect the actual stage background. Thus, in *The Golden Age*, 67, we have, "Enter the foure old

Beldams, drawing out Danae's bed; she in it," and later, 70, "the bed is drawne in." In *The Silver Age*, when the scene is supposed to be in the Eremanthian forest, the stage directions, 131, refer to the doors and, 139, say "Earth riseth from vnder the stage." In *I Iron Age*, 332, Achilles and Paris are carefully directed to go out so that Achilles may re-enter "with an arrow through his heele." No dramatist writing a mere closet drama would so arrange his scene. In *II Iron Age*, 379, to show a change of scene from outside to inside the city, the stage direction follows stage practice, not at all the imagined action: "They march softly in at one doore, and presently in at another. Enter Synon with a stealing pace, holding the key in his hand." Many of the directions thus describe pantomime and action, but the practical stage is the background. Heywood had to present unusual scenes, and he made use of all the means at his disposal. At that he asks for scarcely more than does Kirke in *The Seven Champions of Christendom* or Dekker in *If It be not Good*. We must, therefore, accept the directions in the *Ages* as statements of what the author, a practical man of the theater if there ever was one, expected the stage manager to provide for.

How effective those provisions were is another matter; the actual accomplishment may have been sadly lacking in realism in a way which would carry very little illusion to us. But that is scarcely the point. Heywood's audience was also that which watched *The Two Noble Ladies*, the methods of which, described in chapter III, show how much was left to the imagination. The bonfires and thunder-bolts and gods ascending and descending, may have been inadequately presented in the *Ages*, but something was done at the Red Bull to correspond to or suggest these directions. And it was something in the staging, not merely in the speeches; often the speeches give no suggestion of the pantomime described. It had to be carried out.

My own opinion is that the evidence of all the *Ages* is of equal authority, but to adhere to our classification, *The Silver Age*, because of its possible production at court before publication, and the two parts of *The Iron Age*, because of late publication are placed on the *B* instead of the *A* list.

(4)

Edward Alleyn (*Account Book*, quoted in Young, *The History of Dulwich College*, II, 51) records that on October 1 and 3, 1617, he visited the Red Bull; on the second visit he says he received for *The Younger Brother* (a play not now known, though one with this title was entered in *The Stationers' Register* in 1653) but £3 6s. 4d. Adams,

p. 299, says these references, the only ones to the Red Bull in the
Alleyn papers, "do not necessarily imply, as some have thought, that
Alleyn was part owner of the playhouse; possibly he was merely
selling to the Red Bull Company the manuscript of an old play." Dr.
Gerald Bentley, on the basis of this entry and other evidence which
he has been kind enough to call to my attention but whose publication
I do not wish to anticipate, suggests the possibility that the Prince's
men were for a short time at the Red Bull. I have, therefore, included
in my list four plays of theirs given about 1620, but as their connection
with the Red Bull is only a possibility, the plays are on the C list.

(5)

At the death of Queen Anne, Beeston in 1619 joined Prince Charles'
men at the Cockpit in Drury Lane (the Phoenix), but, Adams thinks,
the other members of the company continued at the Red Bull as the
Red Bull company, and Lawrence, *op. cit.*, p. 225, says they received
a warrant as such on February 24, 1620. *The Two Merry Milkmaids*
(1620) has a Prologue obviously, from a reference to the "yard,"
intended for the audience at the Red Bull. This prologue, with its
aspersions on the audience's expectations, gives considerable information on what they had been getting and on their own behavior:

> This Day we entreat All that are hither come
> To expect no noyse of Guns, Trumpets, nor Drum,
> Nor Sword and Targuet; but to heare Sence and Words
> Fitting the Matter that the Scene affords.
> So that the Stage being reform'd, and free
> From the lowd Clamors it was wont to bee
> Turmoyl'd with Battailes; you I hope will cease
> Your dayly Tumults . . .
> We hope, for your owne good, you in the Yard,
> Will lend your Eares, attentively to heare . . .
> . . . we haue in't a Coniurer, a Deuill
> And a Clowne too, but I feare the euill . . .
> Of wanting Squibs and Crackers at their taile.

Perhaps this change in style was due to the fact that Beeston when
he left, according to the papers in the Smith-Beeston lawsuit (1619-
20), took away "all the furniture and apparell." That would certainly
curb spectacle at least for a while. Also reflecting conditions at the
Red Bull is the forecast for April in *Vox Gracvli or Jack Dawes'
Prognostication* (1622):

About this time, new Playes will be in more request then old: and if company come currant to the *Bull* and *Curtaine,* there will be more money

gathered in one after-noone, then will be given in *Kingsland* Spittle in a whole moneth. Also, if at this time, about the houres of foure and fiue, it waxe cloudy, and then raine downeright, they will sit dryer in the Galleries, then those who are the vnderstanding men in the yard.

A riot in April, 1622, arising from the injury, by the sword of one of the actors, to an apprentice sitting on the stage, need only be mentioned as another reminder of the theatrical surroundings for which these playwrights wrote.

On July 8, 1622, a license was issued to the company "to bring up children in the quality and exercise of playing," under the name of the "Children of the Revels." This makes possible some doubt as to the assignment to the proper company and theater of plays perhaps given in these general years and acted according to their title-pages by "the company of the Revels." Conceivably this might mean in certain circumstances not this Red Bull company, but perhaps the various companies of Children of the Revels (Murray, I, 353-363), 1604-17; or the King's Revels company (Murray, I, 279-281), which played at the Salisbury Court Theater in the Whitefriars from perhaps 1629 to 1632, or even the various provincial Revels companies (Murray, II, 8-13). Usually the assignment of such a play depends on the date decided upon as that of its production. According to Adams, the company at the Red Bull was dissolved in the summer of 1623. By July the theater was occupied by Prince Charles' men, who had been at the Curtain. Herbert licensed *The Duche Painter and the French Branke* to them at the Curtain in June, 1622; and July 30, 1623, *The Bellman of Paris* for them at the Red Bull. (But see Murray, I, 237 n.) Also it is interesting to note that a strange company gave a play at the Red Bull in September or November, 1623. At King James' death (1625) some of the actors joined the King's company; the others continued as the Red Bull company, but no plays remain which were likely to have been given in the next few years at the Red Bull.

About this time the Red Bull, was, says Dr. Adams, seemingly rebuilt and enlarged. The evidence as to date is not very clear. Adams, p. 302, cites from *London's Lamentation for her Sins*, by W. C. (1625), the following: "Yet even then, Oh Lord, were the theaters magnified and enlarged," which, he thinks, refers to the rebuilding of the Fortune in 1622 and of the Red Bull. And Prynne in *Histrio-mastix* (1633) speaks of the Fortune and the Red Bull as "lately reedified [and] enlarged." Dr. W. J. Lawrence, *Fortnightly Review*, CV (May, 1916), 824, suggests that the Red Bull would have been rebuilt shortly after the Fortune, which was burned in 1621 and restored as soon as possible thereafter at nearly four times the original cost. Dr. Hotson, p. 86, quoting some notes from *Mercurius Fumigosus*, shows that Lawrence is mistaken in thinking the theater was roofed at this rebuilding, for a Turkish acrobat had because of wind and rain to abandon performances which seem to have been announced 1654, 1655 for the Red Bull. I see no force in this connection in Lawrence's question, *The Physical Conditions of the Elizabethan Public Playhouse* (1927), p. 128, concerning the pillar brought in for *The Virgin Martyr*. Why should a pillar be brought in in this play of 1620, he asks, unless in some reconstruction of the theater the pillar assumed as present in *The White Devil* (1610) had been removed. But this is to assume that these pillars were necessarily the same, or that that in *The White Devil* was not also placed on the stage without direction as many properties were. He himself agrees 1620 is too early a date for the reconstruction spoken of above.

Because of the definite break in the list of plays at the Red Bull and because of this reconstruction, we close our study with, roughly, 1625. That means we have to consider plays given by the Red Bull company, also called on the title-pages the company of the Revels, 1619-23, and by Prince Charles' men, 1623-25.

This account of the Red Bull should not close without quoting Edmund Gayton's comment, p. 24, in *Festivous Notes upon Don Quixote* (1654), though whether this applies or not to the period of the Red Bull we are considering is uncertain:

I have heard, that the Poets of the Fortune and red Bull had alwayes a mouth-measure for their Actors (who were terrible teare-throats) and made their lines proportionable to their compasse, which were *sesquipedales*—a foot and a halfe.

And a similar disparaging attitude toward the Red Bull authors appears in Leonard Digges' commendatory verses to Shakespeare's Poems (1640); see Chambers, *William Shakespeare* (1930), II, 233. The poet urges upstart writers not to pollute Shakespeare's stage with their verses:

> But if you needs must write, if poverty
> So pinch, that otherwise you starve and die,
> On Gods name may the Bull or Cockpit have
> Your lame blancke Verse, to keepe you from the grave:
> Or let new Fortunes younger brethren see,
> What they can picke from your leane industry.
> I doe not wonder when you offer at
> Blacke-Friers, that you suffer.

In this connection also it should perhaps be noted that Lawrence finds the origin of the term "bulls" for theatrical blunders in their supposedly frequent occurrence at the Red Bull; see "The Origin of Bulls," *Speeding up Shakespeare* (1937), pp. 144-158. Extant plays are in no way remarkable for them, however, and Lawrence suggests that the ascription is due rather to the social snobbishness which caused the persistent ridicule of the Red Bull.

Finally the judgment of *Historia Histrionica* (Hazlitt's Dodsley, XV, 407) must be noted, though, published in 1699, it also may not concern the Red Bull of our period. After mentioning the Globe, the Blackfriars, the Phoenix, Salisbury Court, and finally the Fortune and the Red Bull, the author says: "The two last were mostly frequented by citizens and the meaner sort of people. All these companies got money and lived in reputation, especially those of the Blackfriars, who were men of grave and sober demeanor." Are we to conclude that the gravity and soberness of the Red Bull actors were more questionable?

CHRONOLOGICAL LIST
OF PLAYS GIVEN AT THE RED BULL, *ca.* 1605 TO *ca.* 1625[3]

I. PLAYS GIVEN BY THE QUEEN'S MEN BEFORE 1609
(Some of them certainly at the Red Bull)

Number	Title	Reference to	Date of Production
B 1	SIR THOMAS WYATT	Dekker, III	1602

P. 1607, as it was played by the Queen's men; another edition, 1612. If Chambers' identification of it, III, 294, with one of the parts of *Lady Jane* (Henslowe, Oct., 1602) or a combination of them is sound, we cannot be sure what performance the existing text represents; therefore, a *B* play. Kirschbaum lists it among the "bad" Elizabethan quartos.

---

[3] The following abbreviations and short references are used in this list:

A, B, C, are explained in the text above; *L* indicates a lost play. Lost plays have duplicate numbers. The date of production is from Chambers' discussion of the plays in *The Elizabethan Stage,* unless otherwise stated.

B. M.	British Museum
Brooke, C. F. Tucker	*The Shakespeare Apocrypha,* 1908
Chambers, E. K.	*The Elizabethan Stage,* 1923
Clark, Arthur M.	*Thomas Heywood,* 1931
Dekker, Thomas	*Dramatic Works,* Pearson edition, 1873
Fleay, F. G.	*A Biographical Chronicle of the English Drama,* 1891
	A Chronicle History of the London Stage, 1890
H.D.	Hazlitt's Dodsley, *Old English Plays,* 1874-76
Herbert	*The Dramatic Records of Sir Henry Herbert,* edited by Joseph Quincy Adams, Cornell Studies in English, 1917

C 2   THE FAIR MAID OF THE EX-   Heywood, II   *ca.* 1602
      CHANGE

S.R. April 24, 1607; p. 1607; other editions, 1625, 1637. Chambers, III, 106, n., lists it as probably a Red Bull or Curtain play. The title-page does not connect it with the Queen's men or with the Red Bull, but I include it because of Chambers' suggestion, based presumably on Heywood's authorship. See also Chambers, IV, 13.

Heywood, Thomas   *Dramatic Works,* Pearson edition, 1874
H.   Huntington Library
Hunt, M. L.   *Thomas Dekker, a Study,* 1911
Kirschbaum, Leo   "A Census of Bad Quartos," *The Review of English Studies,* January, XIV [1938], 20-43
P.   Date of publication
Schelling, Felix E.   *Elizabethan Drama,* 1908
Sibley, Gertrude M.   *Lost Plays and Masques, 1500-1642,* 1933
S. F. E.   Students' Facsimile Edition of Old English Plays, 1907-14
S.R.   *Stationers' Register*
Stork, Charles Wharton   *William Rowley,* 1910
Webster, John   *The Complete Works of,* edited by F. L. Lucas, 1928
Wiggin, P. G.   *An Inquiry into the Authorship of the Middleton-Rowley Plays,* 1897

Alphabetical Finding List

(The numbers show the position in the chronological list)

C 34   All's Lost by Lust
L 41b Antonio and Vallia
C 12   Appius and Virginia
L 43a The Bellman of Paris
C 13   The Birth of Merlin
A 22   The Brazen Age
       The City Gallant, see
         Greene's Tu Quoque
       Come see a Wonder, see
         The Wonder of a Kingdom
C 42   The Costly Whore
A 31   The Devil's Law Case
B 30   Edward II
L 44b The Fair Foul One
C 2   The Fair Maid of the Exchange
C 33   A Fair Quarrel
L 46a The Fairy Knight
L 44a A Fault in Friendship
B 11   Fortune by Land and Sea
A 26   The Four Prentices of London
L 44c The Four Sons of Aymon
A 20   The Golden Age
L 38a Gramercie Wit
B 18   Greene's Tu Quoque
B 25   The Hector of Germany
A 38   The Heir
A 39   Herod and Antipater

A 27   The Honest Lawyer
B 3   How a Man May Choose a Good Wife from a Bad
       How to Learn of a Woman to Woo (see The Wise Woman of Hogsdon)
A 19   If It Be Not Good the Devil Is in It
B 6, 7 I, II If You Know Not Me You Know Nobody
B 23, 24 I, II Iron Age
L 44e Jugurth
L 46b Keep the Widow Waking
L 44d The Madcap
C 43   A Match at Midnight
B 17   Match Me in London
C 45   Nero
C 15   A New Wonder, a Woman Never Vexed
C 8   Nobody and Somebody
       The Parricide, see
         Revenge for Honour
L 43c The Peaceable King
L 41a Philenzo and Hippolyta
L 43b The Plantation of Virginia
A 10   The Rape of Lucrece
C 46   Revenge for Honour

B 3   How a Man May Choose   SFE and Before Aug. 17, 1602
    a Good Wife from a   HD IX (Chambers, IV, 20)
    Bad

P. 1602 as acted by Worcester's men; six other editions by 1634. Chambers, III, 106 n., says, "probably a Rose or Boar's Head play"; but its numerous editions suggest its continued popularity and its consequent performance at the Red Bull. Chambers, III, 342, says, "generally assigned to Heywood."

B 4   A Woman Killed with   Schelling, *Typical Eliza-*   1603
    Kindness   *bethan Plays*; and Heywood, II

Chambers III, 341; p. 1607; 1617, third edition, as "oftentimes Acted" by the Queen's men. Henslowe paid Heywood £6 for the play and £7, 3 sh. for two costumes for it, 1603. As the stage directions of the editions are the same the text probably represents the performance at the Curtain. But the play's popularity suggests its presentation also at the Red Bull.

C 5   The Wise Woman of Hogsdon   Heywood, V   *ca.* 1604?
Chambers III, 342; *S.R.* March 12, 1638; p. 1638, as "sundry times Acted with great Applause. Written by Tho: Heywood." Fleay, I, 292, suggests this may be *How to Learn of a Woman to Woo*, given before the king by the Queen's men, Dec. 30, 1604. But this is one of the much disputed so-called Cunningham forgeries; see Samuel Tannenbaum, *Shakspere Forgeries* (1918), pp. 22, 75 n. 10. Tannenbaum condemns the record as forged and also asserts Fleay's identification has nothing to support it. If Fleay's identification is correct and the record is authentic, then the extant text may represent a Curtain performance or that at Court. In any case, this play, "sundry times acted," may have been at the Red Bull, and so may be admitted to the *C* list.

B 6, 7   If You Know Not Me You   Heywood, I   1605
    Know Nobody

Chambers, III, 342; *S.R.:* Part I, July 5; Part II, Sept. 14, 1605. Part I, p. 1605; seven more editions by 1639; Part II, 1606; three more editions by 1632: 1632 ed. has a different version for Act V. Included as Red Bull plays because written by Heywood when he was connected with

---

C 32	Richard III	B 40	The Welsh Ambassador	
B 28	The Royal King and the Loyal		(The Welsh Traveller?)	
	Subject	A 16	The White Devil	
B 14	A Shoemaker a Gentleman	L 46c	The Widow's Prize	
B 21	The Silver Age	C 5	The Wise Woman of Hogsdon	
A 29	Swetnam the Woman Hater	B 4	A Woman Killed with Kindness	
B 9	The Travails of Three English	B 44	The Wonder of a Kingdom	
	Brothers	C 35	The World Tost at Tennis	
B 36	The Two Merry Milkmaids	B 1	Sir Thomas Wyatt	
A 41	The Two Noble Ladies	L 32a	The Younger Brother	
A 37	The Virgin Martyr			

the Queen's men and because they passed to the Cockpit repertory. Their numerous editions point to continued popularity. However, the texts may represent performances at the Curtain, or no performances in this form at all; therefore, *B* rather than *A*. See discussion, chapter III, section 2.

C   8   Nobody and Somebody   SFE and Simp- 1616 (Chambers)
                               son, *The School* 1592 (Schelling)
                               of Shakespeare

Chambers, IV, 37; *S.R.*, March 12, 1606; p., undated, as acted by the Queen's men. Greg, *Henslowe's Diary*, II, 230, suggests it is the "Albere Galles" for which Henslowe paid Heywood and Smith in 1602. This might make it a *B* play, but it had no other editions, and it seems safer, therefore, to put it in the *C* list.

B   9   The Travails of Three   Day, Part V,   1607
        English Brothers   Bullen, ed.

Chambers, III, 286: II, 446; *S.R.* June 29, 1607, "as yt was played at the Curten"; p. 1607 as "now play'd" by the Queen's men. A *B* instead of a *C* play because alluded to in *The Knight of the Burning Pestle* as "stale" from performance at the Red Bull. *The Knight* (Chambers, II, 446) was "almost certainly produced in the winter of 1607."

A   10   The Rape of Lucrece   Heywood, V   Between 1603
                                                  and 1608

Chambers, III, 343; *S.R.* June 3, 1608; p. 1608, as acted by the Queen's men "at the Red Bull, neare Clarkenwell. Written by Thomas Heywood." Other editions, 1609, 1630 "the fourth impression," 1638 with songs inserted. At court, 1612 (but a doubtful record; see Tannenbaum; *op. cit.*, p. 18)); at the Cockpit, 1628.

B   11   Fortune by Land and Sea   Heywood, VI   *ca.* 1607 ?
                                                   1609 (Stork, pp. 14, 26)

Chambers, III, 343; *S.R.*, June 20, 1655; p. 1655, as "Acted with great Applause" by the Queen's men. "Written by Tho. Heywood and Wm. Rowly"; *B* because of late publication.

C   12   Appius and Virginia   Webster, III   *ca.* 1608 (Chambers)
                                               1625-27 (Lucas)

Chambers, III, 508; *S.R.*, May 13, 1654; p. 1654. Chambers says: "There is much to be said for the view . . . that the play is Heywood's own . . . and may have been written, at any date not long after the production of *Coriolanus* on the stage (*ca.* 1608) for Queen Anne's men." It has no certain connection with the Red Bull, but it belongs later to the Cockpit repertory, and its possible Heywood authorship forms another connection with the Queen's men in their Red Bull period.

C 13   THE BIRTH OF MERLIN   Brooke   ?, (Chambers)
                                            ca. 1608 (Stork, p. 58)
                                            After 1621 (Howe)

Chambers, III, 474; p. 1662, as "by William Shakespear and William Rowley." Very dubious connection with the Red Bull and late publication barely admit this to the C list.

B 14   A SHOEMAKER A GENTLE-   Q. 1638   ca. 1608 (Chambers)
       MAN   B.M. and H.   1609 (Stork, p. 13)

Chambers, III, 473; S.R., Nov. 28, 1637; p. 1638, "As it hath beene sundry Times Acted at the Red Bull and other Theaters, with a generall and good Applause. Written by W. R. Gentleman." The epistle says "it is a Play that is often acted" and "as Plaies were then, some twenty yeares agone, it was in the fashion." Listed as B because of late publication and performance at other theaters.

C 15   A NEW WONDER, A   H.D., XII   ?(Chambers)
       WOMAN NEVER VEXED Q, 1632, H.   ca. 1609 (Stork, p. 26)

Chambers III, 474; S.R., Nov. 24, 1631; p. 1632, as "sundry times Acted; never before printed. Written by William Rowley, one of his Maiesties Servants." Stork, p. 26, says, "I should place its date at ca. 1609, or the same as that of *Fortune by Land and Sea,* for at that time Heywood and Rowley were together in the Queen's company." The possible connection with the Red Bull is very uncertain; late publication also places it on the C list.

II. PLAYS GIVEN BY THE QUEEN'S MEN AT THE RED BULL, 1609-19

A 16   THE WHITE DEVIL   Webster, I   1609-12

Chambers, III, 509; p. 1612, as acted by the Queen's men.

B 17   MATCH ME IN   Dekker, IV   ?(Chambers)
       LONDON   1612-13 (Hunt, p. 160)
                                    ca. 1611 (Adams, Herbert, p. 25 n.)

Chambers III, 297; S.R., Nov. 8, 1630; Herbert, p. 25, Aug. 21, 1623, "For the Lady Elizabeth's servants of the Cockpit; An Old Play, called, *Match Me in London* which had been formerly allowed by Sir G. Bucke." P. 1631, "As it hath beene often presented; First, at the Bull in St. Iohn's-Street; and lately, at the Priuate-House in Drury-Lane called the Phoenix. Written by Tho. Dekker." Late publication places it as a B play.

B 18   GREENE'S TU QUOQUE or THE   SFE, and   1611
       CITY GALLANT   H. D. XI

Chambers, III, 269; p. 1614, as "diuers times acted" by the Queen's men; "Written by Io. Cooke, Gent." Given at court, 1611, Dec. 27 and 1612, Feb. 2. On the B list because the text may represent the court performance.

A 19   If It Be Not Good the   Dekker, III   Between 1610
       Devil Is in It   and 1612

Chambers, III, 297; p. 1612, "As it hath bin lately Acted, with great
applause, by the Queenes Maiesties Seruants: At the Red Bull. Written
by Thomas Dekker."

A 20   The Golden Age   Heywood, III   Before 1611

Chambers, III, 344; S.R., Oct. 14, 1611; p. 1611, as "sundry times
acted at the Red Bull" by the Queen's men.

B 21   The Silver Age   Heywood, III   Before 1612

P. 1613; presented at court 1612, Jan. 12. Chambers, III, 345, "the
text presumably represents the play as given at court." But see Tannenbaum, op. cit., pp. 18, 23, 25, 26.

A 22   The Brazen Age   Heywood, III   Before 1613

P. 1613.

B 23, 24   The Iron Age   Heywood, III   ca. 1613 ?

Part I, p. 1632; Part II, 1632.
(For discussion of the Ages, see text, above.)

B 25   The Hector of Germany   Q, 1615, H.   ca. 1615
                                  Payne, ed.

Chambers, III, 493; S.R., April 24, 1615; p. 1615, "As it hath beene
publikely Acted at the Red Bull, and at the Curtaine, by a Companie of
Young Men of this Citie. Made by W. Smith, with new Additions." On
the B list because acted by amateurs and because also given at the Curtain
and published with additions.

A 26   The Four Prentices   Heywood, II   1592 ?
       of London   At the Red Bull
                                                      before 1615

Chambers, III, 340; S.R., June 19, 1594; "Godfrey of Bulloigne with
the Conquest of Jerusalem"; p. 1615, "As it hath bene diuerse times
Acted, at the Red Bull, by the Queenes Maiesties Seruants. Written by
Thomas Heywood."

A 27   The Honest Lawyer   Q, 1616, H.   Before 1615
                                  SFE

Chambers, IV, 19; S.R., Aug. 14, 1615; p. 1616, as acted by the
Queen's men. "Written by S.S" (? Samuel Sheppard).

B 28   The Royal King and   Heywood, VI   1602
       the Loyal Subject   ca. 1618 (Clark, p. 29)

Chambers, III, 341; S.R., March 25, 1637; p. 1637, "As it hath beene
Acted with great Applause by the Queenes Maiesties Servants. Written

by Thomas Heywood." The epilogue describes the play as "old." Possibly the "Marshall Osric" of Worcester's, Sept., 1602. *B* because of late publication.

A 29   SWETNAM THE WOMAN HATER   SFE, H.   1618-19
                                                   (Schelling)

P. 1620, "Acted at the Red Bull, by the late Queenes Seruants."

B 30   EDWARD II   Q, 1594 and 1622   *ca.* 1592
                          Schelling, *Typical*   At the Red Bull
                          Elizabethan Plays   before 1619

Chambers, III, 425; *S.R.*, July 6, 1593; a possible edition, 1593; other editions 1594, 1598, 1612; 1622: "As it was publikely acted by the late Queene's Maiesties Servants at the Red Bull in S. Iohns streete." The stage directions of 1594 and 1622 are the same; they probably represent the early performances; therefore a *B* play.

A 31   THE DEVIL'S LAW CASE   Webster, II   *ca.* 1620 (Lucas)

P. 1623, "As it was approouedly well Acted by her Maiesties Seruants. Written by Iohn Webster."

C 32   RICHARD III   1592-93 At the Red Bull
                                      probably before 1619

In 1637 Heywood (Pearson, VI, 352) published a prologue and an epilogue with this explanation: "A young witty Lad playing the part of Richard the third at the Red Bull: the Author because hee was interested in the Play to incourage him, wrot him this Prologue and Epilogue." Chambers, II, 448, says, "This was probably, and certainly if the play was Shakespeare's, some quite exceptional performance." Certainly not more than a *C* play.

III. PLAYS GIVEN BY THE PRINCE'S MEN POSSIBLY AT THE RED BULL, 1617-19

(For discussion of this group, see text above)

L 32a   THE YOUNGER BROTHER   1617

S.R. November [December] 29, 1653. Alleyn (*Diary:* Young, II, 51): Oct. 3, 1617: "I went to *ye* red bull and *Received* for *ye* younger brother but 3. 6. 4. water 4*d*."

C 33   A FAIR QUARREL   Bullen, Middleton, IV.   1617
                          Q 1617 H.   (Stork, p. 39)

P. 1617, "As it was Acted before the King and diuers times publikely by the Prince his Highnes Seruants. Written by Thomas Middleton and William Rowley, Gentl."

C 34 ALL's LOST BY   Morris, ed., "Belles   1619 (Schelling)
      LUST   Lettres" series   *ca.* 1623 (Stork, p. 30)

P. 1633: "Written by William Rowley. Divers times Acted by the Lady
Elizabeth's Servants. And now lately by her Maiesties Servants, with
great applause, at the Phoenix in Drury Lane." A *C* play because of the
chance that it may have passed to the Phoenix repertory from the Red
Bull.

C 35   THE WORLD TOST AT   Bullen, Mid- 1620 (Stork, p. 41)
       TENNIS   dleton, VII
                            Q 1620, H.

S.R. July 4, 1620, "A booke called a Courtly Masque or 'the world
tossed at tennis' acted at the Princes Armes by the Prince [Charles] his
highnes seruants." P. 1620; "As it hath beene diuers times Presented to
the Contentment of many Noble and Worthy Spectators, By the Prince
his Seruants. Inuented, and set downe, by Tho: Middleton & Wm. Rowley Gent."

IV. PLAYS GIVEN BY THE COMPANY OF THE RED BULL AND REVELS, 1619-23

B 36   THE TWO MERRY MILKMAIDS or   SFE   1619 (Schell-
        THE BEST WORDS WEAR THE GARLAND   ing)

P. 1620, as "Acted before the King, with generall Approbation, by the
Companie of the Reuels. I. C.[umber]"; Murray, I, 196, lists J.
Cumber as a Queen's company actor, 1619. Another edition, 1661. A
B play because first published after performance at court.

A 37   THE VIRGIN MARTYR   Dekker, IV   *ca.* 1620

Chambers, III, 298; *S.R.* Dec. 7, 1621; p. 1622, "As it hath bin divers
times publickely Acted with great Applause, By the seruants of his Maiesties Reuels. Written by Phillip Messenger and Thomas Deker." Chambers continues: "The play is said to have been 'reformed' and licensed by
Buck for the Red Bull on 6 Oct. 1620 (Herbert, p. 29)." Other editions, 1631, 1651, 1661.

A 38   THE HEIR   H. D. XI   1620 (Schelling)
                   Q. 1622, 1633, H.

P. 1622, "As it was lately Acted by the Company of the Reuels. Written
by T. M. Gent. [Thomas May]" 1633, "As it was Acted by the Company of the Revels, 1620. Written by T. M."

L 38a GRAMARCIE WIT   1621: Dec. 30

Murray, II, 192-193; "2° Marcii. A warrant for allowance of XX^{tie}
nobles for one play acted by Ellisworth and his fellowes late servaunts
to Queene Anne and now the Companie of the Revells the play called

gramarcie witt on of 30th of December 1621 and 3 *li* 6*s* 8*d* by way of reward." Called to my attention by Dr. Gerald Bentley.

A 39   HEROD AND ANTIPATER   Q, 1622, H.   1621 (Schelling)

P. 1622, "The true Tragedy Of Herod and Antipater. . . . As it hath beene, of late, diuers times publiquely Acted (with great Applause) at the Red Bull, by the Company of his Maiesties Reuels. Written by Gervase Markham and William Sampson Gentlemen." Another edition, 1622.

B 40   THE WELSH AMBASSADOR   Malone Society   1622 (Herbert)
                                               1623 (Malone Society)

Herbert, p. 23, allowed in 1622 a new play, *The Welsh Traveller,* for the players of the Revels. Adams suggests that this may be *The Welsh Ambassador.* In 1920 the Malone Society published *The Welsh Embassador,* dating the play 1623 on the evidence of a definite textual allusion. That the MS is the work of a scribe does not invalidate this date for this stage copy. The play is certainly prepared for presentation as shown by the prompter's directions, and since mistakes in entry are probable enough, it may reasonably be identified with the play Herbert licensed, and may be given at least a *B* rating. Lawrence's suggestion that this play is one of those arranged for a company traveling in the country is discussed under the next play. Here may be noticed its scene, II. iii, which requires a balcony with a curtain. Could traveling companies plan on such equipment in their playing places?

A 41   THE TWO NOBLE LADIES   Malone Society   1619-23
       AND THE CONVERTED CONJURER   (Malone Society)

Title in MS.: "Often times acted w*th* approbation At the Red Bull in S*t*. Johns Streete By the Company of y*e* Reuells." First published, Bullen, *Old English Plays,* 1882-85; by the Malone Society, 1930. See also F. S. Boas, "A Seventeenth Century Theatrical Repertoire" in *Shakespeare & the Universities,* 1923; the introduction to the Malone Society reprint, 1930; Greg, *Elizabethan Dramatic Documents,* 1931, 274-279; Lawrence, *Review of English Studies,* VIII (1932), 224-228, and Greg, in the same volume, 457-458. Because of the interlacing of abbreviations of minor actors' names in the stage directions of *The Two Noble Ladies, The Captives, Edmond Ironside,* and *Thomas of Woodstock* (called *Richard II* in the Malone Society reprint), Boas suggested that all these plays were for the same company, perhaps a London company making a provincial tour. Lawrence is confirmed in this opinion because none of these manuscripts bears the censor's license for performance, and for the same reason he groups with these plays *The Welsh Ambassador* and *The Parliament of Love.*

If these arguments are sound, *The Two Noble Ladies,* in its present state, may represent an arrangement for country performance only, and be of little use for our purpose. But Greg, answering Lawrence, says there is no authority for supposing that plays for the country did not require official sanction. Absence of the censor's approval on these manuscripts is not significant concerning their place of performance. *The Two Noble Ladies* and *The Welsh Ambassador* are thus not necessarily arranged for use in the country, and we need not consider *The Parliament of Love* as associated with them.

The interlacing of actors' names in the four other plays and the possible occurrence of the same prompter's handwriting in the stage directions of some of them have been taken as showing that these plays were given by the same company. Not too much should be made of this, however; the manuscript of *The Two Noble Ladies* states definitely that the play was given at the Red Bull, and *The Captives* was licensed by Herbert for performance at the Cockpit, September 3, 1624, where the Lady Elizabeth's men were playing. Perhaps the prompter's directions were added at some later time. For our purpose it is sufficient to note that every one agrees that the manuscript of *The Two Noble Ladies* is in the author's hand. It therefore represents the play as it was given at the Red Bull; the prompter's changes, no matter when they were made, modify the staging in no important particular. The introduction to the Malone edition differentiates it from the three other plays and leaves it as the only one likely to have been given at the Red Bull before 1625.

L 41a   PHILENZO AND HYPOLLYTA   1619-23
                                             (Fleay, *Stage*, p. 307)

S.R. June 29, 1660, by Massinger. Warburton's list of burned plays had *Philenzo and Hippolyta* by Massinger. Fleay, I, 213, suggests it was Dekker's *Philipo and Hipollita* at the Rose, 1594, altered about 1620 for the company at the Red Bull.

L 41b   ANTONIO AND VALLIA   1619-23
                                             (Fleay, *Stage*, p. 307)

S.R. June 29, 1660, by Massinger. Warburton's list of burned plays includes this title. Fleay, I, 213, thinks it Dekker's *Antony and Vallia*, given at the Rose, June 20, 1595, and altered by Massinger.

C 42   THE COSTLY WHORE   Bullen, *Old*   1613 (Bullen, on
                          English Plays,   basis of allusions)
                          IV   1629-32   (Fleay,
                                               Stage, p. 342, at
                                               Salisbury Court)

P. 1633, "Acted by the companie of the Revels." If either of the dates suggested for this play is correct, it is too early or too late for our period, but there is a slight chance that this Revels company is the one at the Red Bull.

C 43   A MATCH AT MIDNIGHT   Quarto,   *ca.* 1607 (Stork, p. 13)
                             1633, H.   1622-23 (Wiggin)
                                        1629-37 (Chambers,
                                           III, 474, for later
                                           Revels company)
                                        1623 (Schelling)

S.R. Jan. 15, 1633; p. 1633. "As it hath beene Acted by the Children of the Revells. Written by W. R." [William Rowley]. Only if the 1622-23 date is right does this play concern us.

V. PLAYS GIVEN BY THE PRINCE'S MEN AT THE RED BULL, 1623-25

(The production date for these plays is from Herbert unless otherwise stated.)

L 43a   THE BELLMAN OF PARIS   1623, July 30

Herbert, p. 24: "For the Prince's Players, A French Tragedy of *the Bellman of Paris,* written by Thomas Dekkirs and John Day, for the Company of the Red Bull."

L 43b   THE PLANTATION OF VIRGINIA   1623, August

Herbert, p. 24: "For the company at the Curtain: a Tragedy of *the Plantation of Virginia, the profaneness to be left out,* otherwise not tolerated."—There is no reason to include this here except that Adams says that after the Prince's left the Curtain, that theater was not used dramatically. Perhaps Herbert momentarily forgot that the Prince's company had moved.

L 43c   THE PEACABLE KING OR   1623, August 19
        THE LORD MENDALL

Herbert, pp. 24-25: "For the Prince's Servants of the Red Bull; an Oulde Playe, called, *The Peaceable King; or The Lord Mendall* which was formerly allowed by Sir George Bucke, and likewise by me."

B 44   THE WONDER OF A KINGDOM   Dekker, IV   1623

Chambers, III, 299; *S.R.* May 16, 1631; p. 1636, "Written by Thomas Dekker." Herbert, p. 25, 1623, September 18, licensed "For a Company of Strangers; a new Comedy, called, *Come see a Wonder.* Written by John Deye." Preceding the entry is one as follows: 1623, September 12, "For the Lady Elizabeth's Players; a new Comedy ,called *The Cra . . . Marchant, or Come to my Country house;* Written by William Bonen. It was acted at the Red Bull, and licensed without my hand to itt; because they were none of the *four* Companys." The Lady Elizabeth's company was really at the Cockpit. Adams suggests that the last sentence of this

entry really belongs to *Come See a Wonder*, and says that play is probably *The Wonder of a Kingdom*. There seems to be, therefore, sufficient
reason to put *The Wonder of a Kingdom* on the B list.

L 44a   A FAULT IN FRIENDSHIP   1623, October 2

Herbert, p. 26: "For the Prince's Companye; a new Comedy, called, *A
Fault in Friendship:* Written by *Young* Johnson, and Broome."

L 44b   THE FAIR FOUL ONE   1623, November 28

Herbert, p. 26: "For a Strange Company at the Red Bull *The Faiyre
fowle one, or The bayting of the Jealous Knight,* Written by (William?
[Adams]) Smith."

L 44c   THE FOUR SONS OF AYMON   1623-24, January 6

Herbert, p. 27: "For the Prince's Company; *The Four Sons of Amon;*
being an Old Playe, and *not of a legible hand.*" See Sibley, p. 59: Bought
for the Admiral's men, Dec. 10, 1602. Heywood, *An Apology for Actors,*
pp. 58-59, shows its last part was given in Amsterdam, probably *ca.* 1610,
and tells part of the story.

L 44d   THE MADCAP   1624, May 3

Herbert, p. 28: "For the Prince's Company: A New Play, called *The
Madcap:* Written by *Barnes.*"

L 44e   JUGURTH   1624, May 3

Herbert, p. 28: "An Old Play, called *Jugurth, King of Numidia,* formerly allowed by Sir George Bucke." Adams says this is apparently the
play by Wm. Boyle on which Henslowe lent 30s., Feb. 9, 1600. See also
Sibley, p. 86. Adams says further: "Elsewhere Chalmers writes (*Supple-
mental Apology,* 1799), 'On the 3d of May, 1624, Sir Henry Herbert
states, that he had licensed, without a fee, *Jugurth,* an old play, allowed
by Sir George Bucke and *burnt, with his other books.*' " Alfred Harbage
(*LTLS,* 1936, June 20) suggests a possible connection between these
items and Bodleian MS Rawlinson poet. 195, *Jurgutha or the faitless
Cosen German.* Chambers (*William Shakespeare,* I, 104) says *Jugurth*
was a Fortune play, and suggests it might have burned with the theater.
I see no reason for including it among Red Bull plays, but see Maas on
Nero, next item.

C 45   NERO   Mermaid ed.   1624, May 15
                             Quarto 1624, H.

1624, May 15, "The Tragedy of Nero was allowed to be printed." P.
1624. Maas suggests, p. 112, this is a Prince's play because its entry follows two [*Madcap, Jugurth*] to that company, hardly a convincing
reason, especially since *Jugurth* is doubtfully ascribed to them.

C 46 THE PARRICIDE   Chapman, *Tragedies*   1624, May 27
Parrott, ed.

Herbert, p. 28: "For the Prince's Company; a Play, called *The Parracide.*" *S.R.*, Nov. 29, 1653, *The Parracide or Revenge for Honour* by Glapthorne. P. 1654, *Revenge for Honour* by George Chapman; Adams, p. 29, thinks there is no doubt Glapthorne is the author; Parrott, pp. 713-720, says the play was revised by Glapthorne.

    F. T. Bowers, *MLN*, LII (1937), 192-196, presents arguments to show that *Revenge for Honor* is a version of an unnamed play witnessed by the Venetian ambassador, Dec. 31, 1619, as given by the Prince's company before James I, exciting James "in an extraordinary manner both inwardly and outwardly." C. L. Shaver, *MLN*, LIII (1938), 96-98, thinks the ambassador's account fits Greville's *Alaham* (p. 1633) more closely, and dates the present version of *Revenge for Honor* about 1640, though he says it may have been based on a Jacobean play, written by Glapthorne, 1627-41. In any case *Revenge for Honor* can be no more than a *C* play.

L 46a THE FAIRY KNIGHT   1624, June 11

Herbert, p. 29: "A new play, called, *The Fairy Knight* Written by Forde, and Decker." Adams adds a note that the play was presumably licensed to the Prince's company named just above. Sibley, p. 51, refers to *Huon of Bordeaux*, which Fleay suggested as possibly refashioned into this play.

L 46b KEEP THE WIDOW WAKING   1624, September

Herbert, p. 29: "A new Tragedy, called, *A Late Murther of the Sonn upon the Mother:* Written by Forde, and Webster." "Acted at the Red Bull during the autumn of 1624, by Prince Charles' Company." (Sibley, p. 92.) See C. J. Sisson, *Lost Plays of Shakespeare's Age* (1936), pp. 80-110. The full title is given in a Star Chamber document: "The late Murder in White Chappell, or Keepe the Widow Waking." The authors were Dekker, Rowley, Ford, Webster.

L 46c THE WIDOW'S PRIZE   1624-25, January 25

Herbert, p. 30: "For the Prince's Company: A new Play, called, *The Widow's Prize,* which containing much abusive matter, was allowed of by me, on condition, that my reformations were observed." Adams adds: "*S.R.* Sept. 9, 1653, as by William Sampson."

    Herbert, p. 48, licensed a contest in fencing at the Red Bull, 21 March, 1622; another is mentioned, p. 47, but the date is not clear.

    In 1627, April 11, Herbert, p. 64, received £5 "from Mr. Hemming in their company's name to forbid the playing of Shakespeare's plays to the Red Bull Company." This is the last reference to the Red Bull in Herbert's records before 1640.

The following plays have, for one reason or another, been considered, but finally rejected as not sufficiently likely to be included even on the *C* list. For example, there is T. Rawlins' *Rebellion*, played by his Majesty's Revels; but it was written in 1639, and is therefore too late. On the other hand, Machen's *Dumb Knight*, also played by his Majesty's Revels, was written in 1607-08 (Chambers, III, 418) and published in 1608; it is therefore too early. Other rejected plays are:

The Knight of the Burning Pestle	The Jew of Malta
Messallina	A Cure for a Cuckold
Cromwell	The Captives
Dick of Devonshire	Thomas of Woodstock*
Edmond Ironside*	The Fatal Contract
Lust's Dominion	The Thracian Wonder
The Seven Champions of Christendom	King John and Matilda
The Honest Whore	A Maidenhead Well Lost
The City Night-Cap	I, II, Fair Maid of the West
The English Traveller	The Inner Temple Masque or the
Love's Mistress	Masque of Heroes
Stuckley	The Witch of Edmonton

* After this manuscript was in the hands of the printer, the implication of one slight piece of possible evidence concerning these plays seemed to me to have been overlooked; they demand at last brief further consideration.

As has been stated in the note on *The Two Noble Ladies*, the same prompter's handwriting has been supposedly discovered in the manuscripts of *The Two Noble Ladies*, *The Captives*, *Thomas of Woodstock*, and *Edmond Ironside*. The editor of *Thomas of Woodstock* for the Malone Society disagrees with this opinion, and, quite properly, points out that the designations for the actors—"G.oad" and George—offer too slight evidence without the support of the prompter's identity to connect this play with the others. We may, therefore, disregard it.

There remain, however, the other plays. How did it happen that the same prompter and that actors designated in the same way occur in a play given at the Red Bull and a play given at the Cockpit? The usual explanation is that they had to do with these plays not when these were originally produced, but some time later when they had been acquired by another company.

But the editor of *Two Noble Ladies* suggests, p. ix, that its stage directions in their corrections and recorrections show that this prompter was working with the author. If this suggestion is sound, then this prompter was connected with the production at the Red Bull, and there is more reason for supposing that *Edmond Ironside* might also have been presented at that theater. However, since he was also concerned with *The Captives* at the Cockpit it is just as likely to have been given there. Certainly it is no more than a *C* play; maybe it is not even that.

It offers a few interesting points, but nothing to modify our conclusions. It has no scenes demanding a curtained space: it opens with the entrance of seven, who then "sitt about a table"—this perhaps was discovered; but the first scene of the second act, which could conveniently have been discovered, quite certainly was not; the directions read, "The Drumme and Trumpetts sound: Then Enter" six persons, and at least four sit. Doors are mentioned in the directions several times and the balcony is used once. There it represents the walls of a city, two persons standing in it speak altogether

Among lost plays, which have been suggested for the Red Bull, but which do not have sufficient evidence of presentation there, are:

The Dutch Painter and the French Branke
The Man in the Moon Drinks Claret
A Vow and a Good One

---

sixteen lines, and then a direction, l. 914, demands, "assayle the walls." What happens the text does not make clear.

So much for the parts of the stage. There are also some interesting directions on business, etc. Line 700 begins a torture scene in which the hands and noses of two boys are cut off before us. The directions read, "Hee cutts offe one hande"; "Hee cutts offe the other hande"; "Hee Cutts his hands and Nose." Several heavenly phenomena are described; l. 786, "the Sunne lookes paile the moone shines red The starres appeare," but there are no directions to suggest that anything really happened on the stage. A Chorus, "attired in blacke," describes, ll. 965-1018, a battle, while the actors perform more or less what he is saying. One detail is, "Edricus takes a dead m.. head vppon his swords poynt holdinge yt vppe. . . ." Paper and inkhorn are brought, l. 1148, for a man to write with, and he sits to do so; other scenes also demand a seat or two. A man disguises himself by changing clothes with his servant, but uses some other means as well, for a person whom he is trying to deceive "pulls of the velvet patch of his face"; l. 1313. The conclusion of the play is a somewhat formalized battle: "They march a longe the stage. . ."; "They trayne theire souldio . . . the stage [many of the directions are mutilated]; "The Armies make towards one another when Edricus standing betwene sayeth"; "The Trumpitts sound the Armies doe Compasse the Twoe kings in the middest, they fight"; "they fight againe Edm: driues Canute backe aboute the Stage"; "They goe hande in hand out off th . . . Edricus leadeinge the Drumme."

CHAPTER III

THE EVIDENCE AND ITS TREATMENT

(1)

THE GREATEST difficulty in the study of the Elizabethan stage is to determine how to treat the evidence about it. That evidence is of three kinds: contemporary pictures of the exteriors of the theater and especially of the interior; contemporary contracts, descriptions, and allusions outside the plays; and the evidence furnished by the plays themselves.

Four contemporary pictures of Elizabethan stages have long been known, and there is no need to repeat here the discussion concerning them; see Chambers, *The Elizabethan Stage* (1923), II, 519. Of these pictures the most informing is certainly that of the Swan; we know it represents more or less truly a public theater of about 1596, and it shows more of the theater building than do the others. There is general agreement that the so-called Red Bull picture, the frontispiece to Kirkman's *The Wits* (1672), does not represent that theater when it was still unroofed, as in the years we are interested in. The first known connection of the picture with the Red Bull was made in 1809; see Lawrence, *The Elizabethan Playhouse*, First Series (1912), p. 32, n. 2. Certainly throughout our period the Red Bull was a public playhouse, and the chandeliers of the picture imply a theater illuminated by artificial light. The small curtain conceals the only entrance, an impossible arrangement for most Elizabethan plays. This alone is enough to support J. J. Elson's suggestion in *The Wits* (1932), pp. 424-427, that the picture is "purely a work of the artist's imagination, designed to suggest the possibilities of droll-performances and to promote the sale of the book, rather than to portray the actual settings in which some furtive Commonwealth shows were given." The title-page to Alabaster's *Roxana* (1632) shows a Caroline academic setting, and that of Richard's *Messallina* (1640) is probably of a similar type. In reprinting this last picture for the first time in *Modern Philology*, I (1905), 582, I suggested no definite origin for it because I could find no real evidence, and the various arguments to show that it represents the Fortune (Skemp in his edition of *Messallina* [1910], p. 32), the Red Bull (Albright, *The Shakespearean*

Stage [1909], p. 45), or the second Globe (Hille, Shakespeare *Jahr-buch*, LXVI [1930], 25-78) are in the case of Albright, definitely wrong (see J. Q. Adams, *JEGP, X* [1911], 331); or do not carry conviction. Chambers (*op. cit.*, 519) thinks that if it is a real stage it is more likely to be that of Salisbury Court, where the company which gave the play did most of its productions, and Adams (*op. cit.*, p. 331) that it is a poor copy of the Roxana engraving. But the differences are too many to allow Adams' explanation. The curtains in the *Messallina* picture are not plain like those of the *Roxana* picture, but are painted or embroidered with figures; the *Messallina* window above is single and curtained, while in the *Roxana* there are two windows with people looking out; most important of all, the *Messallina* curtained space projects instead of being flush with the (not-shown) back-wall. An ineffectively drawn detail above the lower curtains is another distinctive feature. To many students it appears merely a sloping narrow cornice, but Albright (*op. cit.*, pp. 63, 66) thinks it an upper stage with the curtained window at its rear. This would be very inconvenient and impracticable because it would allow no concealed passage-way from side to side behind it, and so narrow a shelf would be ludicrously dangerous.

I did not venture to connect the *Messallina* picture with any special Elizabethan theater, but in its projecting curtained space it does have a resemblance to the pictures of Terence's *Phormio*, published at Lyons in 1493. These pictures, according to Max Herrmann, *Forschungen zur deutschen theater-geschichte* (1914), p. 354, show the influence of academic productions in Flanders. The stage for *Phormio* might be explained as merely an artist's conception, but the picture of *Andriae*, I. i, shows the stage as resting on apparently temporary scaffolding, a detail which no artist would include in an imaginary setting. The *Andriae* concealed space does not, like that in *Phormio*, project, but is otherwise in general like it. Such a projecting structure as is shown in the *Messalina* and the *Phormio* pictures would be a practical way to provide a curtained space in an ordinary hall, and this may be the explanation of the Messalina's principal distinguishing feature.

Not listed by Chambers among the pictures of Elizabethan theaters, and generally disregarded by scholars, are the pictures on various title-pages showing only part of the stage. Among these is that on the title-page of *Swetnam the Woman-Hater* (1620). This, as a Red Bull play, presumably shows a part of the Red Bull stage, and we shall return to it later. But as it is only a small part, the Swan picture, however inaccurate in itself and however untypical its theater, remains the best pictorial representation of the interior of an Elizabethan public theater which we possess. Pictures of the exteriors of the theaters offer little of use to us. A list may be found in Chambers (*op. cit.*, II, 353-354, 520).

Certainly not evidence but of unavoidable influence on our thinking are the numerous pictorial representations and models which have been made in recent years.[1] The practical agreement of all of these except Miss Porter's on most important points has an inevitable and cumulative effect on our opinions. We have to remind ourselves continually that in all details in which these pictures and models differ from the Swan picture they are as likely to be wrong as right. Of course, when one makes a model or a pictorial representation of the Elizabethan theater he cannot leave uncertain points vague: space must be filled; details must be supplied. But this unanimity of supposition must not be thought of as evidence, nor their details as for that reason established. Notable illustrations of this need for caution in spite of this unanimity are the rear stage and the obliquely placed doors.

Contemporary allusions to the Red Bull have been listed in chapter II; they contribute little to our knowledge of the construction of the theater. Other contemporary material is the contracts for building the Fortune and the Hope, and such generalized descriptions as the well-known chapter VI in *The Guls Horn Booke*. Perhaps this last is mainly remarkable for the extraordinary variety of interpretation it has en-

---

[1] Among those most often copied is W. H. Godfrey's, well reproduced in the Shakespeare *Jahrbuch* (1908); another is George Westcott's in Albright's *The Shakespearean Stage* (1909), unfortunate in its imitation of the narrowing front stage of the *Roxana* and *Messallina* pictures. Less varied from the Swan picture is that in Quennell's *History of Everyday Things in England*. Others to be mentioned are: A. Forestier's in the *Illustrated London News*, August 11 and September 9, 1911; George Varian's in the *Century* Magazine, LXI, 1912; W. Noel Hill's, issued as a wall picture by the Oxford Press, no date; G. T. Forrest's in the London County Council's pamphlet, *The Site of the Globe Playhouse* (1921); Joseph Q. Adams' in his *Life of William Shakespeare* (1923); S. B. Marston's in Nicoll's *Development of the Theatre* (1927); Tannenbaum and Lawrence's in Lawrence's *Those Nut-Cracking Elizabethans* (1935); G. W. Small's in the *Shakespeare Association Bulletin*, January, 1935; John C. Adams' in the *Theatre Arts Monthly*, October, November, 1936. An interesting but unreliable reconstruction of the interior of a private playhouse by M. Hauschild, 1836, is reproduced in the Shakespeare *Jahrbuch*, LII (1916), 188. Among models of public theaters are H. E. Conklin's, Charlotte Porter's, illustrated in the *Shakespeare Association Bulletin*, April, 1935; and that constructed under my direction by Herbert Nelson, and illustrated in *Theater Arts Monthly*, November, 1930, *Shakespeare Association Bulletin*, October, 1931, and *English Literature in Fact and Story* (1929). The last two are alike in showing simultaneous settings, but Miss Porter's are permanent structural features, and are so far removed from our only sure basis, the Swan theater, that her model cannot be accepted. Notable stages are that in the Folger Library and that used in T. W. Stevens's Globe theater at the Century of Progress in Chicago, 1934, and more recently in other expositions.

dured. Of course, such allusions and descriptions differ in value and must be considered each by itself.

The evidence offered by the plays themselves remains the most important at our disposal and the most tantalizing. It is of three kinds: that of the stage directions, that of the allusions in the dialogue to the stage and its furnishings, and that obtained by studying each play as a whole. By this last I mean evidence secured by noting the staging of successive scenes and of scenes of like situations. The alternation theory of staging rested largely on such evidence. The stage directions can most conveniently be considered first, since some points concerning the other two types of evidence can be cleared up in the discussion.

(2)

The value of the stage directions as evidence differs with their origin. Of course the only directions of any weight are those occuring in the original editions; modern directions are mostly attempts to adjust the plays to the eighteenth-century stage. Sometimes more recent ones try to show how the play was given on the Elizabethan stage. In neither case, of course, have they any authority, and unless they are clearly marked as interpolations, they may be very misleading. Even when so marked, any new directions are likely to give the plays a modern appearance and an apparent orderliness of arrangement far removed from the playhouse versions. It may seem unnecessary to mention all this, but some students have not remembered it.

An original stage direction may have been written: (1) by the author as he composed his play, or by some literary reviser of it; (2) by the prompter as he arranged the play for performance; or (3) by some person—editor is often too pretentious a name—preparing the play for readers. A single play may conceivably illustrate all three, and the second is always accompanied by the first. To these may be added as a fourth type the directions occurring in texts prepared by outsiders, perhaps for stolen copies, where the stage directions may be descriptions of what had been seen on the stage.[2]

The Red Bull plays offer a possible conspicuous example of the fourth kind of directions. Heywood in a prologue, 1632, says of *I If You Know Not Me*, published 1605, "Some by Stenography drew The plot: put it in print; (scarce one word trew)." If this is the full ex-

---

[2] On the general subject of the authorship of stage directions see Chambers, *William Shakespeare* (1930), I, 117-125; Greg, *Elizabethan Dramatic Documents* (1931), pp. 213-221; Lawrence, "Early Prompt Books" in *Pre-Restoration Stage Studies* (1927), pp. 373-413; J. Q. Adams, "Elizabethan Playhouse Manuscripts," *The Johns Hopkins Alumni Magazine*, XXI (1932), 21-52.

planation or G. N. Giordano-Orsini's further idea in *LTLS* [Dec. 4, 1930], 1037, is true that in part, at least, the text was supplied from the memory of some actor or actors, the stage directions would be not the work of the author or prompter before the play was given, but of some one who presumably had seen it in performance. Thus they might individually be pretty close to first-hand directions of what was actually done, though the play as a whole might, as Orsini suggests, suffer from misplaced or omitted passages. If Miss Madelaine Doran's theory is true, tentatively advanced in the introduction to the Malone Society reprint, Part II [1935], xvii-xix, that the two parts as we have them in the first editions are made up of a pirated copy of Part I and a playhouse copy of Part II, further modified by the publisher, we can scarcely be sure who wrote the directions. The directions in *I If You Know Not Me* are pretty complete, especially concerning the dumb shows; they give often the precise numbers engaged ("Enter six with torches," 216; "Enter three poor men," 221, only two of whom speak; "Enter four torches," 234); actions are specified ("He lookes backe, he kills him," 225); and so on.

(3)

The preparation of a play for readers may have been carried so far as seriously to weaken its value as evidence. Editing may cause difficulty by the removal or the addition of material. Jonson's folio of 1616 is an example of a text in which hints of the performance have mostly been removed to bring the play into accordance with classical models. Many plays have either been deprived of important directions, or their staging was much simpler than students have been assuming. Elizabethan theatrical manuscripts show author's directions usually in the right margin and the prompter's usually in the left (Chambers, *op. cit.,* I, 121). It has been suggested (Lawrence, *op. cit.,* p. 385) that some printed plays have so few directions because the printers ignored the marginal material, but this explanation is not very well substantiated. It may be there never were many more directions. The omission by the author and the prompter of directions for the exits of actors and for the removal of properties may be understood; the dullest actor might be expected to get himself off at the end of a scene, unless he was supposed to be "dead," and a table or stool no longer necessary could be removed by a stage-hand without any special notice for it. But properties had to be at hand when they were needed, and if the curtain was to be employed at all it had to be used at the right moment. If such directions are lacking it may mean, despite our theories, that the curtain was not used, and that the table, stools, etc., could be assumed to be present on the stage. In any case, all theories of staging based on supplying a large number of directions are highly questionable. One reason for using the Red Bull plays as a basis for study is that, generally speaking, they have the necessary directions and show few signs of editing by removal.

Additions which weaken the evidence of the plays may be of two kinds. Even if Jonson's *Sejanus* were more fully equipped with directions, it would not be completely useful, because in the address "To the Readers" Jonson says:

> I would inform you, that the book, in all numbers, is not the same with that which was acted on the public stage; wherein a second pen had a good share: in place of which, I have rather chosen to put weaker, and, no doubt, less pleasing, of mine own, than to defraud so happy a genius of his right by my loathed usurpation.

How much these substitutions have changed the acting "plot" of the play, who can say? Among the Red Bull plays an example of such claimed revision after performance and before publication is the title-page of *The Hector of Germany:* "As it hath beene publikely Acted at the Red Bull . . . Made by W. Smith, with new Additions."

How questionable is the evidence of plays of which some printed parts were omitted in performance? The well-known statement by Humphrey Moseley prefixed to the 1647 folio of Beaumont and Fletcher shows that such omissions were made. Moseley says: "When these comedies and tragedies were presented on the stage, the actors omitted some scenes and passages, with the authors' consent, as occasion lead them . . . now you have both all that was acted, and all that was not; even the perfect full originals, without the least mutilation." The cutting of plays for performance, discussed by Alfred Hart in *RES*, VIII (1932), 19-28, 139-154, 395-413, and X (1934), 1-28, with much supporting evidence, must receive some consideration in any study of staging.[3] But even if existing texts were cut, it would not

---

[3] Hart concludes, X, 1, that two hours was the customary time allowed for performance in the important London theaters, that not more than 2300 or at most 2400 lines could be acted in that time, and that longer plays must customarily have been cut to fit these limits. Granville-Barker's caution in his Preface to *Hamlet* (1937), p. 21, is to be noted:

In estimating the acting-time of a play one must always consider the nature of the subject and the method of the writing; mere line measurement can be deceptive. A *Comedy of Errors* and *Love's Labour's Lost* will move far more swiftly than *As You Like It* or *Twelfth Night. Hamlet* moves at very varying speeds.

Hart's measure is, then, only roughly applicable but is usefully objective. He calls attention to two curious points concerning our Red Bull plays: Dekker, in the epilogue to *If It Be Not Good*, speaks of its "three howres of mirth"; Hart comments, VIII, 398: "This is the only dated reference to a three-hour performance prior to 1616. The

seriously weaken their evidence on staging, for where omissions had to be made they would be rather of the poetic embroidery within scenes than of action involving the stage directions. Individual directions in such plays are, therefore, still generally to be relied on. And, indeed, since the main problem in plays considered as wholes is to provide for "split" scenes or their equivalents in time, it is not so much omissions as possible insertions that we must allow for. Thus *The Devil's Law Case* must be provided with an interval between III. ii and III. iii, or we must assume that there were two concealed spaces on the stage. That

play runs to 2700 lines and could be acted without any abridgment in two hours and twenty minutes; perhaps second-class theaters such as the Red Bull gave longer performances in order to attract an audience." On the other hand, Heywood, Hart says, VIII, 399, apologizes for the length of *II Iron Age*, though it is not more than 2300 lines in length. Ulysses, at the end of the play, says:

> If you thinke he hath done your patience wrong
> (In teadious Sceanes) by keeping you so long,
> Much matter in few words, hee bad me say
> Are hard to expresse, that lengthned out his Play.

It is not clear, Hart says, why Dekker should call a performance of less than two hours and a half one of three hours, nor why Heywood should feel called upon to excuse a performance of normal length. But Hart's estimates here raise questions. The Pearson editions run 38 or 39 lines to the page. Accordingly *II Iron Age* with its 76 pages would have between 2800 and 3000 lines, and *If It Be Not Good* with 96 pages about 3700 lines. Even allowing for half lines in the printing, which may account for some of the extra 600 lines in *II Iron Age*, still *If It Be Not Good* is considerably longer, perhaps enough to justify Dekker's statement. Also it is to be noted that both plays have a good deal of pantomime and spectacle, which would lengthen them appreciably.

Hart's surmise that Red Bull performances were longer than two hours is perhaps borne out by the following table. It does not pretend to accuracy, but only to allow a rough comparison of the length of the plays on the *A* and *B* lists. *II Iron Age*, by Hart's count, with 2300 lines, and 76 pages in Pearson's edition, furnishes a convenient measure for those of Heywood and Dekker in the same edition:

	pages		pages
Sir Thomas Wyatt	47	The Golden Age	74
A Woman Killed with Kindness	64	The Silver Age	79
If You Know Not Me, I	54	The Brazen Age	85
If You Know Not Me, II	92	The Iron Age, I	80
The Rape of Lucrece	87	The Four Prentices	89
Fortune by Land and Sea	72	The Royal King	78
Match Me in London	81	The Wonder of a Kingdom	65
If It Be Not Good	96	The Virgin Martyr	86

For plays not included in the Pearson reprints the following estimates, based on the number of pages in the original quartos and the average number of lines to the page, may serve our purpose:

	lines		lines
How A Man May Choose	2754	The Honest Lawyer	2701
The Travails of Three English Brothers	2294	Swetnam the Woman Hater	2952
A Shoemaker a Gentleman	2752	The Two Merry Milkmaids	3552
Greene's Tu Quoque	2988	The Heir	2220
The Hector of Germany	2232	Herod and Antipater	3002

the play as printed is too long for performance certainly does not weaken the force of this evidence.

Another form of editing may have consisted of dressing up stage directions for readers, presumably by adding details not present in the actual performance. Or of course, the author in the heat of composition may also have indulged in imaginative flights in his original stage directions. Or he may have written with readers in mind rather than the stage. Something like this, I suppose, is what Adams means by his objection that the *Ages* are edited for closet reading and are therefore not to be relied on (see discussion, chapter II). I see no way to distinguish between "literary" directions by the original author and those written by an editor, nor can I see that this much matters. "Literary" directions certainly exist and have led students into untenable suggestions. But it does seem that anybody going to the trouble of preparing a play for readers by rewriting directions to make them more appealing would scarcely leave the sort of illusion-destroying items I have cited from the *Ages* in chapter II, allusions, for example, to doors in a forest scene.

(4)

Directions written by the prompter appear most clearly in plays existing in manuscript. Two such are in our list, *The Two Noble Ladies* and *The Welsh Ambassador*. But the quartos also sometimes preserve signs of his hand. Chambers (*op. cit.*, I, 120-123) and Greg (*op. cit.*, pp. 213-221) summarize the characteristics which the prompter's directions are likely to show. Sometimes he supplies the name of the actor who is to play a special part—usually a minor one. In *The Two Noble Ladies* (see below, section 7) though the author planned the actual unromantic way in which his very romantic scene was to be carried out, the prompter changed certain details. He displaced literary directions for sounds by technical ones, and specified what the author had left vague. If this play had been given an Elizabethan printing, it

---

For other of our plays the line lengths are as follows:

The Welsh Ambassador, 2284, of which 2255 were spoken (Hart, *op. cit.*, X, 3).
Edward II, 2670 (*ibid.*, X, 14).
The White Devil, 3013 (*ibid.*, VIII, 410).
The Two Noble Ladies, 2111 (Malone Society).
The Devil's Law Case, 3146 (sum of Lucas' line numbers).

Though these line numberings are not made exactly on the same basis—broken lines are, for example, treated differently in different texts—they are sufficiently alike to allow comparisons. Of the thirty-one plays seventeen run appreciably over the length of *II Iron Age*, and none is longer than *If It Be Not Good*. If *If It Be Not Good* was allowed to run for three hours, perhaps the others were not cut either.

is likely that the evidence of these changes would have been omitted. But the manuscript has preserved them. It used to be said that directions in the imperative mood show the realistic hand of the prompter, but Chambers (*op. cit.*, I, 118) rightly points out that this is not necessarily so. Among the sure signs of his participation which carry over into the printed copies are what Greg calls (*op. cit.*, p. 217) anticipatory directions, as for the entrance of an actor some lines before he takes part in the action; and warning directions, as for an actor or for some property to be placed in readiness for appearance later. These signs of playhouse usage make the evidence of any play especially valuable for staging, for they bring us very near the actual performance.

(5)

Most of the directions in any text—except, of course, a stolen one—are the author's. There is no need to repeat Chambers' description (*op. cit.*, I, 118-120) of the characteristics of authors' directions. What matters for us is how far they can be depended upon as statements of theatrical fact. And with this may be considered the similar problem of the weight to be given to allusions in the dialogue to the stage and properties. Both questions amount to asking how much the Elizabethan stage left to the imagination of the audience.

One misleading consideration must be guarded against. There is little use in arguing as to what would have been most satisfactory imaginatively. Properly appealed to, the imagination can create more dramatic illusion (a quite different matter from an illusion of reality, though historians of drama often forget the distinction) than can any amount of realistic scenery and properties. To say that the storm in *King Lear* can be better imagined than presented is no doubt true, but has little bearing on what the stage manager actually attempted. Not what we should like, but what the Elizabethan theater did is what investigation, so far as possible, has to determine.

The well-known complaints and apologies of the Elizabethan dramatists concerning their theater give little real assistance in showing what degree of realism they expected. Jonson's scorn of ineffective spectacle expressed in the prologue to *Every Man in His Humor* might still be provoked by some of our modern practices; the chorus's apologies for the inadequacy of the stage effects in *Henry V* would be almost as necessary in most theaters of to-day as in the "wooden O" of the Elizabethan Globe. Less well known, perhaps, but to the same effect is Heywood's in *I The Fair Maid of the West*, 319, where the Chorus says:

Our Stage so lamely can expresse a Sea,
That we are forst by *Chorus* to discourse
What should have beene in action.

And John Kirke in *The Seven Champions of Christendom,* chorus,
Act III, makes the frank appeal:

Then let your fancies deeme upon a stage,
One man a thousand, and one houre an age.

It is not often that Heywood exercises such restraint; though he shows
he was aware of the deficiencies of his stage, he like Kirke seldom re-
frained from attempting unrealizable situations. How else could he
have dramatized all mythology? The burlesque of rural methods in
A Midsummer Night's Dream has no more bearing on the usages of
the professional London stage than the second act of *The Torchbearers*
has on those of Broadway. Only in Theseus' "The best in this kind
are but shadows," was Shakespeare thinking of his own stage as he
might well think of our own to-day.[4]

(6)

We return to the question, How literally are stage directions and
allusions in the dialogue to stage and properties to be taken? The prevailing idea is, I think, that they are to be taken very literally indeed.
Certainly Chambers bases his elaborate study of the stage very de-
cidedly on such evidence. To take a single illustration: When
confronted with the presentation of a river bank, he suggests (*The
Elizabethan Stage,* III, 51, 107) "the edge of the stage, with steps
into the auditorium taken for water stairs, seems most plausible." By
such literal interpretation he has built up carefully documented theories, and Lawrence has proceeded in much the same way, with scrupu-
lous consideration of nomenclature and regard for the minutest scraps
of evidence. He argues, for example in *Those Nut-Cracking Elizabethans* (1935), p. 106, that because in *The Tempest,* IV. i, there are
three allusions to grass—"this grass-plot," "this short-grass'd green,"
"this green land"—the writer expected a green stage cloth to be used.
These theories are, I suppose, those generally accepted, though it

[4] Lee Simonson in *The Stage is Set* (1932), p. 239, interprets the staging of *The
Knight of the Burning Pestle,* "in which an inn is made to serve for a castle and a
barber-shop for Barbaroso's cave and the court of Moldavia" as "a parody on the
scenic inadequacies of the open-air public theaters." These details, I suspect, rise
from the general plan of the piece rather than anything especially amusing in the
staging. To have aroused laughter here the staging usual at the private theater for a
castle must have differed from that for an inn. I know of nothing to suggest that it did.

must be noted that William Archer, *Quarterly Review*, CCXLI (1924), 408, objected to Chambers' insistence on visual verisimilitude and modernity of point of view, and Granville-Barker from his practical experience in the theater questioned Lawrence's reasoning in *RES*, IV (1928), 229-237: "The terminology of the theater has always been tiresomely inexact," he says. "The theater is inconsequence itself. It laughs at logic." His objection is also substantiated by such practical adventures with the Elizabethan stage as Stevens' at the Century of Progress or as others of us have tried in actual performance. The nonchalance of reference to absent settings as present, the easily shifting imagined location, the facility with which properties are moved about on the stage or ignored, all show how far removed the Elizabethan stage is from the rigidity of our modern realistic theater and are not easy to allow for in our speculation. Care and thoroughness, logic and consistency, are surely not out of place in any field of inquiry, but in such a one as this can land us only too easily in pedantic absurdity. Because I have myself emphasized textual allusions to properties as proofs of their presence, I am all the more anxious in view of the evidence I am about to describe, to re-examine these assumptions.

There can be no doubt that the Elizabethans did at least in some particulars delight in realism to an extraordinary degree. The evidence for this literalness of staging has been forcefully presented by Lawrence in his essays, "Elizabethan Stage Realism" and "Platform-Stage Spectacle" in *Pre-Restoration Stage Studies* (1927). It need not here be repeated, except perhaps one type of item to serve as examples of the fact that the Elizabethans were in some respects even more insistent on visual presentation than we are. Even the wandering company that put on *Cambises* in the 1560's had "a little bladder of vineger prickt" to represent the blood of a wound, and according to the "plot" of *The Battle of Alcazar* (1591) "3 violls of blood and a sheep's gather" (liver, heart, lungs) were provided to make, Greg suggests (*op. cit.*, p. 148), the butchery in the induction to the third act of the play more realistically horrible. These instances are early in our period.[5] Lawrence cites (*op. cit.*, pp. 238, 247) another bladder of blood used, according to directions, in *The Rebellion of Naples* (1640), for a decapitation, and a bloody sponge made a wound more convincing in Killigrew's *Princess*, late in the sixteen thirties. Montague Sumners in *The Restoration Theatre* (1934), pp. 201-202, gives other ex-

---

[5] A cut on the title-page of *The Maid's Tragedy* (1619), shows blood spurting from the wound in Aspatia's breast, but this picture with its landscape background can scarcely be taken as representing performance in the theater.

amples. So this trail of blood runs through the whole period and beyond. It must have been a messy nuisance; but what of that, we may hear the stage manager saying, if he could give the "understanding gentleman" a deeper thrill.

A Grand Guignol taste for horror may account for this particular realism; the simple desire to see for its own sake is gratified in such cases as *The White Devil*, V. i, where Brachiano, Vittoria, and others cross the stage as visual indication of their marriage, which is then commented on. Innumerable instances of this sort of thing could be cited. Certainly the Elizabethans wanted to see whatever could be represented and not merely to be told about it.

More important evidence of the Elizabethan attempts to visualize even slight hints in the texts appears, if Greg is right, in the item "j dragon in fostes" in Henslowe's inventory of the properties belonging to the Admiral's men in 1598. This is connected by Greg, *Henslowe Papers* (1907), p. 118, with this remote hint in *Dr. Faustus* (1604 ed., Chorus before sc. vii):

> Learned Faustus . . .
> Did mount himself to scale Olympus' top
> Being seated in a chariot burning bright,
> Drawn by the strength of yoky dragons' necks.

If the company went to the trouble of visualizing something so difficult and so entirely unnecessary as this, we cannot say the Elizabethans were indifferent to what they saw and that they asked only for something to imagine.

This dragon car and the bloody wounds really are to furnish spectacle; a manager might go to some trouble for this who would not bother to secure merely suggestive background. Such properties suggestive of background occur in the commonly known items from Henslowe's inventory; "j rocke, j baye tree, j tombe, j Hell mought, ij mose banckes," etc.—though these may also really have been used in the action. To these may be added his question-raising "The sittie of Rome" and "the clothe of the Sone & Moone."

Omitting the other commonly cited evidence for Elizabethan approaches to scenery, I cite for what it may be worth a passage in Heywood's *The English Traveller*, acted at the Phoenix and published in the early sixteen thirties. In it, 63-64, a house is being commented on: "What a goodly Gate . . . what braue caru'd poasts . . . what goodly faire Baye windowes . . . what a Gallerie, How costly Seeled, what painting round about . . . Terrast aboue, and how below supported."

Most readers, I am sure, would take these details as either entirely imaginary, like the "temple-haunting martlets" around Macbeth's castle, or as perhaps more or less descriptive of the front of the tiring-house. But in the margin of the quarto occurs, as if a direction to remind the stage manager of something to have in place, the single word "Bayes." Of course there may be other explanations, but if it really is a direction for settings, the implications for background settings are fairly important.

Among possible background settings are trees. They are often used in the action, but sometimes, like woods and forests, are only scenic. I shall not here repeat much evidence for this sort of setting, but cite only a few instances. Woods and forests are spoken of as present several times, 182, 185, 188, etc., in *The Four Prentices of London*, In *A Woman Killed with Kindness*, V. iii. 45, there is a single allusion to woods: Wendoll, watching Mrs. Frankford on her way along the road to the manor-house to die, says that he "asham'd of day, liue[s] in these shadowy woods," and in *II If You Know Not Me*, 303, Hobson, lost in a mist, appeals for help to Tawniecoat; "If thou beest acquainted in these woods, Conduct me to some town." We need not stop to decide now how literally these single allusions to woods are to be taken, but they are an important item in the problem.

Scenic properties are also suggested by the cuts on the title-pages of *Friar Bacon and Friar Bungay* (1630) and of *Dr. Faustus* (1616). Both seem to show the study settings of their respective plays. In both, certain suitable furnishings are pictured which are not referred to in the text nor necessary for the action.

(7)

Thus a considerable amount of evidence can be collected in favor of a visual realization of textual allusions and even for the presence of properties not mentioned in the text or the directions. But since this seems the prevailing view, these citations may be enough to submit at the moment. For evidence of the opposite method—the appeal to the imagination without much support in the way of settings—I turn, first, to an incident furnished by our Red Bull plays which is singularly clear in its implications; it has not, I think, been previously brought up in this connection.

Chambers, following his method of literal interpretation, has, as noticed above, been forced into supposing some sort of representation of a river on the stage. A scene in *The Two Noble Ladies*, printed by Bullen and by the Malone Society from a manuscript used by the prompter at the Red Bull, where the play was given between 1619 and

1623 by the Revels company, shows only too clearly how such a scene was handled there. In Act III, sc. iii, two soldiers enter, dragging in a young woman. The first soldier says:

Come, now w'are allmost at our iourney's end;
This is swift Euphrates, here cast her in . . .
2nd soldier: Come this way, this way, heare the streame is deepest.
1st: I am enforc'd I know not by what pow'r
     To hale her this way.
2nd: what strange noise is this?
1st: dispatch, the tide swells high.
2nd: what feind is this?
1st: what furie ceazes me?
2nd: Alas, I'm hurried headlong to the streame.
1st: And so am I, wee both must drowne and die.

Meanwhile, a young hero has rescued the lady.

Obviously this would be a difficult sort of thing to give realistically on any stage, but if a river was ever represented in any special way it should have been here. How it was actually managed is shown by the prosaically practical stage directions. When the soldiers exclaim, "What strange noise is this," "Dispatch, the tide swells high," the directions read, "Thunder. Enter 2 Tritons with silver trumpets;" and when one soldier says, "What feind is this," the direction explains, "The tritons ceaz the souldiers;" and when they say they are "hurried headlong to the streame," the direction is, "The Tritons dragge them in sounding their trumpets."

Thus no staging could be simpler. Not even the trap door was used nor the space at the side of the stage. Yet the sounding trumpets show that the stage manager was not neglecting the means of emotional appeal he did have at his disposal. We cannot therefore dismiss the whole scene as being given as it was from neglect or lack of effort.

Heywood's *The Rape of Lucrece,* a play published in 1608 as acted by the Queen's men at the Red Bull, offers a parallel case but with a difference. In it, 173, Tullia, according to the straightforward stage direction, "treads on her Father ['s body] & staies." But a page later, when the scene is described by Brutus, it is embroidered in this way:

                    when his body
Lay all besmeard and staynd in the blood royall,
Did not this Monster, this infernall hag,
Make her unwilling Chariotter drive on,
And with his shod wheeles crush her Fathers bones?
Break his craz'd scull, and dash his sparckled braines

ON (?) THE STAGE OF THE RED BULL

From the title-page of *Swetnam, the Woman-Hater*, 1620

Vpon the pavements, whilst she held the raines!
The affrighted Sun at this abhorred object,
Put on a maske of bloud, and yet she blusht not.

Had the description occurred without the direction I think even a conservative reader might at least have dallied with the idea of a chariot
if not also a sun.

I shall no more than refer to a passage, F 4-G iv, in *The Hector
of Germany*, since, though given at the Red Bull, *ca.* 1615, it was acted
not by a regular company but by a group of citizens. In this scene the
balcony represents a rock on which stands a young man; a group on
the front stage are supposed to be on a ship which approaches the rock,
anchors there, and finally takes off the young man and sails away.
Imagination could hardly go further on less, but possibly this may be
explained by the amateur nature of the performance.

Perhaps even more significant is a scene in *Swetnam the Woman
Hater*, a play given by the Queen's company at the Red Bull in 1618-
19 and published in 1620. The court ladies, tired of Swetnam's attacks
on their sex, decide to punish him. One of them engages him to meet
her in an orchard. There a banquet is commanded to be set forth for
him; when he enters he does not at first see it; he says, "Is this the
orchard"; then, he and perhaps two or more of the ladies sit. But then
the ladies begin to plague him. One of them says, "Bind him to this
Post," and presently another suggests that they try him. To the Queen
she says:

> Madame, we make you
> Ladie Chiefe Iustice of this Female Court,
> Mistris Recorder, I. Loretta, you
> Sit for the Notarie; Crier, she....

Then she continues:

> We want a Barre. O, these two foyles shall serue:
> One stucke i' the Earth, and crosse it from this Tree.

With these arrangements Swetnam is brought to the bar and the trial
proceeds.

From this text one would seem justified in supposing a table and
chairs or stools for the banquet, a post, a formal chair for the justice,
at least two seats for the other officials, a foil stuck in the ground to
support the other foil used as a bar, and a tree—not necessarily a large
one, but a tree of sorts—to support its other end. One might even suppose more than one tree to suggest the orchard setting.

But *Swetnam* has on its title-page a cut obviously intended to represent this scene. There stands Swetnam before the Justice, with his name inscribed beside him that there may be no mistake about it. As we should expect, there are a somewhat elaborate chair raised two steps for the Queen-Justice, a foil stuck in the ground, and another supported by it as the bar. But at the other end is not a tree at all but a turned post. Does that mean a post was used here on the stage? The picture does not exactly represent the stage setting. Table and stools for the banquet are lacking, but perhaps they were in another part of the stage, or had been removed; there still remain, also, the differences that the "Notarie" has no seat and is standing by the Justice's chair, and that there is also a barrier about the throne, unhinted at in the text. Yet the picture is not a freely imaginary one. The background shows a wall with two windows, and there is an artificial flooring of regular blocks, neither suitable for an orchard. It is of course possible that the artist read or observed the scene carelessly and confused the tree and the post. But he has been so careful with the foils that this hardly seems likely. Or, of course, the word *tree* may conceivably have been used to mean *post*—the dictionaries still give *post* as a meaning for *tree*—but the text is otherwise perfectly straightforward in its diction, and *tree* for *post* seems scarcely probable in language, though post for tree in the staging seems likely enough. Certainly the picture suggests that the tree in this scene was indeed only a post, perhaps the same post to which Swetnam was previously bound. Probably what happened was that the playwright, remembering his scene was an orchard, wrote "tree"; that the stage manager, with the post already there, used it instead—after all, one was as suitable as the other for the action; and that the artist drew what he saw.

Are the other textual allusions to trees in the Elizabethan drama similarly to be explained? Trees, as I pointed out in 1907—" 'Trees' on the Stage of Shakespeare," *MP*, V, 153-168—raise perhaps the most significant questions about Elizabethan staging of any of the properties. Allusions to them, especially if we interpret the forests and woods of the plays as made up of them, are so numerous and often so unexpected and apparently unnecessary, and the presentation of them with any approach to realism so bothersome, that if they really were used on the stage as often as they are called for, the whole problem of Elizabethan staging is fundamentally modified. Among the evidence I cited in support of the use of a forest-setting were the descriptions by Dr. Forman of performances in 1610, 1611 of *Macbeth, Cymbeline,* and *The Winter's Tale,* in which he mentioned woods as used, though the text suggests nothing of the kind. Now that the authenticity of these descriptions has been questioned—by J. Q. Adams, *Macbeth* (1931), pp. 293-298; Klein, "The Case of Forman's Booke of Plaies," *P. Q.*, XI (1932), 385-395, and Tannenbaum, *Shakesperian Scraps* (1933), pp. 1-35—the evidence for the use of trees is certainly weakened, and this *Swetnam* picture raises further doubt. Not only concerning the trees but other properties as well; for if a post could stand for a tree, a door might be the approach to a cave, stairs could be a hill to be climbed, and so on. This would be to approach almost oriental theatrical symbolism but might be no less true on that account.[6]

The importance of these passages from the Red Bull plays must not be overestimated. What was done at the Red Bull was not necessarily done at the Globe. But neither can they be ignored. The plays they are from were given well down in the century; the theater was no obscure, inadequately equipped one, but one of the most prominent in London, and rather given to spectacle than avoiding it. So far as any plays allow generalization about the Elizabethan theater, these do, and their evidence would seem strongly on the side of imaginative rather than of literal presentation.

So far I have mainly been discussing textual allusions. But stage directions were also sometimes expressed in dramatic instead of strictly technical theatrical terms. This is especially clear, for instance, as regards the balcony (see chapter V), variously called in the directions by its theatrical designation, uncolored by any dramatic significance, "aloft" or "above," or with dramatic suitability to the scene in which it occurs, "the walls" in battle scenes, "the window" or "the casement" where it represents the front of a house. Sometimes the directions are carefully accurate to the discomfiture of editors who ignorantly presume to change them, as in "Enter and knockes," (*Greene's Tu Quoque*, B, 188), which exactly describes the necessary action on the Elizabethan stage, rather than the—in modern conditions—more

---

[6] Perhaps to be noted here is the letter of Philip Gawdy concerning an accident which occurred at a performance by the Lord Admiral's men in London, November 16, 1587. This letter, presented by Chambers in *The Elizabethan Stage*, II, 135, describes how the players, "having a devyse in ther playe to tye one of their fellowes to a poste and so to shoote him to deathe" missed their aim and killed two members of the audience and wounded another. In a letter to *LTLS*, Aug. 28, 1930, Chambers connects this incident with *II Tamburlaine*, V. i, where according to the text the Governor of Babylon is hung in chains "vpon the citie walles," shot, and later in the scene his body removed. Of course the identification of the incident with *Tamburlaine* is not sure. And perhaps the balcony had posts, though I know of no other allusion to them. If one of the front stage posts was used as the walls in this play, we have another illustration of the loose way in which textual allusions were carried out.

logical sounding "Knock and enter." Sometimes they seem to use words in a special sense, for example, the familiar "Enter" to mean "Discover," as in "Enter a Shoemaker sitting upon the stage at worke," *George-a-Greene*, sc. xi. If prevailing theories of text transmission are correct, the same play may contain directions written some of them by the author, some by the prompter, and some by an "editor" with readers in mind; some of them must be taken literally and some more or less imaginatively. In short, the directions are about as difficult evidence to deal with as can be imagined—always excepting the allusions to staging in the dialogue, which are a little more slippery still.

(8)

The evidence at our disposal may thus seem to offer so dubious a basis that no sound conclusions are possible, but the case is not quite so bad as that. Certain procedures can be followed, and certain checks made use of to make results more sure. I have already emphasized the necessity of studying each play as a whole, and, though I do not print the complete staging for many plays, this has been planned for all of them. Also, by studying only the plays given at a single playhouse in a definite term of years, we can check one play against the others. The result shows, not the consistency we might expect, but that similar scenes were not always staged similarly (see below, chapter IV, on beds and thrones). By this study of all the plays at a given theater, we also learn what properties were in the storeroom and what effects were most in demand.

Much, however, must remain conjectural, and in that conjecture we are a good deal at the mercy of our basic assumptions, assumptions of which we may be scarcely conscious until we force ourselves to formulate them. They should, so far as we are able, be based not on our modern ideas of taste or propriety or even probability, but on what we can learn about the Elizabethan theater and its immediate past. We have noticed that the Elizabethans, though willing enough to imagine, were also on occasion keener even than we are to insist on realism and literalness in their performances. We cannot explain this contradiction by saying—as we might about ourselves, in view of recent plays without scenery—that one staging would be satisfactory at one time and one at another. The Elizabethans show few such signs of self-consciousness in their attitude toward the theater. As a matter of fact the greatest trouble for literalness seems to have been taken in plays most—from a modern point of view—inconsistent in staging.

In short, it must, I think, be clear from the Red Bull plays I have already cited that the dominant ideals of their staging are different from those which we are familiar with and which we tend to assume unconsciously in our study. We are on the wrong track when we look in Elizabethan staging for the consistency we demand to-day. Students have in the past been misled into trying to impose upon the Elizabethan stage the customs of their own theater. Rowe began it in his eighteenth-century stage directions, and the habit of mind has continued ever since. Thirty years ago scholars were mainly anxious to find a place in the Elizabethan theater for a front curtain; they seemed unable to imagine any stage without one. Then, when that attempt was shown to be unnecessary, the idea of imposing the orderliness of the alternation theory was taken up, but it also proved untenable. And now consistency and suitability seem the least we can ask. In doing so we are still committing the same error which has haunted this study from the beginning, that of reading the present into the past. Granville-Barker in his notable review of Chambers, *RES*, I (1925), 68, says Elizabethan illusion was one not so much of *seeing* as *hearing* and therefore did not require the clarity Chambers works so hard to attain. This is certainly true, though Granville-Barker's statement that the people in Shakespeare's theater were an "auditory" and almost nothing besides, must not be accepted too unreservedly either. A few of the Elizabethans expressed dissatisfaction with inconsistency of staging or inadequacy of spectacle, but only a few. What most of them seemed to work for and delight in was a—to us—strange mixture of realism and imagination. Many properties were employed and often a greater literalism insisted on than we demand to-day. Sometimes the effects secured were certainly inadequate, and sometimes—when realization was quite impossible—the Elizabethans said they were doing one thing and really did something quite different. Indeed, the conclusion is inevitable that the fuller their description the less likely is it to have been actually carried out. Properties could be referred to as present which were not there at all—as probably when there is in a play a single reference to a wood; or symbolized by something else —as a tree by a post. Sometimes, on the other hand, I think we may assume the presence of a suitable and easily obtainable property, such as a throne, in a scene where it is not mentioned at all, but for which it is especially appropriate.

This, however, suggests another important check. Though we may with propriety assume a throne even when it is not specifically mentioned, we are not usually justified in thinking that because something could have been done, it was done. Thus, it is unsafe to imagine the

balcony employed unless there is some definite suggestion of it; properties are, we know, often assumed in the text without any direction
for their being put in place; there is no sure case, at least in these plays,
of such a neglect to mention the balcony. And, further, we are also not
warranted in imagining what might have been, unless there is some
definite Elizabethan evidence for it somewhere. Take, for instance, the
removable stairs used by Stevens for entrance directly from the stage
to the balcony. For his purpose such an innovation was highly desirable, but it is surely questionable in historical investigation to build upon
such mere possibilities.

(9)

The final judgment on the questions raised in this chapter must be
that each piece of evidence has to be evaluated for itself. We cannot
generalize that all directions in even a text showing the prompter's
hand are to be taken literally, nor can we say that even all "literary"
directions have no basis in fact. Their trustworthiness varies with the
point under investigation. I suspect, too, that we must admit that
the same text and directions may have been given at some time with
a greater literalness than at others. Where a door served on the public stage, the court may have had a house setting. But whether all
properties were always materially present or not, the principle of the
staging was at least always the same; a play planned for simultaneous
presentation remained so even if a tree was represented by a post or a
cave by a door. Our main difficulty is to be conscious at all times of the
assumptions we are making, and so far as we are able, to think of the
stage as the Elizabethans did, uninfluenced by modern conceptions.

One more point must be mentioned—the system of reference I have
adopted. The usual designation by act and scene is not convenient
since many of these plays exist only in editions not so divided. Moreover, as Granville-Barker has emphasized in his Preface to *Hamlet*
(1937), p. 22, n., the very idea of act and scene division is wrong
as applied to most Elizabethan plays. Even if Lawrence's argument in
Speeding up Shakespeare (1937), pp. 1-16, convinces us that act divisions were customary, still scene divisions were, everyone admits, not
even momentary pauses. As one group of actors left the stage the next
entered. Even a mental scene division always carries with it an unfortunate connotation of a slight pause in the action though none really
occurred, and sometimes of change of location as well. Scene divisions
are not always easy to apply in the text, as, for instance, in battle scenes,
where there is much running in and out. A better division of the plays
than into scenes would be into sections based on the phases of the story,

but as different readers might not agree, such a basis for reference, especially in unfamiliar plays, would not be practicable. I have, therefore, not tried to be consistent. When plays exist in commonly accessible editions my references are made to them either by line or page, or sometimes by act and scene if that is most convenient for the point under discussion. For plays existing only in the old quartos I have used the signatures. In every instance where references are made to a modern edition which does not accurately represent the original directions, I have, of course, confirmed the references by the old copies.

CHAPTER IV

THE PROPERTIES

(1)

BEFORE considering the various parts of the stage, we shall find it advantageous to notice the properties used in the theater, especially the larger ones. This will serve to correct one or two general assumptions frequently made about the Elizabethan stage. The evidence connected with the properties shows clearly that the terminology of the stage directions is not at all exact; the same word at different times means different things. This evidence also makes it quite clear that we cannot assume that because a certain scene in one play was staged in a certain way, a similar scene in another play was staged in the same way. Few such customary procedures can be proved. Almost the only generalization we may be sure of is that since the Elizabethans were human they probably went to no extra labor without some good reason for it; ease and speed of performance are usually desirable considerations at any time.

Elizabethan plays have almost a stock list of imagined locations—palace scenes, parliaments and senates, bedrooms, studies, shops, tents, forests, caves, gardens, etc. Some of them center about large properties not much moved about in real life, or really immovable, such as beds, thrones, trees, tombs, great rocks. Others are various sorts of enclosures—shops, tents, caves, and the like. The latter obviously can be classed as structures analogous to the medieval "mansions," and the former are quite as eligible to be so considered as, shall we say, the sea of Galilee on the Valenciennes stage.

What did these various properties and backgrounds look like and how were they employed? Some were, it would seem, varied arrangements of an interior—the study, for example. Some suggest as well different exteriors of which the interior was also visible—the shop and, at least sometimes, the tent. Others were separate properties that symbolized rather than represented definite scenes—the bed, the throne, trees. It is not always easy, nor is it necessary, to discriminate between these classifications.

Very few directions occur for putting any of these properties in place, except the bed when some one is brought in in it. Usually the properties are simply referred to in the directions or dialogue as present. Does this mean they were already in place when the play began or that they are brought in by the stagehands as wanted?

(2)

Of the larger properties the throne has perhaps caused the most discussion, partly because of the frequency of its occurrence in the plays and partly because of differences of opinion concerning the interpretation of the evidence about it.

The most famous allusion to it is Jonson's complaint in the prologue to *Every Man in His Humor* of the "creaking throne [which] comes downe the boyes to please." Henslowe's *Diary*, Greg, ed. (1904-08), I, 4, also has a record: "Jtm pd for carpenters worke & mackinge the throne Jn the heuenes the 4 of Iune 1595 vij *ll*, ij *s*." On the principle that the simplest explanation is usually to be preferred, I have connected these allusions with the formal seat used so often in the plays. Lawrence disagrees with this identification, and thinks the Elizabethans kept the term "state" for the raised seat with a canopy used by exalted personages, and the term "throne" for the chair let down from above for gods and goddesses, or, to note a specific case, the throne which, according to the 1616 quarto of *Dr. Faustus*, descended and ascended before him in his last moments to show the heavenly seat Faustus had lost forever. Lawrence quotes in support of his idea, *Pre-Restoration Stage Studies* (1927), p. 315, the epilogue to Lovelace's lost play, *The Scholars*, published 1649:

> His *Schollars* school'd, sayd if he had been wise
> He should have wove in one two comedies.
> The first for th' gallery, in which the throne
> To their amazement should descend alone,
> The rosin-lightning flash and monster spire
> Squibs, and words hotter than his fire.
> Th' other for the gentlemen o' th' pit
> Like to themselves all spirit, fancy, wit.

"Why," Lawrence asks, "should the occupants of the gallery be amazed to see the throne descending unoccupied, if regal thrones commonly descended from above? The reference is surely to the surprise that would be felt on seeing the car come down without the usual god or goddess." But references to any descending throne, occupied or unoccupied, are not common in the plays, and when such a descent took place, it would, it seems to me, have been quite enough to amuse the boys and amaze the gallery. In any case, the amazement suggested by this quotation is not necessarily caused by the throne alone; there were also lightning, squibs, and oratory to arouse it. But I do not wish to press the point that the throne was necessarily stored in the hut above and manipulated from there. When it consisted of a seat shaded by a canopy and fastened on a dais I still think it would have been easier to lower it from the heavens than shove it in through the doors. But as will be shown presently, the formal seat was not always of this kind; when it consisted of a movable chair on a dais, or of several chairs, certainly one cannot imagine it lowered from the "heavens" with either safety or solemnity.

Specific mentions of the formal seat in the directions of the Red Bull plays are very few. Of the *A* plays, *Herod and Antipater* has a precise direction, in a dumb show, I 4v, "Augustus ... sets [Antipater] in his Chayre and Crownes him," and *If It Be Not Good*, 271, "Enter Alphonso (King of Naples) Crownde, wearing Robes Imperiall, Swordes of State, Maces &, being borne before him. . . . He takes his Seate; All kneele." *If You Know Not Me*, Part I, a *B* play, in its last scene, after a formal procession in which Queen Elizabeth enters under a canopy borne by four gentlemen, has "Queen takes state." Also in *The Royal King*, another *B* play, 25, II. iii, two banquets enter, at one "The King and the Prince in their State," but here "state" may refer to their general formality rather than specifically to their sitting on a raised throne. *Richard III*, IV. ii, quartos, a *C* play, has a direction, "here he ascendeth the throne," and in *The World Tost at Tennis*, D 3, another *C* play, Jupiter, who earlier in the masque descended from above, is directed to leave his "State." As there has been no direction for him to take his seat in some other place, "state" here seems to refer to the chair in which he descended from above.

Even these few directions show that Lawrence's careful distinction between throne and state is not supported by Elizabethan usage, and the textual allusions to the formal seat are equally varied in terminology. To cite a single instance: *The Costly Whore*, a *C* play, in less than twenty lines, V. i, calls the same piece of furniture, "this tribunall seate," "imperiall chayre," and "this state throne." It is also interesting to notice in this connection that in the passage from the *English Wagner Book* of 1594, which Chambers, *The Elizabethan Stage* (1923), III, 72, suggests as "the nearest approach to a pen picture of an Elizabethan stage," the seat for the King is called a "high Throne" and not a "state." Must we not conclude that "state" and "throne" may refer generally to the same property?

But it does not follow that the formal seat and the descending chair were always presented in the same way. What such a seat actually was is made fairly clear by its use in the various plays. The essential feature was a chair or arrangement of chairs or a bench able to seat one, two, or even three people, and elevated two or more steps. Lawrence (*op. cit.*, 312) say there was a canopy for the state, but there is no mention of a canopy attached to the throne in any of the Red Bull plays, even in scenes concerned with kings. The throne actually used by Elizabeth on a visit to Kimberley House, Norfolk, in 1578, exhibited in London at Christie's and pictured in the *Illustrated London News*, October 8, 1932, 533, consisted of a bench-cover and canopy all of a piece. The canopy and seat are definitely connected also in the picture of Gascoigne presenting his book to Elizabeth as she sits in a highly carved chair (J. D. Wilson, *Life in Shakespeare's England,* frontispiece). But a comic scene in *If You Know Not Me*, Part I, B, gives a different idea. Between two scenes with no set properties occurs a scene of less than a page, 223-224. In it Beningfield says to Barwick, "Is this the chair of state?" "I, sir, this is it." "Take it downe, and pull off my boots." Apparently Barwich removes the chair from its raised position and says, "Come on, sir." But the clown, who has overheard the conversation, says as Barwick struggles with the boots, "What a saucy companion's this? to pull off his boots in the chair of state," and then "pulls the chair from vnder [Beningfield]," who "beats him out." Quite clearly, this chair was elevated but not connected to dais or canopy. This chair had been used near the beginning of the play, 195, when Mary, after a formal entry, says:

> By God's assistance and the power of heaven
> We are instated in our Brothers throne.
> . . . Here we may sit secure.

And it is used again at the end of the play, where a direction reads "Queene takes State." A contemporary pictorial representation of a formal seat is given on the title-page of *Swetnam the Woman Hater,* A, where the queen, as Lady Chief Justice in the mock trial, sits in a large carved chair raised two, possibly three, steps; there is, I think, no canopy, though it is possible that what looks like a carved decoration may be one.

The seat in *Swetnam* is really for a mock judge; are we to imagine such a property used for judges in serious trial scenes? The direction already quoted from *If It Be Not Good* and the phrases employed in *The Costly Whore* suggest such an association. But it is hard to think that the six commissioners in *Sir Thomas Wyatt*, B, 120-124, or the six ambassadors who sat as judges in *The White Devil*, A, III. ii, occupied a set of chairs like that in the *Swetnam* picture. I mention the trial scenes in this discussion because of the above associations, but they belong, I think, rather by themselves. It is, perhaps, more important to include Parliaments, Senates, and the like in which a seat for some special person occurs. *The Rape of Lucrece*, A, has a raised seat, called "a regal throne," for Tarquin in its "parliament" scene, 168-174; *Appius and Virginia*, C, in I. iv, 50, a meeting of the Senate, speaks of a judgment seat, and probably used it also in IV. i, for that scene is later described, in V. ii. 73, as having a judgment seat, "an ivory chair."

It may also not be out of place to notice here the use of the word *pulpit* to designate a formal seat. *I Iron Age*, B, V, begins with the direction, "Enter Thersites with Souldiers, bringing in a table, with chayres and stooles plac'd aboue it"; these are for the hearing about Achilles' armor. Thersites says, "Come, come, spread, spread, vp with the pulpets straight, Seates for the Iudges." And this in turn suggests *Julius Caesar*. When Metellus kneels before Caesar, III. i. 33, Caesar is sitting. In the next scene Brutus, we are told, "is ascended," 11, he "goes into the pulpit," and a little later Anthony is directed by the third Plebeian to "go up into the public chair," 68, and clearly takes Brutus' place. Does it not seem likely that both Brutus and Anthony spoke from the raised dais of the formal seat, not, as is usually said, from the balcony, which would have removed them ineffectively from their audiences?

The unvarying feature of these formal seats is the dais with two or more steps on which the seat stood. Even in *Sir Thomas Wyatt*, B, 120-124, where there are two states, one for Guilford and one for Lady Jane Grey, Guilford at the bar calls to the six judges:

> Come downe, come down, heere at a Prisoners barre
> Better do so than iudge yourselues a misse.

It would appear, then, that there were not only the two regal states for Guilford and Lady Jane but also six raised seats for the judges. Perhaps in spite of the instances cited in which judges' seats, thrones, states, and formal seats of other kinds are alluded to by similar terms, the judges' seats and the public chair did not usually have a canopy and the throne or state usually did. But clearly we cannot be dogmatic about it. The Red Bull may have used different arrangements at different times—a bench, an elaborate chair, a chair with a canopy—each is possible.

The question of greatest interest about the formal seat is where it stood on the stage. Lawrence, while admitting a few cases of "states" on the front stage, thinks that normally they were placed on the rear stage[1] (*op. cit.*, p. 317). He does not see the awkwardness of a raised chair, especially when surmounted by a canopy, in the restricted height of the rear stage as it is usually imagined. But he does recognize, as Chambers (*op. cit.*, III, 89) does not, that no such chair with a dais could be quickly put in place or removed. When the throne recurs in two or more scenes in the same play, it seems likely it remained wherever it was, at least as long as there was use for it; and—if not too much in the way—perhaps longer. For instance, I suspect that the "hill," against which the bodies of the Tarquins were "reared" near the end of *The Rape of Lucrece*, is a dramatic way of alluding to the steps of the "regal throne," which had stood in place throughout the play. What else is it likely to have been?

Examination of the Red Bull plays shows that it is simpler on the whole to place the formal seat for one or two persons on the front rather than on the rear stage. Only two cases suggest a rear stage position, both are only inferred uses of the throne, and both raise considerable difficulties. In *The Golden Age*, A, II, where the direction reads, "Enter Saturn with wedges of gold and siluer, models of ships and buildings, bows and arrowes, &c.," it might be easier for Saturn to be discovered sitting in state, so that these properties could be arranged in place about him. But if so, then the next scene, which begins "Enters Sibilla, lying in child-bed, with her child lying by her, and her Nurse, &c.," would cause a "clash,"[2] for according to the same theories that would require the throne to be on the rear stage, surely this bed should be. Moreover, the throne occurs again in later scenes, where it seems certainly to stand on the front stage: in II. iv, Diana in "these shadowie glades" proceeds to "ascend our state," 29, and almost immediately Jupiter in the course of the hunt which follows, gets Calisto, 32, into

a place

Remote, an Arbor, seated naturally
Trim'd by the hand of nature for a bower,
Skreen'd by the shadowy leaues . . .

---

[1] Throughout this chapter I assume the existence of a permanent rear stage, as do most other students of the subject. Of course, if there was none, the various structures and properties stood exposed on the front stage, and the argument for simultaneous staging would be all the stronger.

[2] A "clash," in the technical jargon of this subject, occurs when two rear stages using different settings occur in succession. Theoretically they are impossible. "Clashes" may have been avoided by short unmarked intervals in the action, by "split" scenes, or by the use of two separate discoverable spaces instead of one. Each of these devices is discussed later.

All realistic theories of staging would have this arbor in the rear stage or an arrangement of it. To have first the throne and then the arbor in the curtained space would cause a great scurrying about, especially as the throne occurs again, 47, when Tytan is about to force Saturn "to be our foot-pace now To ascend our high tribunall." Such placing and replacing of an unwieldy property like the throne seems to me incredible, especially as almost the only reason for it is some fancied consistency. After all, the throne for Saturn, 11, is only inferred, not hinted at in dialogue or directions, and the assumed discovery of the enumerated small properties is prompted only by convenience. Perhaps Saturn was not seated but did really enter as the direction says, and the properties were borne in by the supers. Not much, then, can be built on this instance.

Edward II, a *B* play of dubious applicability, does have a scene, I. iv, in which it would be effective to have Edward and Gaveston discovered sitting on a throne. In the midst of the scene, without any explanation, comes a direction, "Enter King, Gaveston"; when the King says to the nobles who have been on in the former part of the scene, "What, are you moved that Gaveston sits here?" Lancaster replies, "Your grace doth well to place him by your side," and a little later Edward says, "Here, Mortimer, sit thou in Edward's throne." The King and Gaveston could, however, have entered and sat. The coronation scene, V. iv, in which a throne might also well be used, though there is no definite allusion to it in the text, follows a scene requiring a seat, and precedes a scene using a bed. This last "clash" could be avoided by a "split" scene of forty lines, but even that means a quick shift of large properties. The evidence of *Edward II* is mildly for a discovered throne, but aside from it and the still more dubious *Golden Age*, 11, just discussed, all formal seats for one or two persons can, according to Chambers' and Lawrence's methods of staging, as well be placed on the front stage as on the rear, and often better be so placed. This appears in the list below of "clashes" based on their theories; the conflicting rear stage scenes are placed in brackets. That not all of these scenes were, in my opinion, really rear stage scenes is not important.[3]

---

[3] In this list *A*, *B*, *C*, indicates the list to which the play belongs; *d* means that the formal seat is definitely required by the old directions; *t* that it is called for in the text of the dialogue but not in the directions; and *i* that it is only inferred from the general character of the scene as an appropriate setting. References in this list are to scenes even when I have had to use my own scene numbering. This allows briefer citation of evidence than by pages and shows more clearly the relations of the different sections of the play to each other. It will also, I think, cause little difficulty of verification if the reader wishes to consult the text. This list does not include all uses of the formal seat but only those in which "clashes" occur.

B *I If You Know Not Me:* sc. ii, throne (t); [sc. iii, a bed sounds as if discovered, but a "split" scene[4] is possible. Sc. v, seats for six]; sc. ix, throne (i); sc. xii "chair of state" (t); sc. xxiii, throne (d).

B *II If You Know Not Me:* sc. xv, throne (t); sc. xiii is the exterior and [sc. xiv the interior of a house]. I am not sure whether Lawrence and Chambers would for this reason make sc. xiv a rear stage scene or not.

B *The Travails of Three English Brothers:* sc. i, throne (i?); sc. iv, throne (i); sc. v, Papal seat, raised several steps; also raised seats for cardinals (t); [sc. x, banquet, seats for several]; sc. xi, throne (i?); sc. xii, a possible "split" scene [and then stocks, racks, assumed as present].

C *The Birth of Merlin:* I. ii, throne (t); [V. i, a rock on which a man stands and which incloses him; "Thunder and Lightning in the Rock." A "split" scene possible]. V. ii, throne (i).

A *If It Be Not Good:* [sc. i, a sleeping devil discovered (t); then a "split" scene possible]; sc. ii, throne (d); [sc. iii, has a table and seats for seven or more]; sc. iv, throne (i); [sc. v, a table "set out" with seats for three or more]; sc. ix, throne (i); [sc. xi, tree (d), and grove (t); sc. xiii, a table seems discovered; sc. xv, bed, perhaps discovered; sc. xvii, four discovered (d); curtains closed (d), followed by a "split" scene of two pages]; then three judges of hell "each take his state" (t), and presumably Pluto does also.

A *The Golden Age:* I. ii, throne (t); sc. iv, throne (i); [sc. v, bed; II. ii, banquet, seats for 6]; sc. iv, throne (t) in a forest (t); [sc. vi, arbor (t)]; III. vii, throne (t).

A *The Brazen Age:* II. x, throne (i); [sc. xi, a discovery of "two fiery bulls" (d)].

A *The Honest Lawyer:* in the last scene, a raised seat for a judge; a tree, which is climbed (d), and bushes (d); bar (t) for a trial.

---

[4] The term "split" scene, used frequently in this list and elsewhere, is well illustrated by this instance. Scene ii begins with a formal entry by Queen Mary, and in the second line of the scene she says, "We are instated in our Brothers throne." This line may be taken figuratively, but the scene which follows is a formal hearing in which a throne might fittingly be used. In this scene a commission is dispatched to visit Elizabeth, and in the next they arrive at the place where she is confined. Her attendant tries to persuade them not to trouble her, but one of them says, "Presse after her my Lord," a direction reads, "Enter Elizabeth, in her bed," and the first speech following is by Elizabeth, "We are not pleased with your intrusion, lords." This occurs some thirty-five lines after the beginning of the scene. Elizabeth may well have been discovered, though Elizabethan usage permitted her actual entrance. These thirty-five lines, then, could have been given on the front stage, thus forming a "split" scene, during which the throne could have been removed from the rear stage and the bed substituted. Of course, the fact that a "split" scene can be arranged does not prove that it was, and I have not much belief that the device was often used. It is really a hold-over from the argument for the alternation theory of staging, according to which no setting could stand on the front stage and which made such a device necessary. My impression is that these thirty-five lines were actually given on the front stage, but rather to allow the effective business of pressing into Elizabeth's chamber than for a quick change of settings.

B *The Royal King:* II. iii, throne (t?); III. ii, throne (i); V. iii, throne, perhaps figurative—"the State 'fore which I stand"; in the same scene a study; moreover, a bar is set out for a trial, seven sit, and a block and scaffold are ordered.

A *The Virgin Martyr:* [V. i, a study; "split" scene possible]; V. ii, throne (i).

B *The Welsh Ambassador:* III. ii, throne (t); [III. iii, begins with an almost certain discovery; no hint of a "split" scene]; V. ii, study (d); "split" scene possible; V. iii, throne (i).

In this list there is no instance where the formal seat *must* have been discovered, there are several where the seat could have been on the rear stage only if a "split" scene was used, and there are five: *II If You Know Not Me, The Brazen Age, The Honest Lawyer, The Royal King,* and *The Welsh Ambassador,* all *A* or *B* plays, in which this arrangement is not applicable, and in which the throne, if used at all, seems to have stood on the front stage.

Placing the formal seat for one or two on the front stage also permits an easy staging for plays in which this setting occurs several times:

B *Sir Thomas Wyatt:* sc. ii, two "chairs of state" (t), but possibly figurative; [sc. v, sounds, 92, as if discovered—a council]; sc. ix, throne (t), but possibly figurative; sc. xiv, two chairs of state (t), also [six seats, raised, for judges (t)].

B *II If You Know Not Me:* see above.

C *Nobody and Somebody:* sc. i, throne (i); sc. ix, throne (t); sc. xiii, formal seat for king and two others (t).

B *The Travails of Three English Brothers:* see above.

A *The Rape of Lucrece:* sc. ii, throne (t), [also benches for senate; sc. v, Apollo's temple; sc. vii, Lucrece's; sc. ix, (last part) in tent; sc. x, Lucrece's; sc. xiv, bed, discovered; sc. xviii; Lucrece's; sc. xx, in tent]; sc. xxi, a hill (t). The staging of this play is especially interesting and will be commented on later more fully. This full schedule belongs here only if the tentative suggestion made above is true that the steps of the throne are the hill of sc. xxi.

A *The Golden Age:* see above.

B *The Hector of Germany:* sc. iii, throne (i); [sc. vii, garden bank]; sc. xix, throne (t?); sc. xxvii, throne (t), also lists (t).

B *The Royal King:* see above.

A *Swetnam the Woman-Hater:* III. i, two judges seated, a bar (d); sc. iii, seats apparently for King, two judges, two champions; [IV. vi, probably discovery of a hearse and body]; V. ii, the scene discussed in chapter III, laid in an orchard, using a bar, a post, judge's seat, etc.

A *Herod and Antipater:* I. iii, "tribunal-throne," with seats for three (t); sc. v, throne (i); II. i, "tribunal" (d); sc. ii, throne (d); [IV. ii, rack

assumed]; sc. iii, throne (d); V. ii, a prison, in same scene a scaffold
brought in (d).

This list of recurrences enforces the evidence of direct clashes and
helps to show the impracticability of supposing that the throne always
stood on the rear stage or that it was removed from the front stage
to prevent its presence in scenes in which it was not suitable. *The
Honest Lawyer*, with its judge's chair in the same scene as bushes and
a tree, and *The Royal King*, with a throne in a scene with a study, show
that the stage managers did not think such extra labor necessary. The
conclusion for the Red Bull plays must be that sometimes, at least, the
throne or formal seat for two or three persons stood on the front
stage, and there is little or no evidence that it ever stood on the rear
stage.

How formal seats for more than two or three were managed is less
clear; for one thing, there are fewer examples. Some of these have
been perforce included in the list above; others are as follows:

A *The White Devil:* III. ii, a hearing, at least eight seats; the scene is
almost certainly discovered. Scenes i and iii seem excellent examples of front
stage scenes.

B *The Silver Age:* III. xiv, the last scene of the play; Pluto's "tribunall,
made of sable Iet," and his "chaire" are mentioned, 159, before the scene,
but in the scene itself, which begins on the same page, no seat is referred to,
though Pluto, Proserpine, the Judges of Hell, and the Fates might properly
be seated. If any seats were used they may well have been discovered.

A *The Devil's Law Case:* IV. ii, officers prepare seats for two judges (d);
two bars, with two seats probably at each; a trial by combat; V. v, "The
Lists set up;" three judges sit (d).

B *Two Merry Milkmaids:* III. ii, a study (d); III. iii, "the forme of a
court" (d), a bar, several to be seated; a "split" scene possible.

A *The Heir:* V. iii, a trial, three judges.

Of the cases where several seats are involved, the evidence is uncertain in *Sir Thomas Wyatt, The Devil's Law Case, Swetnam*, III. i.
iii, and *The Heir.* In *The Silver Age*, and in *Two Merry Milkmaids*
indications rather favor a rear stage position, and the trial in *The
White Devil* seems certainly on the rear stage. In such parliament or
senate scenes as occur in *The Rape of Lucrece* and *Appius and Virginia*
the seat for a special person could still have stood on the front stage
while the "forms" or "benches" for the members (since the placing of
them would take some time) might be on the rear stage. *II If You
Know Not Me, The Travails of Three English Brothers, If It Be*

Not Good, The Golden Age, The Hector of Germany, The Royal King suggest a front stage position.[5]

One way of solving this problem of persons discovered on thrones is to suppose that the formal seat had its own curtain. Such a seat is

[5] Lawrence's argument on the position of the state (*op. cit.*, pp. 316-321), should receive some further attention, even though many of the plays he cites lie outside the repertory of the Red Bull. It is true that Davenport's *King John and Matilda*, p. 1655, has explicitly (D 2v), "A Chaire of state discover'd, Tables and Chaires responcible, a Guard making a lane; Enter between them King John, Pandulph [and several others]. After them [three others]. The King (holding the Crown) kneeling on the left side of the Chaire, Pandulph possessing it"; but I cannot follow Lawrence in the conclusion that "this one direction alone establishes the rear stage as the normal position for the state." The Elizabethan theater allows no such sweeping generalizations; one direction does not establish a custom at even a single theater. Lawrence cites fifteen other instances of a state, which, he thinks, corroborate his opinion.

Of these fifteen *If It Be Not Good, The Birth of Merlin,* and *Edward II* have already been discussed; none has the throne surely on the rear stage. Of the remaining twelve, one, *The Death of Robert, Earl of Huntington,* offers a clear case; (Hazlitt's Dodsley, viii, 252) "Draw [i.e. open] the curtain; the king sits sleeping" and characters ascend to him. In *King John,* IV. ii, the king opens the scene: "Heere once againe we sit: once against crown'd," and the scene might well use a throne. It follows the scene in which Arthur was to be blinded, and the executioners hid behind the arras, but which also used a chair. In sc. iii Arthur jumps from the walls. The throne may have been behind the arras, but there is no clear indication that it is. But of the ten other instances five seem to give no sure indication as to the position of the throne: *Look About You,* last scene, does have a throne seating a king, two queens, and, lower down, two lords, but the position is not indicated. *Henry V,* I. ii, has "here in presence" and "this Imperiall Throne," and *Cymbeline,* III. i, might appropriately use a throne, but there is no hint in dialogue or directions and the position is left uncertain. Lawrence thinks *Antonio and Mellida,* II. i, 643, pretty decisive: it does mention a state and says the attendants "make a ranke for the Duke to passe through," but this could equally well be done if the throne stood on the front stage. *The Coronation,* II. iii, Lawrence thinks is a clear case of a discovery, perhaps because the modern direction begins the scene, "Sophia crowned and seated under the state"; but the direction in the 1640 edition reads, "Enter Queen" and six others. At line 11 she says, "This crowne sits heavy Vpon my brow," and four pages later a direction reads, "She comes from the state." Perhaps she was discovered, but she may have entered and taken her place on the throne, and once again the place of the throne is not made sure. Nor is there any clear indication where the Queen's seat stands in *The Dumb Knight,* I. iii: "Place there the queen's seat, And there and there chairs for the combatants," and "Place here the lists; fix every joint as strong, As 'twere a wall." Certainly none of this sounds like a rear stage arrangement. Later the Queen "descends"; so her chair was raised above the stage level.

The remaining four cases which Lawrence cites to support his view that the state stood on the rear stage, seem rather to controvert it:

Antonio's Revenge: V. v; here it is doubtful whether a formal seat is required, for a throne or state is not mentioned. Piero, the duke, is to feast with the masquers. He says, "Here Piero sits; Come on, vnmaske, lets fall to." This scarcely sounds formal; he is not like Lady Macbeth, who at a state dinner did "keep her state," and, I think, really sat on the throne. As the scene proceeds, Piero is bound, his tongue is plucked out, he is murdered. Then "The curtaines are drawne, Piero departeth." Thus his chair is, it is true, behind curtains, but it is not necessarily, or even probably, a throne.

perhaps shown in a picture of a simultaneous setting at Cologne, 1581, reproduced in Cheney, *Stage Decoration* (1928), plate 21. Such a property would serve well with other separate structures, such as are shown in this picture, though I must confess I do not see how an actor

---

The Prophetess, IV. iv, is cited by Lawrence. It definitely used a formal seat for two persons, but there is nothing to show whether this stood on the front or the rear stage. The same play, II. iii, has two persons, one the Prophetess, "Enter in a Throne drawn by Dragons." They "hang" as spectators, while on the stage below Diocles is raised "to the tribunal" and made emperor. The persons below exeunt; the prophetess says, "Mount up, my birds," and the direction says, "Ascends throne," which means, I think, that the throne rises. In this scene the throne and the tribunal are certainly separate properties, but the throne is not on the rear stage and the tribunal need not be.

The Devil's Charter: I do not understand Lawrence's citation of this play for this argument. At least one and perhaps two tents and a study are on the stage at the same time; if in such circumstances we can talk at all of a rear stage, Lawrence would, I suppose, identify it with the study, and this identification seems likely since the study recurs throughout the play. The play offers many problems, but I shall note here only the arrangements for Act V, since that is what Lawrence refers to. In its fourth scene there is "a cuppord of plate brought in," and then "enter a table spread, Viandes brought in . . . enter Alexander in his pontificalls . . . the Pope taketh his place, three Cardinalls on one side and captaines on thother." Near the close of the scene comes the direction, "Alex. to his studie," so this table with its seats must be outside the study and hence on the front stage. Sc. vi shows "Alexander vnbraced betwixt two Cardinalls in his study looking vpon a booke, whilst a groome draweth [opens] the Curtaine." After Alexander makes a short speech, "They place him in a chayre vpon the stage, a groome setteth a Table before him." This scene is therefore on the front stage. A little later "Alexander draweth [opens] the Curtaine of his studie [it must have been closed during the intervening action] where he discouereth the diuill sitting in his pontificalls." But this is clearly the seat in the study, not the throne at all. For that we must turn to the Prologue where there is "a chaire on midst of the Stage," around which a magic circle is drawn and in which Alexander, dressed as Pope, is, it would seem, finally seated, and to Act II, l. 1114, where Alexander, after defying Charles from the walls, "marcheth solemnly through" and "being set in state" receives him. Charles, "being presented vnto the Pope, kisseth his foote, & then advancing two degrees higher, kisseth his cheeke." This throne could not have been in the study, and there is no hint that it is concealed by curtains in any way.

Nor can I see why Lawrence refers to *The Downfall of Robert, Earl of Huntington*, IV. i. Here—"Enter Iohn crowned"—perhaps a throne is employed. If so, it would seem to be on the front stage, for in the preceding scene, four pages before, a direction says, "Curtaines open, Robin Hood sleepes on a greene bancke." Possibly the bank was removed in the act interval—if there was one—but there is no hint that this was done. And in Act I there is the direction, "Ely ascends the chaire . . . [Robin and Marian] sit downe within the curtains . . . drawing [opening] the curteins, all (but the Prior) enter, and are kindely recieued by Robin Hoode. The curteins are againe shut." And Skelton continues the induction. Here the formal seat is surely *before* the curtains, an interesting opposition to the clear case of its being *behind* the curtain in *The Death of Robert*, already commented on.

Thus of Lawrence's sixteen citations to prove the position of the state, three do definitely show it was concealed by a curtain, eight are indefinite as to its position, three do not concern a state at all, and two seem to me clearly to place the state *outside* instead of within the rear stage. The other instances he cites of the uses of

could scurry into this particular seat without attracting considerable attention. In any case, it hardly seems necessary to suppose such a property to have been generally used, since in the total number of throne scenes so few instances of certain discoveries are called for.

A hint on the position of the throne is found in the sixth chapter of Dekker's *The Guls Horn-Booke:*

Whether therefore the gatherers of the publique or private Play-house stand to receive the afternoones rent, let our Gallant (having paid it) presently advance himselfe up to the Throne of the Stage. I meane not into the Lords roome (which is now but the Stages Suburbs): No, those boxes, by the iniquity of custome, conspiracy of waiting-women and Gentlemen-Ushers, that there sweat together, and the covetousnes of Sharers, are contemptibly thrust into the reare, and much new Satten is there dambd, by being smothred to death in darkness. But on the very Rushes where the Comedy is to daunce, yea, and under the state of *Cambises* himselfe must our fethered *Estridge,* like a piece of Ordnance, be planted valiantly (because impudently) beating downe the mewes and hisses of the opposed rascality.

The implications of this passage seem to me clear enough. The gull, wanting to show off, is not to go to the stage box ("the Lords roome"), but to plant himself on the stage in full view, where the comedy dances, right by the throne. Lawrence, in his article on the throne, *Texas Review* (January, 1918), 96, says quite properly that "the throne of the stage" is metaphorical, but misses what seems to me the obvious implications of the reference at the end. The gull is to sit by the "state," which stands where the dancing takes place for there he will be most conspicuous and the greatest nuisance. But since the most conspicuous place is surely the front stage and the dancing must take place there, that is where the state must stand. And certainly the gull would not allow himself to be hidden from view by the curtain during all merely front stage scenes, as he must have been if he sat by the throne and it was on the rear stage. If one citation could prove anything, this one, it seems to me, would make the front stage position of the throne conclusive.

But one instance, even a generalized one like this, does not clinch matters. No blanket generalization seems possible; there are too many "perhaps's" and "might be's." Still this dubiousness is something. The

---

a throne or state, but not necessarily to be discussed here since he does not use them to prove the position, show about the same result. One, indeed, *The Valiant Welshman,* III, IV has irremovable "clashes" of the throne with woods, a cave, and a temple. On the whole, then, even Lawrence's picked cases do not show that the throne or state was always or even usually discovered. In three cases it was, but in three others it could not have been on the rear stage. His other examples are either inapplicable or uncertain.

throne or state—I see no reason to distinguish them—did not *always* stand on the rear stage at the Red Bull; of that we are sure. Instead, the evidence of possible "clashes," and especially of the recurring use of the throne in the same play, definitely favors a front stage position.

Finally, then, how shall we picture these formal seats? They were all, as I have said, raised two or more steps. Sometimes, especially as the thrones of kings, they may have had a canopy, though the Red Bull plays do not require this. The seat itself may have been one chair, two chairs, three chairs sometimes at different levels, or sometimes a bench. On the whole the throne seems at the Red Bull to have stood on the front stage and to have remained in place as long as it was needed, perhaps even longer. It was stored, I still am inclined to believe because of Henslowe and Jonson, in the "hut" above and manipulated from there. But in view of its different forms perhaps we should not say "it" but "they," and "they" would naturally be taken care of differently.

I doubt if the seats for judges, commissioners, and the like were really much like the formal seats for kings, in spite of the three or four "states" for the judges of Hell in *If It Be Not Good*. However, sometimes, at least, the seats for judges were raised; when there were several to be provided, they may have been more frequently placed on the rear stage than the front; it would have saved time to do so.

(3)

Beds are among the most commonly used of the large properties; there are in the Red Bull plays seventeen scenes in which a bed seems certain and one doubtful case. One reassuring circumstance is that it is difficult to see how anything else could have been passed off for a bed (as, for example, a post for a tree), but the beds themselves may, of course, have differed in elaborateness.

One form of stage bed is presumably shown in the illustrated cuts of *The Vow Breaker*, William Sampson's play of 1636. It shows a heavy four-poster with curtains, the occupant lying, possibly owing to the lack of skill of the artist, in a most uncomfortable position. Bed curtains are specifically mentioned only in *II Iron Age*, 411; "Enter Egisthus with his sword drawne, hideth himselfe in the chamber behind the Bed-curtaines." But curtains, whether of the bed or of the rear stage, are also alluded to in the dialogue of *The Rape of Lucrece*, 222, and *The Golden Age*, 69. With curtains the bed must have been a pretty sizable and cumbersome property. The Henslowe inventory mentions "j bedsteade," l. 57.

The bed-scenes in the Red Bull plays are significant especially in that they show how unsafe *a priori* arguments are about the Elizabethan stage. One might be pardoned for thinking that the Elizabethans would stage similar scenes similarly, and that bed-scenes, in particular, would always have been discovered on the rear stage; that stage could realistically represent a bedroom, and unceremoniously to shove a bed with a person in it out on the front stage seems to us not merely startling but really a little amusing.

These considerations had no weight with the Elizabethans at the Red Bull as the following list of the bed-scenes shows:[6]

B *A Woman Killed with Kindness:* V. v; *out* then *in;* "Enter Mistress Frankford in her bed;" 100 lines. Rear stage.

B *I If You Know Not Me:* 198-201; *out* then *in;* "Enter Elizabeth in her bed" with two doctors; 75 lines. Rear stage.

A *The Rape of Lucrece:* 221-225; *out* then *in;* "Lu[crece] discovered in her bed," and Sextus comments how she lies "beneath these curtaines"; 115 lines. Rear stage.

A *The White Devil:* IV. ii; *out* then *in;* l. 69, "come, Ile lead you to her" [i.e. Vittoria]; l. 72, "Enter Vittoria" [to these visitors]—she is probably discovered; l. 130, "She throwes herselfe upon a bed"; 68? lines; the next scene uses a window below, and the terrace. Rear stage.

V. iii: *out* then *in;* "Enter Brachiano presented in a bed, Vittoria and others" [with him]; those already on the stage say, "See, heere he comes"; 66 lines; in the earlier part of the scene, barriers are used and a man withdraws to a "cabinet"; the scene following has a discovery behind a "travers"; an interval of 158 lines between the last use of the bed and this discovery is possible. Rear stage, perhaps, but the "heere he comes" suggests the bed was moved out on the front stage; if so, it should have been back at l. 172, "Strangle him in private," for there is no other hint of the removal of the body.

A *If It Be Not Good:* 338-342; in this scene Barterville exits, 340, and seven lines later speaks feebly as though dying; thus the scene is *out* then *in;* he says, "the bed I rise from Count I my death-bed"; 15 lines by the bed; the next scene uses the balcony and a trap. Rear stage.

A *The Golden Age:* 16-19; the scene begins, "Enter Sibilla lying in child-bed, with her child lying by her, and her Nurse, etc."; 152 lines; the scene before may use a throne (i), the following scene, nothing. Front or rear stage.

67-69; the scene begins, "Enter the foure old Beldams, drawing out

---

[6] In this list *A, B, C,* show as usual the relative authority of the play; the phrase "*out* then *in*" means that the scene is supposed to begin outside the bedroom and then changes to it; the number of lines—only approximate—shows how much of the scene is in the immediate vicinity of the bed; the next item notes the settings for the immediately adjacent scenes—if nothing is said, these scenes have no settings of significance; and finally a guess is hazarded as to whether the bed was on the front or the rear stage.

Danae's bed: she in it"; 69, she says, "Before you come to bed, the curtaines draw"; 70, "The bed is drawne in"; 118 lines. Front or rear stage. This is a gate sequence, raising special problems; see chapter VI.

B *The Silver Age:* 152-155; 154, "Enter Semele drawne out in her bed"; 13 lines spoken by her in bed; "As [Jupiter from a cloud] toucheth the bed it fires and all flyes vp, Iupiter from thence takes an abortiue infant." It seems that the bed must have been on the front stage in order for the ascent to be arranged.

A *The Brazen Age:* 235-239; Nymphs "strow faire Venus bed" (t) with flowers in "an obscure cave." Vulcan spreads a net of wire and catches Mars and Venus in it; they are viewed on from above by the gods. It seems therefore that this bed may better be taken as the "violet banke" of 184, and not counted among the true bed scenes. There are approximately 75 lines beside the couch; it stands in the cave.

A *II Iron Age:* 411-414; the scene begins, "Enter Egisthus with his sword drawne, hideth himselfe in the chamber behind the Bed-curtaines"; 55 lines. Rear stage.

B *The Hector of Germany:* sc. i; the scene begins, "A Bed thrust out, the Palsgraue lying sicke in it, [3] entring with him" . . . "The Bedde drawne in"; 36 lines. Front stage.

A *The Devil's Law Case:* III. ii; *out* then *in*, at least this is the impression: after 70 lines in which the surgeons discuss Contarino's affairs, they say, "Here is the Subject you must worke on," and there is a direction, "Contarino in a bed." The scene ends 110 lines later with the men working over him; the next scene opens with an almost certain discovery of two persons sitting by a table. Rear stage.

B *Edward II:* V. v, at line 24 the murderers are told, "Here is the keys, this is the lake," i.e. the dungeon knee-deep with water where the king is confined, or as some amend it, the lock of the dungeon. They apparently bring him out and at line 71 say to him, "Lie on this bed and rest yourself awhile." They murder him on it. Clearly not *out* then *in.* If the "dungeon" was the rear stage, then the bed was on the front stage; if the "dungeon" was a door leading from the rear stage then the bed could have been on the rear stage. Scene before, throne (i); 21 lines by the bed.

C *All's Lost by Lust:* IV. ii, the scene begins, "A bed discovered, on it Lazarello . . . enter [2] with a halter." Morris queries whether Margaretta carries or drags the body out; there is no hint in the text of either. She enters with the body in V. v; 55 lines. Rear stage.

B *The Two Merry Milkmaids:* IV. iii; "A Bed thrust out" in the midst of a scene; the text says, "Zfoote, he shifts his Rome." This hardly sounds like an out scene, followed by a discovery, but rather as if the bed were moved to the front stage; 155 lines.

A *The Virgin Martyr:* IV. i; the scene begins, "A bed thrust out, Antoninus upon it sick, with Physicians about him," and two others; perhaps 150 lines; in the next scene, half way through it, 68, a pillar is set up in the middle of the stage and several seats are necessary. Front stage or rear.

B *The Wonder of a Kingdom:* III. iii; the scene begins, "A Bed discovered. Fyametta upon it. Enter [ten or more] ut antea Fyametta"; 38 lines. Rear stage.[7]

In these seventeen scenes which certainly used a bed, nine, according to the above arrangements, stood on the rear stage and remained there, four seem to have been out on the front stage, and four may have been either on the front or the rear stage. But the ingenuity of modern scholars and the real ambiguity of Elizabethan terminology have given rise to other explanations. Scholars like Albright and Thorndike, dead set against the presence of properties on the front stage, interpret "set out," "thrust out," and so on, as meaning put on the *rear stage.* Lawrence, *Pre-Restoration Stage Studies,* (1927), pp. 304-310, adequately disproves this conclusion, but, warning against the danger of generalization on a few instances, still ventures upon two which, if true, would also change the stagings suggested above: (1) " 'set out' in a direction at the beginning of an act or scene . . . means 'place in position on the rear stage,' "; and (2) "in most scenes where its occupant had to say anything more than a few monosyllables, the bed was thrust out." The Red Bull plays do not support these conclusions. If we take the directions with absolute literalness, with "enter" meaning enter on the front stage and never "discovered" on the rear stage, and "thrust out" in its natural significance, as put out on the front stage, there would be, according to definite directions, three

---

[7] The following are included merely to show they have not been overlooked; no beds were, I think, used on the stage.

B *Greene's Tu Quoque:* 273-279; a bed is mentioned and a man is tied to a post, but the bed need not be on the stage.

C *A Match at Midnight:* H 2—H 4, "Enter in her nightcloathes, as going to bed"; a bed is mentioned in the text, but is "within."

Perhaps the couch of *Revenge for Honor,* IV. i, may best be mentioned here. In this scene Abrahen says,

Take these royal bodies,
And place them on that couch; here where they fell
They shall be embalmed. Yet put them out of our sight.

Abrahen exits a few lines later, and one of the supposed dead comes to life, and goes out after some thirty lines of monologue. Near the middle of his speech he addresses his dead companion. Thus it is not clear whether the bodies were concealed or not. Nothing is said of removing the other body.

In the next scene a man is stabbed, and the servant directed to "help to convey him into's chamber." Sixteen lines later the dialogue shows the body. The scene continues without further reference to the body; it was perhaps again concealed some ten lines after it was disclosed. Whether the couch was used in the second scene, there is no hint, but together the scenes suggest a couch in a concealed space.

instances of beds with occupants discovered (*The Rape of Lucrece*, *All's Lost by Lust*, *The Wonder of a Kingdom*), and one where the direction does not explicitly say "discover" but implies it (*The Devil's Law Case*). Of the two instances of unoccupied beds, that of *Edward II* may be on the front or rear stage and that of *II Iron Age* seems definitely on the rear stage. In four instances the direction says "enter" but seems from the general situation to mean "discovered" (*A Woman Killed with Kindness*, *I If You Know Not Me*, *The White Devil*, IV. ii; V. iii; *The Golden Age*, 16-18 leaves one in doubt). As for "drawn out," "thrust out," etc., *The Silver Age*, *The Hector of Germany*, *The Two Merry Milkmaids* definitely sound as if they meant the bed to be put out on the front stage, while *The Virgin Martyr*, because of the accompanying physicians, would be less awkward if the bed were on the rear stage, and that of *The Golden Age*, 67-69, may also be there.

As for Lawrence's generalizations, "set out" does not occur in connection with the beds at the Red Bull. As to his second, an inspection of the list above raises considerable doubt. Not only should the number of lines spoken by the occupant of the bed be noted, but also how many are spoken close by the bed by anybody. Of the rear stage scenes, *A Woman Killed with Kindness*, *The Rape of Lucrece*, *The White Devil*, IV. ii, *II Iron Age*, *The Devil's Law Case*, *All's Lost by Lust*, *The Wonder of a Kingdom* all have at least thirty lines by the bed, and in all but *The Devil's Law Case* and *All's Lost by Lust* the occupant of the bed says a good deal more than "a few monosyllables." According to Lawrence these beds should have been brought to the front stage, but text and directions do not hint this. On the other hand, the scenes in which beds seem brought out on the front stage do not have unusually long passages at the bed. For instance, in *The Hector of Germany* there is only a page by the bed and in *The Silver Age* hardly more. The latter, in which the bed is set on fire, suggests there are other reasons than Lawrence mentions for putting the bed on the front stage. I do not see that any rigid rule about the bed-scenes is possible nor any single explanation of why beds were thrust out on the front stage. That they were, however, is sure.

The bed scenes in which other persons are said to enter with the occupant (see above: *The Woman Killed With Kindness*, *I If You Know Not Me*, *The White Devil*, *The Golden Age*, *Hector of Germany*, *The Virgin Martyr*) suggest the possibility that a rolling stage like the Greek *exostra* or *eccyclema* may have been employed; see Lily B. Campbell, *Scenes and Machines on the English Stage* (1923), pp. 63-64, 136-140, 212. Awkward as a bed thrust out upon the stage in the midst of the action must seem to us in any circumstances, the awkwardness is surely increased if it trails after it one or more persons supposed to be standing or sitting by it. A rolling stage would certainly make such a presentation much less disconcerting for us. But we are not sure that the Elizabethans were troubled at all by this sort of situation, and there is no definite evidence in the Red Bull plays—nor I think elsewhere—that they actually used any such solution as a rolling stage. We may, therefore, think of this machine as a possibility but hardly as a certain feature of the Red Bull equipment.

(4)

Scenes using trees, forests, gardens, arbors, caves, rocks are curiously and almost inextricably related. They must, therefore, be considered more or less together.

The question of determining what sort of settings served for a single tree and for groups of trees and where these stood on the stage has already been noticed (chapter III). The Red Bull plays are of less help in answering this than one would, in view of their generally spectacular staging, expect. Henslowe, we may note, lists "1 baye tree," "1 tree of gowlden apelles," and "Tantelouse tre," but these hardly sound substantial enough to climb. The Revels accounts—*Documents Relating to the Office of the Revels in the Time of Elizabeth*, Feuillerat, ed. (1908), see index—refer several times to trees: holly is bought for them; canvas, arms of oak and lathes for a hollow tree, etc. Thus it is quite sure that an actual setting was used at court for trees.

That something was also used on the stage of the Red Bull to represent single trees is made certain by the following instances; the "tree" was not merely imaginary:

A *If It Be Not Good:* 325-330; a "blacke tree," standing in a grove, is climbed by Scumbroth. Devils enter and "sits vnder the tree all about him." Then when Lucifer commands, "This Ewe-tree blast with your hot-scorching breath," there is a direction, "Fireworkes; Scumbroth falls."

A *The Honest Lawyer:* C 3, an abbot hides his abbot's dress in "this hollow tree" (t), and near the end of the play, I. ii, "Thirsty climbing vp into a tree" (presumably the same tree) while Rob[in goes] into a bush."

B *I Iron Age:* 300; a direction reads, "Hector takes vp a great peece of a Rocke and casts at Aiax; who teares a young Tree vp by the rootes, and assailes Hector."

A *Swetnam:* the scene, H 4v-K 2, which in the text requires a tree and which on the title-page cut has a post instead, has been discussed in chapter III.

In A *The Brazen Age,* 252-253, several single trees are required; "Enter Hercules from a rocke aboue, tearing downe trees" . . . "All the

Princes breake downe the trees and make a fire, in which Hercules placeth himselfe."

C *Nero:* II. i; Petronius says, "Shroud me, gentle tree."

These references—all there are to single trees—make it sure that the Red Bull represented them in some way or other. It may not have been a realistic way: as the post served in *Swetnam,* so a stage pillar may have been climbed in *If It Be Not Good,* but the hollow tree of *The Honest Lawyer* must have been something else still. What sort of property served for the saplings torn up in the *Ages,* I refuse to guess, but the action is necessary for the story: Ajax threw something; Hercules and the princes went through some sort of pantomime, though, as I have said elsewhere, the effect of reality may have been very unconvincing.

As to where these trees stood on the stage, these examples are scarcely enough to allow any conclusion, and since four of them occur in plays which strongly suggest multiple settings if they have any settings at all, it does not greatly matter. However, we may notice at once that there is no slightest suggestion that the trees were concealed by a curtain or discovered in any other way, and it is quite impossible to conceive a tree big enough to be climbed as standing on the rear stage. Chambers' idea (*op. cit.,* III, 89) that the trees when incongruous to a scene could have been got out of the way by means of trapdoors, is not confirmed by the plays. It is true that in Campion's masque in honor of the marriage of Lord Hayes at Whitehall in 1607, "nine golden trees of fifteene foote high, with armes and braunches very glorious to behold" were used for the entrance of the maskers:

That part of the stage whereon the first three trees stode began to yielde, and the three foremost trees gently to sincke, and this was effected by an Ingin plac't under the stage. When the trees had sunke a yarde they cleft in three parts, and the Maskers appeared out of the tops of them, the trees were sodainly conuayed away, and the first three Maskers were raysed againe by the Ingin . . .

First three sank; then the next three advanced and sank, and then the next three. See Lily B. Campbell, *op. cit.,* p. 169. But this was surely a very special device hardly to be duplicated in regular plays. The magic tree of *Friar Bacon and Friar Bungay* could, of course, as Chambers suggests, be manipulated by a trap-door, and even "the great tree" of *The Warning for Fair Women*—it was not so great that it could not be chopped down a little later. But could the tree climbed in *If It Be*

Not Good and in *The Honest Lawyer?* To be sure, the Devil in *If It Be Not Good* does threaten, 326, that in certain circumstances "Sinck shall these trees to hell," but there is no hint that this actually happens, and no trap-door at the Red Bull is called upon in any play to perform any such maneuver. The only apparent reason for Chambers' suggestion is his desire to avoid the use of incongruous properties on the front stage of the public theaters, and, as will appear later, this is impossible of realization.

The grove-wood-forest-orchard-garden setting may have been quite a different matter—perhaps a group of single trees, or perhaps a painted curtain, or sometimes only imagined. I treat them together because some garden scenes definitely mention trees. The chief difference between woods and forests on the one hand and gardens on the other is that the woods are solitary and wild, the gardens appendages to houses.

The Two Noble Ladies, A, refers to woods as a hiding-place, 241-252, and as a wild place, 1148. In *The Silver Age*, B, 126-130, there are references to "these woods," "the neighbor forest," but not necessarily as actually on the stage. The more frequent allusions in *The Four Prentices*, A, 181-185, 185-196, 220-229, make the presence in that play of an actual wood-setting more probable, especially as it would serve to emphasize the location of the scenes in wild, solitary places. The single references to woods in *A Woman Killed with Kindness*, B, V. iii, 45, and *II If You Know Not Me*, B, 303, have already been called attention to in chapter III. *The Hector of Germany*, B, has a single reference to "the forrest side" in the dialogue of G 2v-G 3v, a scene of solitude, and also a garden scene, B 4-C 2, but no mention in either of single trees. *The Heir*, A, II. i, has a direction "Leucothoe and Psecas in the garden" and an allusion to "that happy shade"; also III. ii is described in III. i, as in a grove by a river's side. If it were not for the explicit direction "in the garden," I should say unhesitatingly that the garden, the grove, and the river were equally imaginary; and indeed, it is very likely that the direction is dramatic rather than theatric—that is, that it arose from the imagined scene rather than from the stage. *Nero*, C, II. i, is in a garden; "these Arbors and trees" are spoken of, and Petronius says, "shroud me, gentle tree"—the last line has already been called attention to in connection with single trees. The only other garden scenes I have noted —I may be omitting some which have no specific mention of trees— are in *Fortune by Land and Sea*, B, 387-392, which speaks of "this garden wall," "that hedge," neither of which need be actually on the stage, and *Match Me In London*, B, 176-184, where the dialogue suggests that the scene is a garden, 177, and that a lady picks a rose, but this is not made very sure; a little later the scene seems a room, 181.

The other instances of woods and forests are associated with arbors and caves and banks and rocks; we may as well take them up as they come and disentangle them later. But some evidence outside the Red Bull may first be noted.[8]

The Revels accounts (see index) show that a forest-woods setting, concocted out of timber and holly, existed at court. They also mention the arbor: "Ivy for the Wylde men*ne* & tharbo*ur* v *s.* x *d.*," p. 200; "Hoopes for tharbo*ur* and topp of an howse, iiij *s.* xj *d.*," p. 203. Then there is the title-page of *The Spanish Tragedy*, which shows the picture of an arbor, presumably that used in the play, a latticed construction trimmed with vines. And, finally, Henslowe lists "ij mose banckes."[9]

Perhaps such a property as the arbor of *The Spanish Tragedy* served in *The Golden Age*, A, 32-35. It is described as

> a place
> Remote, an Arbor seated naturally,
> Trim'd by the hand of nature for a bower,
> Skreen'd by the shadowy leaues from the Suns eye.

As Jupiter asks Calisto to "sit or on the verdure lie," there may have been a bank for her to sit on. Such a bank is precisely mentioned in a direction in *The Hector of Germany*, B, B 4-C 2: two lovers, after a scene outside a garden, which is entered by a door, later locked, are shown as "in the Garden" (d), and "sit on a banke" (d). The bank is also definitely called for in *The Brazen Age*, A, 184, when Venus points out "a violet banke" to Adonis, on which she wants him to "tumble," and on which he may have been laid to die, 193-194. He should at least have lain in a place that could be concealed, because she is left alone with him, with no one to help her remove the body. This bank is also probably the bed of Venus, 235, decked, according to the text, with roses, pansies, and eglantine; the pillow, a violet bank with

---

[8] I repeat only a little of the evidence given in " 'Trees' on the Stage of Shakespeare," *MP*, V (1907), 153-168. As I have pointed out in chapter III, some of it is less certain than I then thought, notably the Forman entries; I gave, also, too much weight to single textual allusions. But the cumulative effect of the evidence is still worth considering.

[9] Mention of the bank suggests comment on Bradbrook's remark in *Elizabethan Stage Conditions* (1932), p. 42, that by the time of *Hamlet* use of the bank "had become archaic and it was relegated to the play within the play." Obviously Miss Bradbrook overlooked these uses in the Red Bull plays, not to mention others.

AN ARBOR

From the title-page of *The Spanish Tragedy*, 1633

lilies. It is variously described as in an arbor, 236, and in "an obscure cave," 226, which has a door from the stage, 227, 230; the "bed" can be spied on by some one on the lower stage "through these chinks," 227, and also by persons above. Mars and Venus enter to it, 228, and come out from it, 230—the point of which remark is that there need be no entrance to this arbor-cave from off-stage. Vulcan arranges a net of iron over this "bed" and catches Mars and Venus in it, so that five of the Gods may "appeare aboue and laugh" as they watch them. This confusion of arbor and cave will be returned to later. Now we may ask whether this cave is also the one in which Lychas, later in the play, 251, hides from Hercules. Perhaps it should also be connected with Omphale's remark, 252, "Beneath this rocke where we have often kist, I will lament," and the stage direction which shortly follows, "Enter Hercules from a rock aboue, tearing downe trees."

All of which makes it necessary to notice what the plays have to show concerning rocks. The rock thrown by Hector, *I Iron Age*, B, 300, the stones used in defense by Sir Thomas in *The Travails of Three English Brothers*, B, 46, the rock carried in at the end of *The Golden Age*, A, 78, as a symbol of the earth, the stone that falls in *The Birth of Merlin*, C, IV. i. 232, and the stone on which Elizabeth sits in *I If You Know Not Me*, B, 213, need only be mentioned to show they have not been forgotten. What concerns us now is real stage settings. Henslowe's inventory specifies "1 rocke," and the Revels accounts (see index) have several entries which mention this property; plates, timber, holly, ivy, etc., were provided for it, also a rock was fetched to court from Bridewell, 309, and "a scalling Ladder that serued at the Rock" is mentioned, 307. The rock to which Hesione is said to be bound in *The Brazen Age*, A, 205, is not made much of as a rock. But that at the end of the play, just mentioned above, was large enough for Hercules to walk on, and so was the rock at the end of *The Birth of Merlin*, C. In V. i, the devil threatens, "On this rock Ile stand to cast up fumes, And darkness ore the blew fac'd firmament"; but Merlin, outconjuring him, causes the Rock to enclose him, while thunder and lightning "in the rock" further enhance the scene. This, as a C play, however, can not be made too much of. In *The Hector of Germany*, B, Fitzwaters stands "aloft" on a "high rocke" F 4-G 1 v, while people below, imagined on a boat, cast anchor, rescue him, and "launch foorth into the deepe" again; thirteen lines are allowed for his exit and reappearance below. Here the descent is made off stage by the usual stairway: in *The Brazen Age* Hercules descends by the rock itself. This suggests the ladder of the Revels records, just cited, and *Love's Mistress*, 100, another Heywood play, where Psyche "climbes up the Rocke" and, 101, Zephirus "takes Psiche from the Rocke." The rocks of *The Brazen Age* and *The Birth of Merlin* are somewhat alike; both are large enough to be stood or walked upon, and both may have caves; we have already noted the cave-arbor of *The Brazen Age*, and Brooke in his stage directions for *The Birth of Merlin*, III. iii, calls for a cave. Sometimes the trapdoor seems alluded to as a cave; so, in *If It Be Not Good*, 333, the Subprior, defying the devils, says, "Downe, downe and sincke into thy damned caue." Finally to be noted is the vague reference to a cave in *The Four Prentices*, 185, where it is associated with woods as in a wild, mountainous country; this cave need not be on the stage at all.

What shall we make of all this? Remembering the frank appeal of the Elizabethan theater to the imagination, shall we say that the un-adorned gallery was the top of the rock and the rear stage the cave-arbor? Perhaps this was true of the amateur-produced *Hector of Germany*, with its purely imaginary ship, but such an explanation hardly fits *The Brazen Age*. There are its trees to be plucked up, there is the veritable arbor of *The Spanish Tragedy*, there is the indisputable rock of Henslowe's list, and the Revels records for constructing rocks. Per-haps the rock in these Red Bull plays was some special structure which rose from the main stage to the balcony level and which included a concealable space used by Heywood now as a cave and now as an arbor, so that it occurred to his mind equally well as one or the other.

My own impression is that, as so often in the directions, the same words refer at different times to different things. After all, Venus' "bed" of flowers in *The Brazen Age* is hardly the same property as Danae's curtained bed in *The Golden Age*, and the removable throne of *I If You Know Not Me* not the same as the formal seat of other plays. So I suspect that the "arbor" of *The Golden Age* may have been a structure like that on the title-page of *The Spanish Tragedy*, and that the arbor of *The Brazen Age* was really the same setting as the cave, which may have been either a decoration of the balcony and rear stage, or a separate structure with a large enough opening to conceal the "violet bank." On the other hand, the bank of *Hector* may not have been concealed at all; it may even have been only two stools on the front stage.

To return to the woods with which the rock, arbor, cave, are so often associated, whatever the cave was, the woods—if they were present at all and not simply imagined—stood outside it. So if the cave-arbor was the rear stage, the woods were on the front stage; if it was a separate structure the woods were still furnishings of the front stage. As a matter of fact I doubt the existence of any woods setting in these Red

Bull plays unless we conclude a wood setting was practically always on the stage ready to be drawn into the imagined scene by a reference to it in the dialogue. Plays of certain periods and theaters do have so many such references as to suggest this. The Red Bull plays have so few allusions to such a setting as to make such a conclusion unlikely for it. But something certainly stood for trees in the plays in which single trees are made use of, and Hercules and the princes must have had something to toss about in *The Brazen Age.*

(5)

Nine plays may be cited as perhaps suggesting the use of tents, but in six of the nine the suggestions are feeble indeed. *Appius and Virginia,* C, II. ii and IV. ii are at camp, but there is not even a hint of tents; indeed, a soldier in IV. ii asks "Is our *hut* swept clean?" *A Shoemaker a Gentleman,* B, F 4-G 2, *The Hector of Germany,* B, C 4v-D iv, D iv-D 2v, *The Four Prentices of London,* A, 208-217, and *II Iron Age,* B, 356, 371, merely mention tents as nearby but not as necessarily on the stage. So *Revenge for Honour,* V. i and III. ii, though in a camp, do not refer to tents. These six plays are therefore uninformative.

But the three others are more revealing. *I Iron Age,* B, 324, has a stage direction, "Achilles discouered in his Tent, about him his bleeding Mermidons, himself wounded, and with him Vlisses." Since the tent is clearly required in this scene, it is likely it was used also where Achilles, 311-315, is said to be keeping his tent while the others fight; the same tent is at least supposed in sight where Achilles is directed to enter "from his Tent," 328; and Hector's body is borne to it, 322. Thus the tent is a feature in the staging of a considerable part of the play.

The most striking use of a tent is in *Richard III,* C, V. iii. Richard orders his tent pitched and forty-six lines seem allowed for doing it; Richmond orders ink and paper in his tent. Then to Richard in his tent, and to Richmond in his, the ghosts of Richard's victims appear. Of course, this is all one continuous scene, and two tents must be suggested in some way at the same time. This example must not be pressed too far, however, for the *Richard III* of the Red Bull may not be Shakespeare's; and, if it was, the performance there, as Chambers says, was "quite exceptional." Yet the play was certainly given at a public theater and shows that such theaters permitted a violation of realistic distance and the use of simultaneous settings.

In any case the scene is not unique. Besides *The Devil's Charter,* only partly discussed above, since it was not a Red Bull play, but sufficiently, I think, to show its simultaneous use of tent, throne, and study, there is also *The Rape of Lucrece*, an *A* play of unquestioned authority. Pages 204-205 are before a tent, 205-209 show seven seated in it at a banquet, 227-247 are before and in the tent, which is furnished with a table and lights. But the second of these scenes, 205-209, is immediately followed by a scene at Lucrece's, where she is seen sitting in her chamber; and 227-234 is followed by a similar scene at Lucrece's. To be noticed also is 221-225, where Lucrece is discovered in bed. Thus the tent recurs pretty much throughout the play and the rear stage can hardly be used both for the tent and for the scenes with Lucrece. Since in *Richard III* the tent is pitched, and since the plot of *The Seven Deadly Sins* (Greg, *Elizabethan Dramatic Documents*) begins with a direction, "A tent being plast one the stage for Henry the sixt he in it A sleepe," we may fairly assume that in *The Rape of Lucrece* the chamber of Lucrece occupied the rear stage, and the tent was another and a removable setting.

(6)

The Red Bull plays of the *A* list have no shop-setting, but four *B* plays definitely require one, as do two *C* plays. As the evidence is in agreement, there seems no special reason to distinguish between them.

C *The Fair Maid of the Exchange:* this play uses a drawer's shop in scenes ii, v, viii, ix, xi. Some of the scenes show this only by textual allusions ("Heere is his shop," sc. ii), but scene xi begins with a direction, "Enter Cripple in his shop." Scene vii is in another shop; it begins, "Enter Boy in a Shop cutting up square parchments." A yardstick is lying by, the stock— lawns, cambrick, ruffs, shirts, waistcoats, etc.,—is mentioned. The boy is directed to open the door, and Phillis goes in from the street and sits and works in the shop (d). The scene closes with her apparently still sitting there; scene viii opens with the direction, "The Cripple at worke"; thus the two shops must be different. In scene xi this shop is spoken of, 66, as "my ungarnished, darke, and obscure Cell."

C *The Wise Woman of Hogsdon:* I. ii, "Enter Luce in a Sempsters shop, at worke vpon a lac'd Handkercher, and Joseph a prentice." The shop may occur again in IV. ii, because it would be a suitable location for the scene, but there is no indication of its use there.

B *II If You Know Not Me:* 256-263 and 282-288 are at Hobson's shop, the first scene shown by allusions in the dialogue, the second by a direction, "Enter in the shop two of Hobsons folkes and opening the shop." Sold in the shop are "pins, points, and laces, Poting-sticks for young wiues, for young wenches glasses." The shop account-books play a considerable part in the scene. In the first shop-scene Hobson enters in the shop and sees his apprentices, supposed to be tending the shop, "at Tauern . . . Now they peepe like Italian pantelowns, Behind an arras." Without leaving the stage, he gets them out and reprimands them. Later in the scene he calls for stools for two gentlemen. The second shop-scene is preceded by this speech, made by a customer looking for the shop: "This is the lane: theres the Windmill; theres the Dogs head in the pot; and heres the Fryer whipping the Nunnes arse. Tis hereabout sure." Then comes the direction quoted above. I suppose the lane, the windmill, and the sign-boards spoken of are imaginary, but the shop can hardly be so.

B *A Shoemaker a Gentleman:* B 4-C 2v "Enter discover'd in a Shop a Shoo-maker, his Wife spinning, Barnaby, two Iournimen." A stool is "reached." The shop also seems likely in E 4v-F 3v. C 2v-C 4 has a well from which an angel rises.

B *Match Me in London:* Act II begins, "A shop opened. Enter Bilbo and Lazarillo." They are keeping the shop and are probably discovered. Lazarillo cries the wares: garters, robes, stockings, gloves, girdles, etc. Male-vento comes and recognizes Bilbo, saying, "step forth." Bilbo replies, "A Counter you see still before me." Tormiella comes in the shop and calls for her workbasket; she probably sits. A passing officer points her out: "What thinke you of yonder parrot i'th Cage." At the end of the scene Bilbo says, "Make fast the shop door," and one goes from the shop into the house to dinner, and another goes away. Scene iv of this act is apparently at the same house, but there is no hint of the shop.

B *Greene's Tu Quoque* opens with the direction, "A Mercers Shop dis-couered, Gartred working in it, Spendall walking by the shop." The shop has satins, stuffs, velvets—more than ten pieces (t). People pass into the house to look at other wares. Near the end of the scene the boy in attendance says, "Shut vp shop"; so something can be closed—the shutter?

These instances are all pleasantly in accordance with each other and with what we should expect. The shop has a counter, and though not mentioned specifically here, a shutter. (In *Arden of Feversham* it has an active part in the play, II. ii. The boy tending the shop says, "Tis very late; I were best shute vp my stall. . . ." The direction follows, "Then lettes he downe his window and it breaks Black Wils head," Will being the murderer waiting outside to kill Arden.) The space in front of the shop is the street, which can be reached from the shop through a door. Another exit at the rear is supposed to lead to the house. Appropriate merchandise is displayed and stools are sometimes brought for customers—into the street?

The discovery of these scenes, specified in *A Shoemaker a Gentle-man* and *Greene's Tu Quoque*, might be taken to mean that the shop was on the rear stage or an arrangement of it. Chambers (*op. cit.,* III,

110) notes the necessity of three shops in *The Roaring Girl*, two in *Two Lamentable Tragedies*, and three in *Bartholomew Fair*, to which our list adds the two shops of *The Fair Maid of The Exchange*. He suggests, 83, that two shops might be placed side by side on the rear stage, but these Red Bull plays hardly support this. The implications of the scene in *If You Know Not Me* are, I think, that the shop was a separate structure outside the arras, here thought of as in a tavern. However, if this shop did stand in the rear stage, the arras, drawn back to display it, might still have been in view beside it. So too much cannot be made of this instance.

The succession of scenes does not help us much. In *The Wise Woman* the scene following the shop-scene is somewhat elaborately described, but may have no settings on the stage after all; and similarly the second shop-scene in *If You Know Not Me* is immediately preceded by one in which a large number of portraits are described as hanging on the walls. But with the possibility of three imaginary walls on which to hang them—instead of, as on the modern stage, only one —I think we can hardly insist on their actual presence. The scene following this shop-scene has the laying of the bricks for Gresham's new exchange, and here it does seem as if the bricks were really necessary. This might cause a serious "clash" if every property had to be thought of as on the rear stage, but as this is surely not necessary, the scene hardly has much bearing on the position of the shop. No more significant are the two or three stools used in the scene which follows the shop-scene in *Match Me in London*.

A conservative conclusion seems to be that the shop was a special structure, sometimes, perhaps, placed on the rear stage and discovered there, but sometimes arranged on the open stage.

(7)

A few larger properties less commonly referred to in the Red Bull plays may be briefly treated. First, the altar:

Henslowe, we may note in passing, lists "j littell alter."

A *The Rape of Lucrece:* 184-186 begins, "Apollo's Priests, with Tapers, after them [3] with their oblations, all kneeling before the Oracle." The text mentions "the Gods, To whose faire altars we have done due right," "the blood of the slaughter'd sacrifice," and also the marble pavement. Since the latter was surely imaginary, Apollo's altar might be thought so also, but as the property room had an altar, it was probably used here. The direction sounds like a discovery. The scene before this one has no settings; the scene following begins, "A table and chaires prepared," and no "split" scene is possible. To the explanation of such "clashes" we must return later.

A *The Brazen Age:* 183, in a dumb show commented on by Homer, comes the direction, "Enter Busyris with his Guard and Priests to sacrifice; to them two strangers, Busyris takes them and kils them vpon the Altar: enter Hercules . . . kils Busyris and sacrificeth him vpon the Altar, at which there fals a shower of raine." Nothing is said of removing the bodies, and though such negative argument must not be given too much weight, the altar may well have been discovered. The next scene alludes in the text to "a violet banke." Also, 247, "Enter to the sacrifice two Priests to the Altar." For full description of this scene see chapter VIII. It uses a rock, trees, perhaps a cave, and the "labors" of Hercules.

B *II The Iron Age:* 390, "King Priam discouered kneeling at the Altar," four others with him. Here the evidence that the altar was discovered is clear. So in 426, one page after the scene begins, though there is a direction, "An Altar set forth," and a character on the stage says, "The Priests prepare the Alter," we may still think of the altar as discovered. This is also suggested by the fact that though eight die, there is no sign of the removal of the bodies.

In these five scenes, then, the altar could most conveniently have been discovered.[10]

"Barriers" and "lists" occur in the Red Bull plays in only two or perhaps three plays. They seem used on the front stage.

A *The White Devil:* V. iii begins, "Charges and shoutes—They fight at Barriers." When Brachiano says he is poisoned by his helmet, Flamineo cries, "Remove the barre"; this remark Lucas, in Webster, *Works* (1928), I, 252, explains as a reference not to the barriers but to the bar of the helmet. His explanation of the barriers as a rod across which the combatants fought is also clear, but not why he places this fight on the rear stage. Aside from the fact that this location would be too cramped for such an action, Brachiano, 40, withdraws into his cabinet and is thirty lines later "presented in a bed." Though one says "See heere he comes," and the bed may have been put forth, it surely was at first on the rear stage, and the barriers could, therefore, hardly have been there also.

B *The Hector of Germany:* in the last scene a fight takes place, and combatants say " we are marcht into this dreadful Lists." "Lists" may be, however, only figurative: if there were real lists, it is interesting to note that the scene gives an impression that a throne was also present.

A *The Devil's Law Case:* the last scene begins, "The Lists set up. Enter [3] as Judges, they sit." Lucas, rightly I think, places this scene on the outer stage.

---

[10] In this connection it may be appropriate to notice the image in *The Virgin Martyr,* I. i, and III. ii, since it would, one would think, be discovered. But this image is brought in, 48: "Enter Priest with the Image of Iupiter, Incense and Censers, followed by Caliste," etc.

The scaffold also seems to have been usually brought in.

The last scene of *The Royal King*, B, begins in a study, therefore on the rear stage. Then a direction says, "A Barre set out" and seven "take their seates." A reference follows, possibly, figurative, to "the State 'fore which I stand," and before the scene is over a scaffold and block are ordered fetched. As women entering say, "Executioner forbeare," it seems the scaffold and block must have really been brought. Possibly the curtains may have closed on the study and reopened later with the stage reset, but there is no hint of this in the text.

A *The Virgin Martyr*, act IV, begins with "a bed thrust out" with physicians about it; it may therefore have been either on the front or rear stage. The next scene has "a scaffold thrust forth" and a split scene is possible but not hinted at. The scaffold is large enough for four or five people to stand upon and is reached by several steps: one of the characters says of Dorothea, "She ascends, And every step, raises her neerer heaven." This scene ends the act; the next act begins in a study.

A *Herod and Antipater*, in its last scene also has a scaffold. Two scenes are represented at once: in a prison with Antipater and in the place where Herod is sick. A direction reads, "Enter . . . Officers with the Scaffold & the Executioner," and an execution follows.

A setting which occurs with some frequency is that for a trial. Its distinguishing feature is the bar. Otherwise it can scarcely be distinguished from council scenes which group about a table, and tables are associated with so many other types of scenes and are treated so variously—sometimes being brought in, sometimes discovered, sometimes assumed as present without explanation—that consideration of them here would not be to much purpose. The bar of the court room must be noted, however. One instance from *The Royal King* has just been cited above, in which the bar is clearly placed on the front stage.

B *Sir Thomas Wyatt*: 120-124, has for the trial of Lady Jane and Guilford, six seats for the judges; and as Guilford tells the judges to "come down," their seats seem raised. Guilford and Jane are also placed "seuerally in chaires of state." The allusions to the bar are only textual: each is told to hold up his hand at the bar, and Guilford says "heere at a Prisoners barre." Because of the large number of special seats required it is likely that at least some of them, with the bar, were discovered.

B *How a Man May Choose a Good Wife from a Bad*, in its last scene has a Justice, who according to the text, sits and directs his hearer to answer "at the barre"; a secretary is told to be ready with pen and ink.

A *The White Devil*: III. ii, has a formal hearing before six ambassadors: eight seats are required. The scene may well have been discovered. Vittoria, on trial, is ordered to "Stand to the table." There is no mention of a bar.

Thus this hearing is really more like a council scene such as *Sir Thomas Wyatt*, 91-95, or a scene where a commission is holding an investigation as in *I If You Know Not*, 204-209, and really does not belong in this list.

A *The Honest Lawyer:* in its last scene, I 3v, Gripe is told to "stand to the Barre." The same scene uses a tree, a bush, and a raised seat.

A *Swetnam*, in the first scene of its third act, a real trial scene, has a marginal reference to "A Barre" and a direction, "The Prisoners brought to the Barre by a Gard." In V. ii, occurs the mock trial pictured on the title-page, where a foil represents the bar. (See chapter III.)

A *The Devil's Law Case:* IV. ii. This scene is unusual in specifically calling in the directions for two bars. Officers prepare the seats for the judges. A man is concealed in a closet and later reveals himself, and a picture is brought in and hung up. Lucas uses the whole stage for this scene, but there is no hint in the scene itself that it is discovered.

B *The Two Merry Milkmaids:* III. iii; this scene follows a scene in a study, but begins with fourteen lines of unplaced conversation, so that a "split" scene is possible. Then at least six enter, the direction reads "the forme of a Court," and a little later comes "Enter Dorigen plac'd at the Barre."

A *The Heir* ends in a trial scene. Three judges take their seats and there is a textual allusion to a bar.

Thus, though several of the allusions to the bar are only textual and could perhaps be interpreted as merely figurative, the directions show there was an actual property. Once, at least, it was brought in, presumably to the front stage. There is no clear instance of a discovery, but two or three are not unlikely.

The position of the rack is also not clear. In *The Virgin Martyr*, A, the last scene, a direction reads, "Some go for the rack," and there are textual allusions to irons cooling, whips, burning pincers, etc. But in *The Travails of Three English Brothers*, B, 75-82, the rack can well be discovered. A jailer, gloating over Sir Thomas' perscution in prison, calls to him, "Where are you here? ha!" and a direction reads "Enter Sir Thomas." A little later a direction says, "Exit Iaylcr leauing Sir Thomas in the stocks," so that it seems pretty clear that Sir Thomas was discovered. In passing we may note that this reference to stocks is the only one in the Red Bull plays. Shortly the great Turk comes to Sir Thomas and orders him tortured. The presence of a rack is assumed, the text reading "Hoist him vp," "Wrinch him againe," and finally "One take him downe and bear him back to prison." This last phrase may, of course, mean that the rack on which Sir Thomas was tortured was on the front stage, and that he was borne back to his prison on the rear stage, but that interprets the "back to prison" very literally. In *Herod and Antipator*, A, I 1-I 4v, the presence of the rack is also assumed: a direction reads "They racke Adda," and there are textual references: "pull home," "higher yet," "giue her ease," "Take her downe." Thus in *The Virgin Martyr*, the rack seems brought to the front stage; in *Herod* it may have been put forth without a direction or discovered; in the *Travails* it seems discovered.

Other properties, usually stationary in reality, are the well of *A Shoemaker a Gentleman*, B, C 2v-C 4, which follows a shop-scene and would, therefore, be on the front stage (the well is used again (t) E 3-E 4v); and the spring in *If It Be Not Good*, A, 303-306, 308-314, of which the position is uncertain. The Revels accounts provide "ffor the Cariadge of the partes of ye well counterfeit from the Bell in gracious strete to S*t*. Johns to be p*e*rformed for the play of Cutwell," p. 277, 1576/7, and "Canvas for a well," p. 365, 1584/5, showing that even at these early dates the well was a real setting and not merely a trapdoor at an innyard playing place.

Henslowe mentions in his inventory one "Hell-mought" and the Revels accounts, p. 140 (1573-74), provide "devices for hell & hell mowthe." Such a property could be used in *If It Be Not Good*, 265-271, 331-334; *The Silver Age*, 159; *The Two Noble Ladies*, 1712-1910; *The Virgin Martyr*, 77-83, 83-91, but would be only suitable, not required. Indeed, since the imagined scene is before Hell only in *If It Be Not Good* and *The Silver Age*, these may be the only suitable uses, and even they are very doubtful examples.

The tomb of *How a Man May Choose*, B, IV. i, must be noted. This scene begins away from a church, then approaches it, and, 64, has this description:

> Now it is night and the bright lamps of heauen
> Are halfe burnt out . . .
> This is the Church, this hollow is the vault
> Where the dead body of my saint remaines,
> And this the coffin that inshrines her body.

The informative nature of this speech would suggest that the settings are imaginary, but a direction says, "Mistres Arthur in the Tombe." Of course the tomb might still have been only the trapdoor, but we must note that Henslowe definitely lists a "tombe" besides the two more dubious entries "tome of Guido" and "tome of Dido." So a definite "tomb" property existed, but I see no way to be sure it was used here, and if it was whether it was discovered. Possibly the shift of place in the middle of the scene suggests the latter.

Possibly, but hardly probably, a property tomb was used in *The Four Prentices*; a corpse is buried in a dumbshow, 178, Christ's sepulchre is referred to as present, 241, and the play closes with all going out: "So in Procession walke we to Christs Tombe." First, however, they are to hang certain trophies in the Temple. Surely a trapdoor was used for the grave, 178, but the tomb of Christ may be, probably was, only imagined.

The "great horse" of *II Iron Age* was discovered and apparently unmoved in the action of the play. It may have given place to the altar or both been in sight at once. See chapter VIII.

(8)

This study of the larger properties leads to the following conclusions: the trees always, the throne often, and the beds sometimes were shown on the open, front stage. The altar was apparently discovered; the scaffold, the barriers, and the lists seem to have been placed on the front stage, as were also the well and spring; the Red Bull plays leave the position of the bar, the tomb, and the rack uncertain. The tent, the shop, and the arbor—perhaps the cave may be mentioned also in the list—were alike in that they were inclosures of which the interiors were visible. Sometimes at least they were structures separate from the rear stage and could stand outside it. The bearing of these conclusions on the general problems of staging will be pointed out in a later chapter.[11]

---

[11] Simply as a matter of some curious interest there follows a list of the small properties which occur in the Red Bull plays. Only those of the *A* and *B* plays are included, and only those which the property man would have to go to some trouble to secure; swords, stools, tables, pens, ink, dishes, etc., are all omitted. So are the references to thunder and lightning and to fireworks, all of which are discussed later. Some properties, referred to only in the text, of which the actual use is doubtful, are marked (t).

Severed heads: Jane's, *Sir Thomas Wyatt*; "a counterfeit head like Shirley's," *The Travails of Three English Brothers*; Mortimer's, *Edward II*; a head struck off, *The Virgin Martyr*; a head of a crowned king, *The Silver Age*. In this connection see Lawrence, "Stage Dummies," *Speeding up Shakespeare* (1937), pp. 127-143.

"Cords in some ugly shapes," *The Virgin Martyr*; whips (t), *ibid.*

Winding sheets, two stuck with flowers, *The Devil's Law Case.*

Hearse: *I If You Know Not Me, Swetnam, Edward II.*

Two coffins, *The Devil's Law Case.*

Two trunks from which people come out, *Herod and Antipater.*

Blood: Winifred bled to death, blood drunk, *A Shoemaker a Gentleman*; a bleeding heart upon a knife's point and a bowl of blood, *The Golden Age*; the limbs of a man in the service (of a banquet), *ibid.*; possibly also in *The Brazen Age*, 222.

An abortive infant, *The Silver Age.*

A "coarse" buried, *The Four Prentices.*

A chain: to bind the Winds, *The Golden Age*; to bind Acricius and later Cerberus, *The Silver Age.*

A red-hot spit (t), *Edward II*; burning pincers (t), *The Virgin Martyr.*

Pots of color of make-up, *The Two Merry Milkmaids.*

Image of Jupiter, *The Virgin Martyr;* the "oracle" of *The Rape of Lucrece.*

A basket filled with fruit and flowers, *The Virgin Martyr;* a cross of flowers, *ibid.*

Lantern: *A Woman Killed with Kindness, Greene's Tu Quoque, If It Be Not Good.*

Wall portraits: *II If You Know Not Me* (t), *The Wise Woman of Hogsdon* (t); a curtained picture, *The White Devil;* a picture hung up, *The Devil's Law Case.*

Three prospective glasses, *The Travails of Three English Brothers.*

A hand in the "heavens," *The Brazen Age.*

Laurel crown: *The Rape of Lucrece, The Hector of Germany, The Royal King;* "guilt laurel," *The Virgin Martyr.*

A crown of thorns, *The Four Prentices.*

Three garlands, *Herod and Antipater;* garlands for Hercules, *The Silver Age;* garlands for satyrs and nymphs, *The Golden Age.*

Naval properties: wheel, sails, etc., all textual, *Fortune by Land and Sea.*

A vaulting horse (athletic apparatus), *The White Devil.*

"Spectacles," i.e., glass masks, *The White Devil.*

"A pot of lilly-flowers with a scull in it," *The White Devil.*

A death's head: *If It Be Not Good, The Devil's Law Case.*

A table of "laws" hung up, *If It Be Not Good.*

Blue (red . . . author and stage-manager disagreed) tables full of silver letters, *The Two Noble Ladies.*

Four men "standing in their torments"—the text names as one a "kettle of brimstone pottage," *If It Be Not Good.*

Barrel-tops, fired, *If It Be Not Good.*

A ladle full of molten gold, *If It Be Not Good.*

A rich cradle, *The Royal King;* cradle for Hercules, *The Silver Age.*

A feather bed, *Edward II* (t).

Distaff and spindle for Hercules, *The Brazen Age.*

A looking-glass, *II Iron Age.*

Royal purse, mace, scepter, cap of Maintenance, the Collar and a George, *I If You Know Not Me;* marshal's staff and key, *The Royal King;* crown and scepter for Jupiter, burning crown for Pluto, *The Golden Age;* the crown of Egypt, *The Brazen Age.*

Canopy carried over a royal personage: *I If You Know Not Me, Edward II.*

"The Silver Oare" in the procession to execution, *Fortune by Land and Sea.*

"A red crossier staffe" for an angel, *The Two Noble Ladies.*

"The order of St. Iago," *The Travails of Three English Brothers.*

Standards, etc.: English, Spanish, *II If You Know Not Me;* a Roman eagle, *A Shoemaker a Gentleman, The Virgin Martyr;* Christian and Pagan, *The Four Prentices;* "A banner full of ruptures," *Herod and Antipater.*

Welsh hooks, *Edward II.*

Shields: with golden letters, *The Two Noble Ladies;* with distinctive insignia on the shields, *The Four Prentices.*

Distinctive properties not classified above: in *The Golden Age:* wedges of gold and silver; models of ships and buildings; peddlers' packs; a rock, thread, and a pair of shears for the Fates; a globe in which they cast lots; thunderbolt for Jupiter, a trident for Neptune; in *The Brazen Age,* Vulcan's net, forge (t), Hercules' labors (enumerated, 247).

A goat led in, *I If You Know Not Me.*

? Falcons (t), *A Woman Killed with Kindness.*

Two snakes strangled by Hercules, *The Silver Age;* a handful of snakes, *If It Be Not Good.*

Lion's head and skin for Hercules, *The Silver Age.*

A bull's head (in trapdoor), *The Brazen Age;* the head of a boar, *ibid.;* two fiery bulls, dragon, the golden fleece, *ibid.*

A cock that crows, *The Brazen Age.*

The sea-horse that carries Neptune away, *The Golden Age.* (The eagle that ascends with Jupiter, *ibid.*, is, one must suppose, a masking of the lift.)

Mention of these various real and artificial animals suggests the query whether real horses were used at the Red Bull. I share Lawrence's doubt of their employment (*Pre—Restoration Stage Studies*, 1927, p. 270 ff). They are conspicuously avoided in *A Woman Killed with Kindness*, and *The Royal King*. In the former, V. iii, Mistress Frankford has considerately stopped her coach off-stage and returns to it at the end of the scene; in the latter, though the talk is all of horses, none certainly is in sight. In the *Rape of Lucrece*, 173, Tullia speaks of treading on her father's body, but, 174, is described as driving her chariot across it; clearly the latter is only a rhetorical flourish. In *Sir Thomas Wyatt*, 85-88, Guilford and Jane are directed to ride to the Tower, but a stage direction shows what they actually did do: "A dead march, and passe round the stage." Thus the Red Bull, for all its spectacle, suggests the use neither of real horses nor hobby-horses.

CHAPTER V

THE STAGE OF THE RED BULL

PRACTICALLY all that is known outside of what the plays can tell us of the construction of the Red Bull theater before the Civil War is the single sentence in *Historia Histrionica* that "The Globe, Fortune, and Bull were large houses, and lay partly open to the weather and there they always acted by daylight." (Hazlitt's Dodsley, XV, 408). The pictures of Elizabethan theaters, except that, perhaps, of *Swetnam*, as has already been pointed out (chapter III), offer no direct evidence concerning the Red Bull.

Some of the plays given at the Red Bull were, according to their title-pages, also presented at other theaters, a circumstance which implies its general similarity to them. Thus *The Travails of Three English Brothers* and *The Hector of Germany* were given both at the Red Bull and the Curtain; *Match Me in London* at the Red Bull and the Phoenix; the *Ages* at three several theaters, presumably the Curtain, the Red Bull, and the Phoenix. These connections are, however, too uncertain to press very far. We may presume that as a public theater the Red Bull had a platform stage projecting into an unroofed yard, and a tiring house with balcony, heavens, and hut above: that, in other words, it was in general of the same type of stage as that shown in De Witt's drawing of the Swan and described in the contracts for building the Fortune and the Hope.

(1)

Concerning the front stage *The Hector of Germany*, B, substantiates one detail by definite information of some interest. In its last scene the clowns see a play is forward, and say, "Begin, begin, we are set." An accompanying direction reads, "Sit on the Railes," the only allusion I know of in Elizabethan drama to the railing about the front stage, though its existence has been known for some theaters from the Messallina and Roxana pictures and an allusion in Middleton's *Black Book*.

(2)

An important feature of the front stage was the trapdoors. For convenience I list together all references to entrances from below the main stage level, though some, perhaps, were not to the front stage, and some possibly not by means of traps.[1]

? B *Sir Thomas Wyatt:* 102-103, a man buries gold. Scene before, in a cabin; scene following, throne (i). Front stage.

? B *How A Man May Choose:* IV. i, "this hollow is the vault" (t), "Mistres Arthur in the Tombe" (d). Scene first away from, then in the church; scene following, n.d. Rear stage.

C *The Birth of Merlin:* V. i. 40, "On this rock Ile stand to cast up fumes" (t), "Thunder and lightning in the Rock" (d); "The Rock incloses him" (d). The easiest way to carry this out would be by a trapdoor. Scene before, n.d.; scene following, throne (i). Above?

B *A Shoemaker a Gentleman:* C 2v-C 4, "Enter, an Angell ascends out of the Well, and after descends againe" (d). Scene before, four people discovered in a shop (d); scene following, n.d. Front stage.

E 3-E 4v, "this sorcerous pool" (t). Scene before, a seat (i); scene following, shop (i). Front stage.

? B *Greene's Tu Quoque:* 257-262, Spendall in prison is transferred to the "hole." He is "on the ground"; told to "Looke vp." Scene before, n.d.; scene following, n.d. Not clear.

A *If It Be Not Good:* The last scene in this play shows that there were several entrances from below outside the curtain; 338 also suggests this position. The trap of the other scenes could be similarly placed.

267-271, "Ruffman comes vp" (d), "Enter Shackle-soule comes vp"; "Lurchall and another Spirit come vp." This scene is the beginning of the play, opening with the possible discovery of a sleeping devil; scene following, throne (d).

303-306, "A golden head ascends . . . Descendit [in a spring or well]." Scene before, table set out; seats for 3 or 4; scene following, n.d.

308-314, Subprior draws gold from spring; "Golden head ascends." Scene before, n.d.; scene following, throne (i).

331-334, Subprior orders devil: "Downe, downe and sincke into thy damned caue." This scene is a discovery; a table, Subprior sitting by it. Scene before, n.d.; scene following, n.d.

338-342, "this vnknowne way, leads to a cellar"; "Zounds, into the dungeon?" . . . "downe, downe, downe"; a bed possibly discovered later in this scene. Scene before, n.d.

342-348, "Enter Friers aboue" as on the monastery walls. The King says they are to die there and orders the building set on fire. The devils, below, say to them, "You shall with vs to hell ride, all in flames." One devil

---

[1] Question marks indicate *very* doubtful cases of a use of the trapdoor. After A, B, C, to show the relative applicability of the play to the Red Bull, come the title, place of the reference to the entrance from below, how this is referred to, significant indications of staging in the scene preceding and the scene following, and the conclusion as to where this trapdoor was placed. "N.d." means no definite indication of properties or part of the stage.

says, "Catch"; then all say, "Come." "Let euery spirit his owne prize beare." Then a direction: "Sinck downe, aboue flames." This sounds as if three devils, each with a friar on his back, go down through the trapdoor.

348-359, "From vnder the ground in seuerall places rise vp spirits," (number not specified). In this scene a later direction for a discovery of four by means of a curtain.

A The Golden Age: "Enter at 4 seuerall corners the 4 winds. Neptune riseth disturb'd: the Fates bring the 4 winds in a chaine, & present them to Aeolus, as their King." This scene is a dumb show presented by Homer at the end of the play. It also uses the lift (an eagle). Front stage, if real traps were used.

B The Silver Age: 137-140, "Earth riseth from vnder the stage." Speaks twelve lines. "Earth sinkes" . . . "The river Arethusa riseth from the stage"; Arethusa speaks nine lines, then "Exit Are." Scene before, n.d.; scene following, a banquet at which thirteen or more are seated; perhaps discovered. Front stage.

156-164, "Hercules [fighting Cerberus before the gates of Hell] sinkes himselfe: Flashes of fire; the Diuels appear at euery corner of the stage with seuerall fireworkes." Scene before, Homer; scene following, Homer. Front or rear stage.

164, "Exeunt three wayes . . . Hercules dragging Cerberus one way; Pluto, hels Iudges, the Fates and Furies downe to hell; Iupiter, the Gods and Planets ascend to heauen." Pluto, etc., may exeunt through a door previously designated as "hell." See the discussion of doors, chapter VI. Only the "sinking" of Hercules suggests that the trapdoor was the entrance to Hell.

A The Brazen Age: 172-182, "When the Fury sinkes a Buls head appeares" . . . "He tugs with the Bull and pluckes off one of his horns. Enter from the same place Achelous with his forehead all bloody." Same scene has a throne (t). Scene before, Homer; scene following, Homer. Front or rear stage.

226-231, "Gallus sinkes and in his place riseth a Cocke and crowes." Gallus is described as "sleeping at the Caues dore." This scene uses a cave-arbor. Scene before, Homer; scene following, Vulcan's forge (t). Front stage.

241-256 (See discussion of balcony, later in this chapter, for full directions.) "His [Hercules] body sinkes." This scene has cave, rock, trees, altar, lift. Scene before, n.d.; scene following, Homer. Front stage.

? B Edward II: V. v, a possible use of the trap for the dungeon, vault, or "lake" in which Edward is mentioned as standing in mire and puddle; twenty-one lines spoken in the dungeon. The dungeon has a key, however, and is described as entered by a door. Later in the scene Edward comes out and is told to "lie on this bed"; twenty-four lines in the scene before the dungeon is opened; scene following, n.d. Front or rear stage.

A The Four Prentices: 175-178, "Enter a Coarse, after it Irishmen mourning, in a dead March. To them, enter Eustace and talkes with with [sic] the chiefe Mourner, who makes signes of consent, after buriall of the

Coarse, and so Exeunt." This scene has a series of dumb shows using possibly throne (i), woods (i). Scenes before and after, n.d. Front or rear stage.

A *The Two Noble Ladies:* 1712-1910, "The Devills sinck roaring; a flame of fier riseth after them." In this scene a woman is discovered in a chair asleep. At l. 1900 there is a direction showing a second thought as to use of the trapdoor: "Throws his charmed rod, and his books vnder [into a] the stage. A flame riseth." Scene following, n.d. Front or rear stage.

A *The Virgin Martyr:* 77-83, Devil "sinks a little" (d) "down, helhound, down." This scene also has "fire flashing out of the study" (d). This scene begins the act. Front or rear stage.

83-91, "The divell sinks with lightning." In this scene a rack used. Front or rear stage.

One cannot always be sure whether the traps were used in certain scenes or not. Doubtful cases are *How A Man May Choose,* where the tomb may be only a special setting concealing Mistress Arthur; *Sir Thomas Wyatt,* where a trap may be used for hiding the gold but is not necessary; *Greene's Tu Quoque,* where the "hole" is really a technical term for the worst part of the prison and may not be visually a hole; *If It Be Not Good,* 338-342, may possibly use only a regular stage door as may also *Edward II,* and *The Silver Age,* 164. For ten persons to descend in this last scene would be a tedious business. The plays with entrances at the corners are also not quite certainly referring to traps.

Of the plays certainly using entrances from below the stage level, only three demand more than one: *If It Be Not Good,* 348-350; *The Golden Age,* near the end; *The Silver Age,* 159. In the last two the "winds" and "diuels" "enter" or "appeare" at the corners of the stage, a normally not very useful place for a trapdoor; also "enter" and "appeare" instead of "rise" cause some doubt. Perhaps the actors scrambled up over the edge of the stage. *If It Be Not Good* does say "rise," but its "several places" is rather vague. Notably only one trap is necessary in the other plays, or at most two will serve, one on the front stage, one on the rear (see below).

The traps need not be large. There is no hint of one sufficient in size to take care of trees, bower, arbor, etc., as Chambers, in *The Elizabethan Stage* (1923), III, 107, suggests. As a rule only one actor uses the trap at a time, but two rise together in *If It Be Not Good,* 267-271, three sink each with one on his back, 348, and an unspecified number of "devills sinck roaring" in *The Two Noble Ladies,* 1860.

Some of these traps may have had special settings: for example, for the well in *A Shoemaker a Gentleman,* and *If It Be Not Good,* 303-

306, 308-314; if the trap was used, for a tomb in *How A Man May Choose;* for a grave in *The Four Prentices,* 175-178; and for the barely possible hell-mouth of *If It Be Not Good,* 267-271, 331-334; *The Silver Age,* 159; *The Two Noble Ladies,* 1712-1910, and *The Virgin Martyr,* 77-83, 83-91. But it must be noted that if such properties were employed, the trap-setting in *If It Be Not Good* would have had to be changed from hell-mouth to a well and back again, or different traps have been employed. Some change in the trap would also have been desirable in *The Silver Age.* This is a possible but, considering Elizabethan methods generally, hardly a necessary staging.

I am not assuming a trap to be necessary for the various river scenes of the plays. Keeping in mind the simple solution in *The Two Noble Ladies* of the problem of portraying a drowning, I cannot follow Chambers (*op. cit.,* III, 107) in demanding a trap for Horatio to jump into in *The Rape of Lucrece,* 244, or Lawrence's *Pre-Restoration Stage Studies* (1927), pp. 159-160, in supposing that a property "bank" to simulate a river bank, masked the trap in such scenes.

The position of the main trap is clearly on the uncurtained space in *A Shoemaker a Gentleman,* C 2v-C 4, *If It Be Not Good,* 348, and *The Brazen Age,* 226-231. In the other instances there is no definite indication; when a trap is employed in a scene using the curtained space, the trap may be there or on the front stage. Probably, however, the fire "flashing out of the study" in *The Virgin Martyr,* 77-83, and the explosions, fire, etc. of *If It Be Not Good,* 350-351, could most easily be managed by a curtained trap.

There is one doubtful case of some interest, *The Birth of Merlin,* C, V. i, where a rock on which the devil stands, opens and engulfs him with thunder and lightning. If the rock is some arrangement of the balcony, this may call for a trapdoor there. It is the only sign of one in that position in these plays. The "aboue flames" of *If It Be Not Good* hardly necessitate one.

(3)

A post is referred to in several plays. This may sometimes have been one of the supports of the "heavens," but not always. The post pictured in the Swetnam title-page is a separate non-structural feature, which could hardly have been permanent without causing great inconvenience. A movable pillar is required in *The Virgin Martyr,* A, IV. ii: "A hangman with cords in some ugly shape, sets up a Pillar in the middle of the stage"; and Hercules brings in two brazen pillars to an altar in *The Brazen Age,* 247. Some mentions of posts and pillars may refer to nothing really on the stage: so in *Match Me in London,*

B, 140, a man is warned to "ware the post" as he turns "down this lane" on his way home; in eleven lines he is before his master's house. No post is really necessary. Perhaps equally imaginary are "the high pumps" of *A Match at Midnight*, C, G 4v-H 1: "Was ferry exceeding darke, but here is high pumps, sure here is two couple of cross wayes." But Swetnam is bound to a post, H 4v-K 2, after a banquet in an orchard; in *The White Devil*, A, V. vi, 184, a man is bound to a pillar and killed, and in *Greene's Tu Quoque*, B, 277 a man who breaks into a lady's chamber is bound to a post (d). These, therefore, are really tangible somethings, whether the structural posts shown in the Swan drawing or presumably movable posts like that on the *Swetnam* title-page. Whether the post stood on the front or rear stage is not clearly indicated in these plays.

The Red Bull plays suggest no other comments on the front stage. The doors leading to it will be dealt with in the next chapter; among its common furnishings, in my judgment, are the throne, trees when required, and seats and tables, so often assumed that they seem to have been almost always present.

Comment on the curtained space I postpone to another chapter.

(4)

The gallery at the rear of the stage raises a considerable number of questions and illustrates once more, if more illustration is needed, the indefiniteness of the stage directions and the astonishing ingenuity of investigators in deriving different significances from a few simple words and pictures: also their interpretation of the directions, and even more unsoundly the dialogue, as statements of fact made in a carefully consistent terminology, when inspection shows that the terms are used with little consistency and that the directions are often as dramatically conceived as the text itself. There seems increasingly manifest a tendency to let imagination play freely about the indications of staging in the directions and text to arrive at interesting results, rather than to determine exactly what the plays demand. Moreover, in doing this the evidence of the contemporary pictures is largely ignored.

Suggested as places for actors to appear considerably above the level of the main stage are: (1) an upper balcony on the level of the second gallery of the auditorium; (2) a place above this on the level of the third gallery; (3) the huts; (4) a sort of shelf in front of the balcony, and (5) balcony windows above obliquely placed proscenium doors.[2]

---

[2] It has also been suggested that the rear stage was elevated a step or two above the

All this is very ingenious and may be true, but it rests largely on literal explanations of the directions and very free treatment of the contemporary pictures. Since none of these pictures, except that on the title-page of *Swetnam*, meager in its information, represents the Red Bull before 1625, they can be taken only as general indications of what the Red Bull theater may have been. The Swan shows only a perfectly straight balcony flush with the back wall of the front stage, the Messallina only a small curtained window in an apparently projecting structure, the Roxana two windows straight above the curtain, and the so-called Red Bull picture a series of small windows, with curtains over the middle portion. The lower curtains in the Messallina hang from what some see as a sort of narrow shelf and others as a sloping coping; this is the only pictorial hint of (4) above. No one of the pictures suggests bay windows above obliquely placed doors, or the third story gallery. It is perfectly fair to object that all the pictures are not large enough to take in some of these items, but it is also fair to note that these items are not supported by the pictures. They may, of course, have existed, but should scarcely be assumed as proved.

When one turns to the evidence of the directions and texts, one finds that this is not as clear as one might wish. It is not always easy to be sure whether the action is placed above or not. Take, for example, the phrase "over the stage." When used to refer to spectators, as in Guilpin's *Skialetheia* (1598), epigram 53:

> See you him yonder who sits o're the stage
> With the Tobacco-pipe now at his mouth,

it may mean that the smoker is in the balcony, as Chambers (*op. cit.,* II, 534) infers, but it can just as easily, and I think more probably, refer to De Witt's "orchestra" in the Swan picture. In *The Woman Killed with Kindness*, II. iii, "Enter over the stage Frankford, his wife, and Nickolas," might be taken to mean in the balcony, since they apparently do not see Wendoll on the lower stage, where he is soon joined by Jenkin. Yet this does not certainly prove that Frankford is above, and in *The Rape of Lucrece*, 203, where seven generals "with souldiers, drums, and colors march over the stage and congee to the King and Queene," the procession would be most ineffective in the balcony, and the phrase seems certainly to refer to crossing the lower stage.

Greg's suggestion in *Elizabethan Dramatic Documents* (1931), p. 119, that "Exit then enter againe" in the "plot" of *The Seven Deadly*

---

main stage level. Whatever may be said for this belongs rather with a discussion of the rear stage than in this chapter.

Sins means an ascent to the balcony may be true, but has no supporting evidence; such a direction usually indicates a change of scene, as in *II Iron Age*, 379. (See "Doors," chapter VI.) And I can see little justification for his supposing (*op. cit.*, p. 99) that the "prysoun" of *The Dead Man's Fortune*, III. i, is in the balcony. Are not these only imaginative guesses?

Miss Bradbrook in *Elizabethan Stage Conditions* (1932), p. 45, illustrates the mistake of too easy generalization in saying that the senate house in *Julius Caesar* is "placed, as usual, above." The remark is based, so far as I know, only on *Titus Andronicus*, and holds for none of our Red Bull plays.

Mr. John C. Adams in the *Theater Arts Monthly*, XX (1936), 903, has created a new difficulty of nomenclature by asserting that the balcony was often called the "chamber." For this, justifiably perhaps in a popular magazine, he offers no evidence, but he would, I think, find it difficult to prove this usage not only "often" but even "now and then" in the *directions*. In the dialogue, of course, the balcony is given its dramatic significance; and, as it often represented the front of a house, the room above is spoken of as "the chamber." Thus, in the text of *The Wonder of a Kingdom*, 275-277 and 280-286, we hear of the chamber, the window, the casement, but the directions use consistently only "above." The only use of "chamber" in the directions of the Red Bull plays occurs in *II Iron Age*, 411, before the murder of Agamemnon:

> Loud musicke. Enter Egisthus with his sword drawne, hideth himselfe in the chamber behind the Bed-curtaines: all the Kings come next in, conducting the Generall and his Queene to their Lodging, and after some complement leaue them, euery one with torches vshered to their seuerall chambers, &.

Even if this did not make it clear that the scene is below, the action later in the scene would do so.[2a]

Because of another danger I have mentioned, that of letting one's imagination run away with one in dealing with Elizabethan staging,

---

[2a] All this has important implications in connection with Adams' correspondence in *LTLS*, Feb. 15, May 23, 1936, about the staging of the bedroom scenes in *Romeo and Juliet*. There he assumes that because Juliet was in her bedroom "above" in one scene, III. v, the bedroom of IV. v, must also be there. This is to show too great a confidence in Elizabethan theatrical consistency. And in his letter of May 23, he argues that because characters speak of others as "below," the speakers must be in the upper stage. I mention Adams' discussion because it so clearly illustrates the mistaken interpretations arising from the idea that the Elizabethan theater was consistent in its usages, and that the textual allusions to place and settings are to be taken literally.

the soundest procedure is to suppose no scene in the balcony which. the contemporary directions do not in some way suggest there. In my own stagings of the Red Bull plays I have permitted myself to place only one other scene in the balcony—that of Althea and the fatal brand in *The Brazen Age*, A, 198-203. The banquet to celebrate the killing of the Calydonian boar is taking place, at least nine seats being necessary. Meantime, unseen by the banqueters, Althea is burning the brand on which Meleager's life depends. When the brand is consumed she is directed to exit and to re-enter twelve lines later to the interrupted banquet. The facts that she is not observed in the first part of the scene, that she does exit and re-enter, and that the interval is of the right length to allow a descent from the balcony at least suggest this arrangement.

The commonest terms applied to acting places above the level of the main stage, and the freest from any dramatic coloring are "above" and "aloft," with which may be noted the unusual "vpper Stage" of *The World Tost at Tennis*, C, 266. Colored by the scenes in which they occur are "on the walls" and "at the window." This use of "window" requires that attention be paid to all mentions of a window or grate, whether above or not. And there are also a few other possible references to the upper stage, as, for example, to the turret, tower, main-top, etc. These may be considered first:

B *Fortune by Land and Sea:* 413-416, a boy is ordered to "Climb to the main-top," and about a page later is directed, "Come, descend." Five lines are allowed for his ascent before he has to speak, when the direction reads, "Above, Boy."

A *If It Be Not Good:* 295-303, "Get thee vp hye Into my Turret where thou mayest espie All commers euery way . . . Fly vp to 'th top ath house. . . . Goe beate a drumme ith garret, that no tongues Of clockes be heard but mine." There is no direction that shows the man addressed did any of these things.

A *The Four Prentices:* 245-246, We are told that Guy and Eustace have "gone to scale a Tower In which our father lies," and then they enter with their father, only to exeunt as the pagans enter, and the Soldan says, "I'le make these Turrets dance among the Clouds, Before the Christians shall inhabite them." This can be interpreted as calling for action in some place above the "walls," i.e., above the balcony, but one cannot be sure that the visible action of these two pages is not all on the main stage.

C *All's Lost by Lust:* III. i. 84, "Now to my turret, To see if the king comes." Twenty lines later the speaker enters to say the king is coming, but there is nothing to indicate that the speaker ever appeared above.

A *The Devil's Law Case:* V. iv, Two people, presumably on the lower stage, are told to go into "that closet." The door is locked; the place is described as "a Turret of the Castle." Presently the two "enter above at a window." They speak of the turret, "the most desolate prison Of all the Castle." One says, "I will leape these Battlements." The scene ends, "Ope the other casement That looks into the citie" and they exeunt.

The last example is interesting because it combines so many terms in one reference. "Turret," "window," "casement," "battlement" are all one and all "above." The references in other Red Bull plays to turrets and tower are all only textual, and are dramatically appropriate rather than technically theatrical. So is the "main-top" of *Fortune by Land and Sea*. As only five lines were allowed for the boy's ascent, he could scarcely have gone higher than the usual balcony. Certainly the hut is quite out of the question; with the "heavens" in the way many of the audience could not have even seen him there.[3] Nor would the hypothetical third story opening add much to the effectiveness of the scene.

In this connection it may not be out of place to notice Mr. John C. Adams' closely reasoned and ingenious article, "The Staging of *The Tempest*, III. iii," *RES*, XIV (1938), 404-409. In it he argues that the "heavens" or stage-cover must have been "not less high than the heads of the highest placed spectator in the third spectator-gallery"; and that, if it was so placed, room would be left for this third story opening, which could have served for the music gallery and for "the top" where Prospero appears "invisible." This is not completely convincing. In the first place *The Tempest* directions may represent the Blackfriars rather than the Globe performance, and the Blackfriars, as an enclosed theater, may have had no stage-cover at all, perhaps even no third gallery; see Adams, *Shakespearean Playhouses* (1917), p. 196 n. How can we be sure, moreover, that Elizabethan theater builders were so considerate of the third gallery spectators as to arrange for them to see all the action on the stage, when in even the best eighteenth-century and early nineteenth-century theaters many seats allowed no view of the stage at all? The "heavens" of the Swan theater is so awkwardly drawn one cannot judge much from it. It seems to start from the level of the roof of the third gallery and to slope sharply forward,

---

[3] Professor Allison Gaw, Shakespeare *Jahrbuch*, LXIV (1928), 182-184, argues that the hut would be visible from most of the theater, and therefore could be used in *I Henry VI*, I. iv, for the English tower. I think he forgets people sitting on the stage itself or standing close to it. But his objection to Brodmeier's idea—referred to in a review of Gaw's book on *I Henry VI*, Shakespeare *Jahrbuch*, LXIII (1927), 203—that the English tower was represented by a box in the theater, is certainly well taken. Brodmeier's suggestion is an excellent example of the impractical theories we academic folk can fall into, when we fail to consider the practical conditions in the theater.

but the slope may be only a poor attempt at perspective. Still, the Swan drawing may leave room for a third story opening, and the familiar pictures of *The Empress of Morocco* (1673)—see Nicoll, *The Development of the Theatre* (1927), pp. 166, 167—with a little music gallery in that position support the idea. Our Red Bull plays certainly offer no sure use of this third story opening and indeed hardly a possible use of it. The passage quoted by Graves from R. M.'s *Micrologia* (1629) as given in Adlington's *A Book of Characters*, 351, "A Player," can apply equally well to the opening in the floor of the hut as to this third story opening:

If his action prefigure passion, he raves, rages, and protests much by his painted Heavens, and seems in the height of this fit ready to pull Jove out of the garret, where perchance he lies sleeping on his elbows or is employed to make squibs and crackers to grace the play.

All the references in the plays to turrets, etc., then, seem either not carried out in action at all or to be easily interpreted as referring to the usual balcony. Thus, so far as the Red Bull plays are concerned, there is no real evidence of any other raised playing place on the stage.

As for references to windows and grates, the case is a little different. The title-page of *Swetnam the Woman Hater*, A, shows the lower part of two leaded windows in the back wall of the lower stage, each window divided in the middle. The windows appear about three feet wide. Similar single windows are shown on the title-page illustrations of *Dr. Faustus* (1624), and *Friar Bacon and Friar Bungay* (1630). The reference in *The White Devil*, A, IV. iii, 35, "You that attend on the Lord Cardinals Open the window and receive their viands," to be discussed just below, is probably to such a window on the lower stage. So I think are the lines in *Sir Thomas Wyatt*, B, 109-110, "Out of this firme grate you may perceiue the Tower Hill," and the reference in *How A Man May Choose*, B, III. ii, "The cushions in the windowes neatly laid, The cupboord of plate set out, the Casement stuck With Rosemary and Flowers, the Carpets brusht," provided any of these were represented and not merely imagined. The very specificness of the last instance makes it all the more suspect. But some references to windows and casements and grates are certainly to the upper stage. Thus in *The New Wonder*, C, IV. ii, there is a direction, "Old Foster, and above at the grate a box hanging downe," and in *The Wonder of a Kingdom*, B, 275-277, where the direction shows the action is "above," the text speaks of window and casement. In *The Heir*, A, II. i, two men enter "at the window" and observe what is going on in a garden. They might conceivably be below, but I think the reference is rather to the window above. There is no evidence whatever in the Red Bull plays to the window which some scholars have advocated as at the *rear* of the balcony—notably Albright, *The Shakespearean Stage* (1909), p. 66; Lawrence, *The Elizabethan Playhouse*, Second Series (1913), pp. 45-50; Chambers, *op. cit.*, III, 96. Chambers and Lawrence definitely suggest that it was a source of daylight. This seems to me not only unproved but also very unlikely. To have no concealed passageway from one side to the other behind the balcony, as such a window implies, would be a very inconvenient arrangement. If the light were only reflected it would be negligible in comparison to light from the front of the balcony itself.

There are a few other directions which may or may not refer to the regular balcony. Sometimes, as in *The Silver Age* and *The Brazen Age*, speeches may be made from the descending-ascending device instead of from the balcony. We have also to consider the possibility that the "rock" of *The Birth of Merlin*, *The Brazen Age*, and *The Hector of Germany*, may be special large properties. (See chapter IV.)

Finally, there is in The *White Devil*, A, one of the few mentions in Elizabethan drama of the "tarras." Act IV. iii, has "Enter [8]. At another dore [1]." At line 20 comes a direction, "Enter servants with severall dishes covered"; they are surely on the lower stage. At line 35 they say, "You that attend on the Lord Cardinals Open the window, and receive their viands"; and we may suppose that a window on the lower stage is referred to. Then, line 40, there is a direction, "A Cardinal on the Tarras," and he is presently described as "On the Church battlements." Why, however, this single mention of the terrace from all the Red Bull plays should be taken as anything but dramatic I cannot see; there is nothing but the word to distinguish the scene from a regular balcony scene.

One argument for projecting bay windows over obliquely placed doors is that this allows characters above to look down into the curtained space of the lower stage. In these Red Bull plays the only scene in which such an action occurs need not be explained in this way. In *The Brazen Age*, A, 235-239, "all the Gods [five are named] appeare aboue and laugh" at Mars and Venus, caught by Vulcan in a place variously described as a cave and arbor. If this cave-arbor is a special structure on the front stage, as seems not unlikely, the gods could act more effectively in the broader space of the balcony itself.

Some indication of how far the spaces used for acting may have been above the main stage level may be found in the number of lines of dialogue allowed to cover the ascents and descents. The shortest allowance for descent in scenes using the usual balcony is the noise of "alarums" in *I Iron Age*, B, 319-320; in this time Hector is not only supposed to pass from "the walls" to the lower stage, but also while on the way down to kill five of his opponents. Other passages covering descent vary from seven lines in *The Hector of Germany*, B, C 2-C 2v, to fifty-four in *Greene's Tu Quoque*, B, 281-289; for ascent from eight in *If It Be Not Good*, A, 342-348, to twenty-eight in *The Devil's Law Case*, A, V. iv. These limits are so loose as to be of little assistance; still, since the boy in *Fortune by Land and Sea*, B, 413-416, is allowed only five lines to climb to the "main-top" it is a pretty sure sign, as has been pointed out, that he did not go beyond the usual balcony. In *The Heir*, A, V. iii, but one line is allowed for a king's descent, but some stage business is indicated in that line, "His Majesty is comming downe; let vs attend."

Thus the Red Bull plays seem to require no other raised acting place than the regular balcony, and no structural departure from what is shown in the contemporary pictures. Different terms are indeed employed to designate this upper stage, but they seem dramatic, rising from the scene, rather than theatric. It is significant, I think, that usually the term "window" occurs only in the directions for house scenes, and "walls" with cities and towers. *The Devil's Law Case*, with the window of its directions and the turret, battlements, casement, of its text, rather confirms than contradicts the identity of these items. The simplest explanation will serve: merely the straight front of the balcony, designated dramatically as "window" or "walls" or "tarras" to suit the situation portrayed, or theatrically as "above," "aloft," or "the upper stage." Of course the more elaborate arrangements which students have imagined *may* have existed, but the plays do not require them.

On the basis of the arrangements so far suggested we may list the uses of the upper stage as follows:

B *Sir Thomas Wyatt:* 116-118, "Enter Pembroke vpon the walles"; participants, 1; lines spoken above, 16; lines to descend, 18. Scene is over Ludgate: Wyatt knocks on the gate below.

B *I If You Know Not Me:* 240-242, "Enter [3] above"; use, as a housefront; participants, 3; lines spoken above, 34.

A *The Rape of Lucrece:* 240-245, "Enter in severall places, Sextus and Valerius above" (see discussion below); participants, 2; lines above, 28.

B *Fortune by Land and Sea:* 387-392, "Climb into that hovel" (t), later called "a hen roost," "hay loft"; no exit is marked; "Enter above" (d) 391; "Forrest leaps down" (d), 395; participants, 1; lines above, 15.

413-416, (see discussion in text above); use, as a main-top; participants,

1; lines above, 18; lines to ascend, 5; after last speech above, thirteen lines before end of scene.

C *The Birth of Merlin*, V. i, use as a rock. Perhaps Joan, the Devil, his assistant spirit, and Merlin are all on the rock, in which case the whole scene of 107 lines is above. Or perhaps the Devil gets up on the rock at line 35 (in which case no lines are allowed for ascent) and speaks 14 lines from above. Or perhaps this scene does not concern the balcony at all. As only a C play, it need not too much trouble us.

B *A Shoemaker a Gentleman:* C 2v-C 4, "Musicke heere descends" (d); (see discussion below).

C *A New Wonder:* IV. ii, "Old Foster and above at the grate, a box hanging downe" (d); use, as a prison; participants, 1; lines above, 16; lines to ascend, 16.

A *The White Devil:* IV. iii, see discussion above. I think the window mentioned is below; and the "tarras" the balcony; participants, 1; lines above, 3.

B *Greene's Tu Quoque:* 203-206, "Enter [2] aloft" (d); "Look up to the window" (t); use, as house-front; participants, 2; lines above, 53; lines to descend, 13 for one, 10 for the other.

224-331, "Enter [1] aloft" (d); "The window is clasped" (t); use, as house-front; participants, 1; lines above, 14; lines to descend, 34.

281-289, "Will Rash aloft" (d); use, as house-front; participants, 1; lines above, 2 or 3; lines to descend, 48.

A *If It Be Not Good:* 342-348, "Enter Friers aboue"; "Sinck downe, aboue flames" (d); (see discussion under Trapdoors, above); use, as Abbey wall; participants, 4, possibly more; lines above, 10?; lines to ascend, 8; friars may jump down.

B *The Silver Age:* 117, "Enter Ganimed aboue" (d); use, as house-front; participants, 1; lines above, 10; lines to ascend, 12; lines to descend, 44; the gate to the house is below.

122, "Iupiter appeares in his glory vnder a Raine-bow, to whom they all kneele"; probably a use of the descending device; (see below).

130, "Enter Iuno and Iris aboue in a cloud"; only Iris is above. Juno asks her to "tell me from the cloud Where I haue plac'd thee to behold the Chace"; use, as cloud; participants, 1; lines above, 16; Iris told to descend, but there is no sign that she does. Perhaps the descending device.

152, "Iuno and Iris plac'd in a cloud aboue"; participants, 2; lines above, 19.

A *The Brazen Age:* 198-203, (see discussion above); use, as a place of observation (by Althea); participants, 1; lines above, 28; lines to descend, 11. If this staging is correct a fire is used above.

203-208, 206, "The Troians on the walles, the Greeks below." In this scene Hesione is bound to a rock; Hercules kills the sea monster—nothing is said about its removal; use, as walls; participants, two or more; lines above, 15; lines to ascend, 10. No hint of gates to the city.

222-225, "Enter vpon the wals [more than 4]" (d); "Telemon first mounts the walles, the rest [more than 4] after"; use, as walls; participants, more than 4; lines above, 1; lines to descend, nothing indicated.

235-239, "All the Gods [5 named] appeare aboue and laugh" (d) at Mars and Venus caught in Vulcan's net in cave-arbor; use, as place of observation; participants, 5; lines above, 17.

241-256, "Enter Hercules from a rocke aboue, tearing down trees" (d); use, as rock (see discussion under Properties); participants, 1; lines above, ?; lines to ascend, 21; lines to descend, ?.

254, "Iupiter above strikes him with a thunder-bolt" (d); participants, 1; lines above, none. Possibly a use of the descending device, not the balcony.

B *I Iron Age:* 298-302, "Enter aboue upon the wals [more than 8]" (d); use, as walls; participants, more than 8; lines above, 14.

319-320, "Enter aboue" (d); use, as walls ;participants, more than 5; lines above, 10; lines to descend, none, but a direction calls for "alarum."

B *II Iron Age:* 379, "Enter Synon with a torch aboue" (d); use, as walls; participants, 1; lines above, 19; lines to ascend, 14; lines to descend, 10; Synon then unlocks the city gate.

B *The Hector of Germany:* C 2-C 2v, "Enter ... above" (d); use, as house-front; participants, 2; lines above, 3; lines to ascend, 16; lines to descend, 7.

F 4-G IV, "Enter aloft" (d) (see discussion above); use, as rock; participants, 1; lines above, 49; lines to descend, 11.

A *The Four Prentices:* 230-234, "Enter vpon the walles [more than five]" (d) ... "Enter some bringing forth [above] old Bullen, and other prisoners bound" (d) ... the Sophy "sets vp his Standard & Crowne" (d) ... "The Christians are repulst. Enter at two seuerall dores, Guy and Eustace climbe vp the wals, beate the Pagans, take away the Crownes on their heads, and in the stead hang vp the contrary Shields, and bring away the Ensignes flourishing them, seuerall wayes." The next scene is inside the city among the Turks. Use, as walls; participants, more than 11; lines above, 45.

240-247, Many references in text: talk of scaling a tower, putting a cross up on the walls, but no directions. Doubtful use of balcony.

A *The Devil's Law Case:* V. iv, (see discussion in text above); use, as prison, turret, casement, battlement; participants, 2; lines above, 25; lines to ascend, 28; lines to descend, 18, also a fight.

C *The World Tost at Tennis:* 266, "The nine Muses (who in the time) are discouer'd on the vpper Stage plac'd by the nine Worthies and toward the conclusion descend, each one led by a Muse"; participants, 18; lines to descend, 14, a song.

A *The Virgin Martyr:* II. iii, "They whispering below enter above [5]" (d); use, as place of observation; participants, 5; lines above, 45; lines to descend, 15.

V. i, "Rise, consort" (d); (see discussion below).

A *The Heir:* II. i, "Enter at the window" (d); use, as window from which to observe garden; participants, 2; a table (is referred to but may be "off"); lines above, 111. This may be a lower window, but hardly seems so.

V. iii, "The King speakes from aboue"; "helpe me to ascend," "ascendant" (d); use, to observe below; participants, 1; lines above, 1; 6 pages between ascent and the speech above, but the king is observing before he speaks; lines to descend, 1.

A *Herod and Antipater:* C 4-D iv, Two "aloft" overhear what is said below; use, to observe below; lines above, 17.

B *The Welsh Ambassador:* II. iii, "above" (d); a tableau of two disclosed; lines spoken above, none, but about 16 while the tableau is observed; lines to ascend, 18. Almost certainly a discovery above.

B *The Wonder of a Kingdom:* IV. iv, "Enter . . . above" (d); "casement," "window" (t); use, as "chamber"; participants, 1; lines above, 24.

V. ii, "above" (d), "chamber" (t); use, as "chamber"; participants, 3; lines above, 53; lines to descend, 8.

C *Richard III:* III, vii, (Q) "Enter Rich. with two bishops alofte" (d); participants, 3; lines above, 55.

C *Nero:* III. iv, "Enter above"; use, point of observance; participants, 1, possibly 3; lines spoken, 32 or 60, depending on whether a 28-line soliloquy is spoken above or not.

Of the forty-six plays we are considering, twenty-five including the dubious case of *The Birth of Merlin,* and the place for music in *A Shoemaker a Gentleman,* employ the upper stage. Of these uses, five are specifically for walls (*Sir Thomas Wyatt, If It Be Not Good, The Brazen Age, I* and *II Iron Age, The Four Prentices*); seven are for windows or a grate above (*I If You Know Not Me, The New Wonder, Greene's Tu Quoque, The Heir, The Wonder of a Kingdom;* here also I count "the hen-roost" and "hay-loft" of *Fortune by Land and Sea,* and the "window" spoken of as turret, battlements, casement, of *The Devil's Law Case*); seven uses are as undescribed points of observation (*The Silver Age, The Brazen Age, The Hector of Germany, The Virgin Martyr, Herod and Antipater, Richard III, Nero*). Besides these there are the main-top of *Fortune by Land and Sea,* the cloud of *The Silver Age,* the terrace of *The White Devil,* the rocks of *The Birth of Merlin, The Brazen Age,* and *The Hector of Germany.*

Some further uses require a bit of comment: one of the most interesting and revealing of Elizabethan ideas is that in *The Rape of Lucrece,* A, 240-245, where the direction reads, "Enter in severall places Sextus and Valerius above"; "severall places" are indeed necessary, for Sextus is supposed to be on a hill outside the city, Valerius on the city wall, and one of the stage doors to lead to the bridgehead which Horatius is protecting. A tent is also on the stage. *The Welsh Ambassador*, B, has a tableau of two persons "above" discovered to observers on the lower stage, and in *The World Tost at Tennis*, C, the nine muses placed by the nine worthies are discovered on "the vpper Stage." These two last instances thus require a special curtain for the balcony, as does also, perhaps, *The Brazen Age*, 198-203 for the fire. It is noticeable in this list of uses that the C plays make no demands not already necessary for the A and B plays.[4]

Though it appears that the balcony served all of these purposes, it is not impossible that it was masked differently for some of them, especially since we know that such maskings existed. The clouds, rocks, battlements at court show the Elizabethans had such constructions, and they may have used them at the public theaters. It is necessary also to remember the curious "bayes" of *The English Traveller*, mentioned in chapter III. If distinctive maskings of the balcony were employed, they are, with the forest settings, the nearest approach to scenery that the Elizabethan theater affords. Against the use of such decorations is the treatment in *The Rape of Lucrece* of the balcony as at the same time a hill and walls, and the looseness of terminology in *The Devil's Law Case*, already mentioned so often. Also such maskings raise difficulties. Usually it would seem that they must have been put in place before the play began and remained throughout, since no one any longer holds that a curtain concealed the outside of the

---

[4] There are two other uses of the balcony which are not clearly illustrated by these Red Bull plays, but which deserve attention. One use of the balcony or at least of the front wall is for hangings. Thus in *II Edward IV*, 136, where Shore is to be hanged, the direction reads, "The while the Hangman prepares, Shore at this speech mounts vp the ladder." This explains the somewhat cryptic business in *The Spanish Tragedy*, III. vi, when Pedringano is to be hanged; he asks, "So then, I must vp," and a little later the direction reads, "He turnes him off" obviously off the ladder. Our Red Bull plays have no hangings, and so do not illustrate this usage.

In *The Virgin Martyr*, A, 78, occurs a curious direction "Rise consort," which Lawrence interprets in *The Physical Conditions of the Elizabethan Public Playhouse* (1927), p. 91, as telling the musicians to take their place above. This may be so, but it gives them very short notice, for they must play by the end of eight lines. Possibly referring to the balcony is a direction in *A Shoemaker a Gentleman*, B, C 2v –C 4, "Musicke heere descends." This may refer to the descending device, but this hardly seems likely. Music has been called for earlier in the scene when an angel rises from a well. Does this direction provide that, this service fulfilled, the music shall return to some position below? If so, it is odd indeed, for usually the directions do not concern themselves with what may happen after a scene is over. Also this would perhaps controvert Lawrence's idea of the usual place of the music as above. Or does it support it? Apparently the music did sound from above in this scene, but then why does it "descend"?

balcony, and to put them in place would have required some time. Generally the balcony has, as the list shows, only one meaning throughout a play. In *Fortune by Land and Sea*, however, it is first a hen-roost, and later the main-top of a ship; in *The Silver Age* it is first a house-front and then a cloud; and in *The Brazen Age* successively an indefinitely imagined place of observation, if my supposition about Althea is sound; then the walls of Troy; then a place of observation outside a house; and finally a rock. Of course one may invoke the principle of simultaneous settings to arrange these various instances. My own impression is that Elizabethan practice was not uniform even at the one theater. I suspect there was something in *The Brazen Age* to suggest at least a rock, and that it was there all the time; that in *The Silver Age* the cloud was lowered into place when it was needed and then withdrawn, and that for the other uses the balcony was not masked at all.

The balcony has usually been imagined as about twelve feet above the main stage level. The only evidence offered by our plays, besides the lines allowed to cover ascents and descents, is that Forrest in *Fortune by Land and Sea*, 395, "leaps down" and runs off. Also it may be that the friars in *If It Be Not Good*, 348, jumped from the balcony into the arms of the waiting devils—the word "catch" suggests this—before they all descended into Hell.

The balcony seems normally to have been reached by some means off stage, presumably one or more stairways within the tiring-room. It is possible that sometimes characters scrambled up the wall of the stage; Forrest may have done this in *Fortune by Land and Sea*, when he is told, 389, to "climb into that hovel"; so may the boy who, 414, went to the main-top. There is no exit direction for either of them, though there is an entrance specified above for Forrest. In *The Four Prentices*, 234, the directions, however, explicitly say, "Guy and Eustace climbe vp the wals." Perhaps they did so with ladders, but there is no hint of them. There is also direct communication between the upper and the lower stage in *The Brazen Age*, 253, when Hercules, having entered "from a rocke aboue, tearing downe trees," descends to the lower stage.

Further inspection of the references to the balcony shows, first, that it is never used by itself, but always in connection with the stage below. The only possible exception is *The Birth of Merlin*, V. i, a *C* play, an instance only if the whole scene is played above. Second, only a comparatively small number of lines is spoken from above. By far the largest number, 111, occurs in *The Heir*, A, II. i, and in the dubious case of *The Birth of Merlin*, C, V. i, with 107 lines; next come the also dubious *Richard III*, C, III. vii, with 55 lines, and then *Greene's Tu Quoque*, B, and *The Wonder of a Kingdom*, B, each with 53. In twenty-six different scenes fewer than 30 lines are spoken above. These two facts are perhaps further evidence that the potion scene in *Romeo and Juliet* would scarcely have been staged in the balcony. The only action of much account "above" is the "beating away the Pagans" in *The Four Prentices* and Hercules' "tearing down trees" in *The Brazen Age*—both, it is fairly certain, pretty sketchy performances. The Red Bull plays confirm Peter Wilhelm Biesterfeldt's conclusion in "Die Oberbühne bei Marlowe," *Archiv*, CLX (1931), 51-59, that the upper stage was more a place for speech than action. The only suggested furnishings "above" besides seats are a table in *The Heir*, A, which indeed may not be in sight, and if my suggestion is correct, the fire for Althea's brand in *The Brazen Age*, A.

Only if the rock of *The Birth of Merlin*, C, was the balcony, is there any definite evidence of a trapdoor in the balcony. In *If It Be Not Good* friars on the wall "sinck" and fire bursts out "above"; but, as I have suggested, they may have jumped to waiting devils before they sank, and in that case the trapdoor would have been that of the main stage. The "fire" above, of course, needs no trapdoor.

Perhaps also to be mentioned among balcony furniture are the pagan standards and the Christian shields set up on the walls in *The Four Prentices*, 233, 234. Curtains for the balcony have already been called attention to. Finally it may be noted that, contrary to some opinion, there is a considerable use of the balcony in our later plays, though little use of it as "walls," because of the change in subject matter from battles to domestic situations.

(5)

The most obvious fact about the use of machinery for ascending and descending—which for briefness of reference I am calling the "lift"—is that it occurs in so few plays, even if one include the doubtful cases. The certain cases at the Red Bull are all in the *Ages*. *The World Tost at Tennis* was very doubtfully at the Red Bull, and the references in *A Shoemaker a Gentleman* and *Swetnam* are only textual.

The means of descent and ascent is never specified as a chair or throne. In *The Golden Age* an eagle is definitely mentioned for Jupiter, and in *The Silver Age* a cloud for Juno and Iris, but Jupiter "in his majesty," Jupiter "in his glory under a rainbow," Medea "with strange fiery-workes" are not after all informing. The "hand" from a cloud in *The Brazen Age* should also be noted. The other descents may have been managed without intentionally visible means of support—a long way of saying the "god" may have been suspended only by a rope and belt. Certainly Mercury, who "flies from above" in *The Silver Age,* could hardly be shown sitting.

The greatest demand upon the lifting apparatus came in *The Silver Age* when Semele's bed "flyes vp." Except for the end of the play, where "Iupiter the Gods and Planets ascend to heaven," only two come down together and one goes up. This direction may mean only to state their final destination.

There is nothing to show precisely where these descents began or finished except the "from the heavens" concerning the hand in *The Brazen Age.* Unless a crane were employed—and for this we have no evidence—the descending characters could not have come from an opening in the front wall of the tiring house. In any case the descent must have landed them on the front stage rather than within the curtained space. The usual opinion that the huts projected over the front stage and so permitted these operations seems a sensible one.

Though not from one of our Red Bull plays, it may not be out of place to notice the passage from *Cymbeline,* V. iv. 120, concerning Jupiter, "The golden pavement closes, he is enter'd His radiant roof," which suggests a trapdoor to the huts. Also Mr. John C. Adams' article (on *The Tempest,* III. iii) referred to above, has a detailed consideration of how Ariel in the guise of a harpy removed the banquet in this scene; it involved elaborate manipulation from above.

A list of the uses of the "lift" follows:

B *A Shoemaker a Gentleman:* C 2v-C 4, "Musicke heere descends." A very doubtful case (see discussion above).

A *The Golden Age:* V, end of play, "Iris descends and presents him [Jupiter] with his Eagle, Crowne and Scepter, and his thunder-bolt. Iupiter first ascends vpon the Eagle, and after him Ganimed."

B *The Silver Age:* 98, "Iupiter discends in a cloude."

121, "Iuno and Iris descend from the heauens."

122, "Iupiter appeares in his glory vnder a Raine-bow, to whom they all kneele." He speaks 16 lines.

130, "Enter Iuno and Iris aboue in a cloud." See discussion above of the balcony.

138, "Mercury flies from aboue." Speaks 10 lines; said to "exit."

154-155, "Iupiter descends in his maiesty, his Thunderbolt burning." . . . "As he toucheth the bed [of Semele] it fires, and all flyes vp, Iupiter from thence takes an abortiue infant." Juno, watching in a cloud, laughs. "Iupiter taking vp the Infant speakes as he ascends in his cloud."

164, "Iupiter, the Gods and Planets ascend to heauen."

A *The Brazen Age:* 217, "Two fiery Buls are discouered, the Fleece hanging ouer them, and the Dragon sleeping beneath them: Medea with strange fiery-workes, hangs aboue in the Aire in the strange habite of a Coniuresse."

254, "Iupiter aboue strikes him with a thunder-bolt, his body sinkes, and from the heauens discends a hand in a cloud, that from the place where Hercules was burnt, brings vp a starre, and fixeth it in the firmament."

A *Swetnam the Woman Hater:* K 2-L, In a Masque "Repentance" is spoken of: "Who's that descends so prosperously With such sweet sounding Musicke?"

C *The World Tost at Tennis:* 148, "Pallas descends."

232, "Iupiter descends."

415, "Iupiter leaues his State."

873, "Iupiter ascends."

CHAPTER VI

THE STAGE DOORS

(1)

PROOF that the Red Bull had at least three doors leading from the tiring-house to the stage is not as plentiful as one might expect. A good many plays require three entrances: for example, *Sir Thomas Wyatt*, B, 109-110, 124-130; *Match Me in London*, B, I. i; *Herod and Antipater*, A, F 4v. At the end of *The Silver Age*, B, exeunts must, according to the directions, be made "three wayes"; but one may be through a trapdoor. Only one *A* play specifies three doors: *The Four Prentices*, Prologue: "Enter three in blacke clokes, at three doores." That two *C* plays make similar demands is worth noting, but, of course, does not prove much: *Nobody and Somebody*, sc. ix, "Enter at one doore . . . Enter at another doore . . . Enter at another doore" in quick succession; *The World Tost at Tennis*, 277, "Enter at the three seuerall doores the nine Worthies, three after three." The *Swetnam* picture shows no door at all, though it would seem the center door should show between the windows; it could hardly be completely hidden by the chair. Still, since the three door arrangement is so natural a plan, we may, I think, accept it, even in spite of the picture, as a feature of the Red Bull.

Three doors suffice for all our plays except perhaps for *The Wise Woman of Hogsdon*, and for certain sequences of gate scenes. These gate scenes will be discussed later. *The Wise Woman of Hogsdon*, as a *C* play, does not carry much weight, but its last act does set an interesting problem. The denouement of the play requires that several different persons, each concealed from the others, observe and comment on what is going on on the stage. They are said, 345, to be "in severall roomes, that looke Into this one." Altogether there are four such groups requiring four separate entrances; a fifth is also necessary as an entrance to the main room from outside. But there need not, of course, be five *doors;* by use of the ends and middle opening of the curtain, the scene could at a pinch be arranged on the usually imagined stage.

We may in this chapter, as in the last, accept the usual idea of a rear stage, and assume that the third door opened into it from the tiring-room. Thus the third door was concealed by the stage curtains when these were closed.

As to the form of the doors and their locks, bolts, etc., the Red Bull plays contribute nothing not noted by Lawrence in his careful discussion in *Physical Conditions of the Elizabethan Public Playhouse* (1927), pp. 13ff, and I shall not repeat his points here.

The size of the doors requires some attention. In chapter IV various large properties—shops, tombs, rocks, etc.,—have been shown to exist. How were they got out on the front stage? If put in place before the play began, they could have been, perhaps, brought on in a "knocked down" state and erected. If brought on in the progress of the play, they must have come through the doors, down from the hut, or up through the trap-doors. Since there is no evidence that the traps were of sufficient size, these may be disregarded. If Semele's bed in *The Silver Age* could have been managed from the hut, other sizable properties could also, but on the whole the most reasonable place for bringing out the large properties would seem to have been through the stage doors. I cannot see that there is any way to determine whether properties were brought in through one door rather than another. Lawrence (*op. cit.*, p. 58) assumes that they came through the rear stage, but the assumption rests on the idea that the middle door was larger than the side doors. Perhaps it was, but no convincing evidence has been submitted to this effect. Also Lawrence's argument that there was a door in one leaf of the gates is scarcely convincing. Of course, such an arrangement is possible, but are not his instances all examples of taking terms used dramatically as if they were literal? At any rate the Red Bull plays offer no certain proof of such a theory.

William Archer in the *Quarterly Review*, CCXLI (1924), 404-406, argues strongly for an oblique position for the side doors:

It is really a darkening of counsel to cling to a pair of doors flatly facing the audience. That they cannot have been in common use we know from the very frequent occasions on which two men or bodies of men enter simultaneously from opposite directions and squarely encounter each other in the middle of the stage. To do this on the De Witt stage, the one party would have to make a right wheel, and the other a left—an impossibly ineffective manœuvre.

Archer's argument seems to me of very little force. In formal entrances right and left wheels would be more interesting than straight forward ones—there would always be the anxiety of a proper "dress" —and in scenes where groups rush in indiscriminately an oblique or straight position of the doors would make little difference. An oblique position for the gallery above the doors offers a greater argument from convenience. Occupants could then look down more convincingly on persons on the rear stage, and scenes in which people below talk to persons above perhaps be staged more effectively. But all such arguments are of little weight against the combined evidence of the pictures, and though the possibility may be admitted of an oblique arrangement of the doors in some theaters, there can surely be no certainty about it.

(2)

One of the striking facts about the Elizabethan stage is that it had to suggest changes of its imagined locations with little if any change in the physical appearance of the stage. The dialogue shows these changes of location, or we should scarcely detect them; but it is doubtful if some of these hints, carefully searched out by editors today, registered with audiences. Moreover, visual signs are more immediately effective than mere statements, and if the Elizabethan playwright could, by exercising care, give the doors some consistent significance it seems he would have done so. Whether he did or not the following pages attempt to show.

It may be worth noting that the significance of the doors in the Elizabethan stage shows little if any influence of the classical convention concerning doors as explained by Vitruvius and Pollux; see Lily B. Campbell, *Scenes and Machines on the English Stage* (1923), p. 17. On the Greek stage certain doors might lead to guest chambers, one entrance to the forum, one to the harbor; the unity of place permitted such continuous allocation. The shifting location of most Elizabethan plays did not permit this, but increased the necessity for clear designation. Hence the problem we are considering.

Some proof that emphasis was placed on the doors in Elizabethan drama is to be found in the items usually quoted concerning locality boards: Sidney's Asia on one side and Africa on the other, Percy's elaborate directions, etc.[1] Greg's curt dismissal of this subject (because of the absence of any evidence for it in the "Plots"), "We can

---

[1] See: Lawrence, *The Elizabethan Playhouse, First Series* (1912), "Title and Locality Boards," pp. 41-71; Chambers, *The Elizabethan Stage* (1923), index under "Labels." Professor Harold N. Hillebrand's "William Percy: An Elizabethan Amateur," *Huntington Library Quarterly*, I, iv (July, 1938), 391-416, with its conclusion that his plays were probably for private performances and mere curiosities, certainly diminishes their importance as evidence on staging. I have never held a brief for the importance of the plays as plays, but I still find it difficult to see how Percy made up his staging without some basis in Elizabethan custom. Perhaps there is enough to suggest it in the conventions I discuss in chapter VII.

. . . no longer believe that the exhibition of locality-boards was a general or even a usual practice of the Elizabethan stage"—see *Elizabethan Dramatic Documents* (1931), p. xi—scarcely disposes of the matter. The real objection to scene-boards is the difficulty of showing their usefulness and of ascertaining how they were managed. If they were placed above the doors, as seems likely from various references, they must in many plays have been frequently changed, business which would have taken time and distracted attention. It is possible, indeed probable, that only general signs were used. In a play like *Macbeth,* for example, if signs "Scotland" were displayed over the two stage doors until Act IV. iii, and then one of them changed to "England," the action would not be delayed and would be somewhat clarified. There is no indication in the text of the location of this scene in England until line 43; before that, if the audience are to know, they must remember that, in II. iii, Malcolm, in the height of the excitement of the discovery of Duncan's murder, had, in a single line, said that he was going to England, and that Macduff, in IV. i, was said to have fled to England. Some of the delayed indications of the locality of important scenes among the Red Bull plays are: *Sir Thomas Wyatt,* B, 91-95, in which the location is not announced until three and one half pages after the beginning of the scene; and 110-116, one and one half pages (but not too much should be made of this "bad" quarto on such a point); *Match Me in London,* B, 150-158, about a page; *The Four Prentices,* A, 196-205, two pages. Locality boards would make such scenes clear at once, but this is, after all, not very convincing evidence. Mostly there is little obscurity of location in scenes where it matters: it is announced in some shortly preceding scene, as in *The Four Prentices,* 175-178, by a Presenter for the next two or three scenes; or, to use more familiar examples, by a regular character in the play, as in *Hamlet,* I. ii. 252, for I. iv, when Hamlet promises to meet his friends "upon the platform"; or the characters when they enter state where they are, as in *Twelfth Night,* I. ii: "This is Illyria, lady"; or the location is shown indirectly but unmistakably by means of some speech or business, as when Brutus, in *Julius Caesar,* II. i, orders Lucius to fetch a taper to his study and we know at once he is at home. Such methods even make clear "journeying" scenes, those scenes which by a survival of medieval custom change the location in the midst of the scene, as in *A Woman Killed with Kindness,* B, the last scene of Act V, presently to be described. (For further discussion of "journeying" scenes in the Red Bull plays, see chapter VII.) Thus, the problem of location was usually managed expeditiously.[2]

(3)

But it must be clear that with the rapid imaginary shifting of scenes, anything that assisted the audience by means of sight would have been invaluable, and it is clear that the Elizabethans also made use of certain conventions no longer customary. One such convention was that by opening a curtain the scene was changed from outside to inside a house, or from one room to an adjoining one. A single example will suffice: in *A Woman Killed with Kindness,* B, V, where the scene begins on the way to the country house, then as a "journeying" scene shifts to before the house, and finally is changed to within the house apparently by the drawing of a curtain when Mistress Anne is discovered in bed. Or it may be the last change was shown by shoving the bed out upon the stage. Either procedure was common enough and is easily understood even by a modern reader.

A little less obvious method of showing a change of scene was a usage I have discussed elsewhere; see "Two Conventions of the Elizabethan Stage," *MP,* XVII (1919), 35-43. It consisted simply in an exit at one door and a re-entrance at another before enough time had elapsed for the place of exit to be forgotten. Examples with explicit directions occur among the Red Bull plays in *All's Lost by Lust,* C, V. i, ii, where the scene shifts from one room to another, and II *Iron Age,* B, 371-385.

This latter scene is worth examination in detail. It begins at Troy with the Trojans before the city congratulating themselves on the departure of the Greeks. On page 372 there is a direction, "The Horse is discouered," and Aneas says, "Soft, what huge Engine's that left on the strond." Presumably the curtain has opened to display it. After Synon's lying tale and Laocoon's death—apparently off stage—there is talk of breaking down the walls and hauling the horse into the city, but there are no directions for such action and certainly no chance for it. But this talk has—imaginatively—put the horse within the city. The Trojans exeunt, 377, Synon soliloquizes on the success of his treachery, produces "the key vnto this machine," and exits, 378; then the Greeks from the fleet enter and hide in ambush—outside the city—awaiting Synon's signal. Next, "Enter Synon with a torch aboue," 379; Ulysses says, "Now with a soft march enter at this breach," and we have the direction, "They march softly in at one doore and presently in at another. Enter Synon with a stealing pace

---

[2] For a longer discussion of some of these phases of the problem of location see: A. C. Sprague's *Shakespeare and the Audience* (1935), chapter II. Of others, especially the conventions about to be mentioned, he seems curiously unaware.

holding the key in his hand," and the other Greeks "leape from out the Horse: And as if groping in the darke, meete with Agamemnon and the rest." Thus, by the conversation about moving the horse and by the use of the convention I am illustrating, the scene had been shown as shifting from outside to inside the city. Nor does it appear that the curtain had closed over the horse after its first discovery. The audience was to suppose the horse first outside, then inside, the city— although it had not moved at all.

On the strength of these explicit directions for exit and immediate re-entrance we may assume a similar method of procedure even where no directions occur. Thus, *The Royal King*, B, III. iii, is before a whore-house and visitors knock for entrance; III. iv, is in the house, but has no signs of being a rear stage scene. A similar situation occurs in II *If You Know Not Me*, B, 307-315. *The Hector of Germany*, B, B 3v-B 4, is before a garden reached by a door; B 4-C 2, is in the garden with a bank to sit on. To discover the bank, the scene may have been placed on the rear stage. In *Edward II*, B, the short scene, I. iii, only five lines in length, separates an exit and re-entrance, which could be managed by this convention to show a change of scene. The last part of Act III of *The Golden Age*, A, could use this convention to show the progress of the hunt. *The Brazen Age*, A, begins, 172, at court; indicates by the dialogue, 179, a shift to the bank of a river; then the river is swum (off-stage), and entrance according to this convention is the obvious way to show the scene has changed to the other side. Other instances could be cited but these may suffice.

Opinions will differ as to how much dialogue may intervene between the exit and re-entrance without rendering this convention inapplicable, but there can be no doubt that it was a custom of the Elizabethan theater.[3]

(4)

With this clear demonstration of the importance of the doors, we are not only justified in thinking the stage doors had a special importance, but we are forced to think so. It mattered where actors went out and came in. It mattered so much that one can but speculate

---

[3] The other convention concerning the doors, discussed in the same article, may be briefly noted here. This convention was that the locking of one door could be taken as meaning the locking of all. Possible examples in the Red Bull plays are *The White Devil*, A, V. vi, *Match Me in London*, B, 208-212, and *The Wonder of a Kingdom*, B, 257-262. In *The Devil's Law Case*, A, III. ii, the doors to the stage are supposed locked, but there is no emphasis on a single door. In some other cases of locking *one* door, the other doors are not supposed locked, for example, *The Devil's Law Case*, V, iv, where two persons are locked in a closet.

whether the significance lasted on from scene to scene: that is, whether a door, because it meant some special place in one scene, did not usually continue to mean the same place in later scenes unless the author went to definite pains to break this significance. Study of this management of the doors has not received much attention, and is indeed a tantalizing business, but is worth some notice.

A play which illustrates more conveniently than our Red Bull plays both the advantages and difficulties of this idea of the significance of the doors is *Arden of Feversham*, easily available in a not too much edited form in Brooke's *Shakespeare Apocrypha* (1908), and Schelling's *Typical Elizabethan Plays*, first edition; references in the following summary are to Brooke.

(5)

Arden is usually dated 1586-92 and was first published in 1592. It is probably much more precise in its realistic details, among them the location of its various scenes and the exact particulars of its crime, than are most plays, because it was dramatizing a well-known story of ordinary life. Thus, some of the stage directions may state the precise fact without any corresponding exactness in the presentation. For example, a direction, V. i. 365, reads: "Then they beare the body into the fields," but "into the fields" certainly arises from the facts of the story and not from something in the staging.

William Poel gave this play with a multiple staging of three sets. We shall assume nothing so unusual, but only a stage with three doors, Right, Center, and Left. The other items of staging are simple. The play calls for a ditch into which Shakebag fell and from which he spoke several lines. The ditch may have been a trapdoor, or perhaps only imaginary and indicated by pantomime. There were also a shop with a front, of which the shutter could be let down, and a discoverable space large enough to seat several persons. The shop front may have been placed in the rear stage for the single scene in which it occurred, II. ii, or a shop setting may have stood beside the curtained space, both reached from the tiring-house by the center door.

The play began in or before Arden's house, indicated at the very beginning by Arden's and Francklin's entrance through the closed curtains. This significance continued throughout Act I (a modern division) the other doors serving the one as "the painter's house"—so labeled in line 245—the other as leading to "the key," line 89, and from line 418 on, toward London; this is stated three times within fifteen lines. At line 361 we may assume that the curtains opened, showing the table set for breakfast for four in Arden's house. The significance of the central curtains, or the door they concealed, became especially effective at the end of Act I, where, if Mosbie and Alice went out that way, not even a deaf member of the audience could miss sensing their treachery to Arden.

In Act II. i, the separate entrances of Greene with Bradshaw and Black Will with Shakebag, the former from Feversham, the latter from no specified place, gave no special significance to the doors, but the scene as a whole served to shift the location of the following scenes to London. Scene ii, in London, used the shop setting but is otherwise of no special interest for staging. Near the end, however, it set with great care the scene for Act III, Michael, Arden's servant, directing his murderers thus, line 188 ff:

> This night come to his house at Aldersgate:
> The dores Ile leaue vnlockt against you come.
> No sooner shall ye enter through the latch,
> Ouer the thresholde to the inner court,
> But on your left hand shall you see the staires
> That leads directly to my M[aisters] chamber:
> There take him and dispose him as ye please.

Just how literally this description was carried out may be doubted; shall we conclude on the basis of this that the stairs were actually visible on the stage of this (unidentified) theater? They are not mentioned in Holinshed; perhaps this detail does come from the stage. However, in view of the Elizabethan usual use of description to take the place of what was not shown, the presence of the stairs need not be insisted on.

At any rate it is not unlikely that the first scene of Act III was in this "inner court," that Arden, Francklin, and then Michael, entered at the door at the (actor's) right, supposed to lead to the street; and that the door on the left hand of anyone entering there, that is the center door, led to the stairs, which took one inside the house. We may note that this arrangement of the doors suggests a theory I advanced in "William Percy and his Plays," *MP*, XII, (1914), 120, that the stairs to the upper stage are usually described as leading from the center door. Arden and Franklin exeunt through this center door, to bed, Michael re-enters from there and after presumably unlocking the door Right, (there is no direction), returns to sit on the Center threshold. Then he goes into hysterics in thinking of the approaching murder, and his cries call back Arden and Francklin (entering through Center). Arden suspects mischief and finds "the dores were all vnlockt."

"Dores" suggests a question. Really only the right door is supposed to lead to the street and is the only one, therefore, to be locked. Does Arden, however, try the left door as well? Or does this plural, like Michael's in Act V. i. 210 (see below), really refer to but one door? In any case, though there is no direction, Arden must lock the street-door, Right, possibly the other front-stage door, Left, and retire to bed, Center.

Now comes an example of a kind of scene not uncommon in Elizabethan drama, and one which, I think, raises real difficulties. In this scene (Sc. ii) the murderers appear, supposedly outside the house, and, trying the house door, find it locked. This happens at line 34, where Shakebag says, "This is the doore; but soft, me thinks tis shut." They must have entered without difficulty though we have just seen all the doors, except the Center one, supposedly locked, and they must be at once imagined outside a house we have just been inside of. Of course, the text soon makes this understood, but how was it visually shown?

Lawrence in *The Physical Conditions of the Elizabethan Public Playhouse* (1927), p. 65, thinks I am unduly exercised about such scenes: "The explanation is simple. The one set of gates did duty for both kinds of scenes, the dialogue conveying to the audience on which side of the gates they were supposed to be." His remark shows I have not made the problem clear. Of course, the doors are the same for indoor and outdoor scenes—that is precisely the difficulty. How was their different significance made visually clear?

Still, perhaps, Lawrence is right and the only means made use of was the dialogue. The entering villains are known as such to the audience, the situation and staging have been carefully made clear. Perhaps the stupidest spectator would not be hindered by even a momentary obscurity. If so, then this chapter is largely concerned with imaginary matters and the doors had no continuing visual significance. But I find this hard to believe. Reading such a scene, of course, raises no difficulty, for in reading we are not hindered by visual memory. On our modern stage the scenes would be definitely different and we should expect the doors to have different significances. But how was this arranged to satisfy a thickwitted groundling, viewing obviously the same doors in the two scenes?

So much more important is sight than words that I suspect even an intelligent member of the audience, not knowing the story, might be momentarily in doubt. Such an interference of the dramatic tension would, especially at this place in the play, be unfortunate. So one wonders if there was not some custom, some conventional procedure— say like our falling curtain, or like the convention of exit at one door and re-entrance at another—which broke the connected significance of the doors, and signalled to the audience that the door they on the inside had just seen locked, was now being viewed from the outside.

A possible means which will at once suggest itself, and which will work satisfactorily for this play, is to have closed the curtains on the rear stage. Since opening the curtains regularly signals the change of locations from outside a house or room to inside it, why should not closing them have the opposite significance? Then the convention would be that closing the curtains would put us outside the house, and it would be natural enough that we should be watching the murderers trying to open the door, Right, locked only a moment before on the inside. A slight hint that the curtains do close is found in Arden's remark, the last line in sc. i, "Michael, farewell; I pray thee dreame no more," as if he were leaving him once more on the stage to guard the gate.

For a while I played with the idea that a real door instead of, or with, a curtain closed the rear stage. The idea of such a door is not a new one. Chambers thinks that gates could have been inserted at will in the tiring-house walls. That this opening should have had some more permanent protection than curtains against the weather seems only sensible. There are also a few hints in the plays of such doors. I have noted in the Red Bull plays only one case of "Enter and knock" as in *Romeo and Juliet*, III. iii, Folio,—that in *Greene's Tu Quoque*, B, 188, "Enter another Messenger hastily and knockes." But the cave-arbor of *The Brazen Age*, A, 227, is definitely described as having a door. So have the shops. But these instances may concern only structures, not the rear stage, and even if such doors to the rear stage could be proved, it would not explain very well the sort of scene we are now considering. The door we saw locked, say stage Right, would not be the door the murderers would be trying to open, which by this theory would be the front center door, if I may term it such, nor would this front center door, of course, be the door Arden locks. If it were, he would have to be *behind* it and speak the five last lines out of sight!

Accepting the convention of a closing curtain as a visual way of changing the significances of the doors, and postponing for a little the consideration of similar scenes in the Red Bull plays, we may examine further the use of the doors in *Arden*. Scene iii of Act III shows Arden, Francklin, and Michael in the morning after the thwarted attack. Arden tells Michael to go make the bed, and so the scene is presumably again in the inner court with the curtains open. Scene iv begins, "Here enters Michaell at one doore. Here enters Greene, Will, and

Shakebag at another doore." The scene is unlocated, except by infer-
ence as a street in London. The important point is that Michael enters
apart from the others to show he has not been with them; the exact
location does not count for much. In the ensuing conversation the
murderers twice mention the scene of their next attempt against Arden
as to be on Raynum Down. To give this information is the real purpose of the scene.

Act III, scene v, is at Feversham. The entrance of Mosbie and Alice,
Arden's wife, shows this clearly enough. Probably they entered
through the center door or the curtains; at least there is nothing that
suggests that this entrance was not the one leading to Arden's house
in all the Feversham scenes. But the doors do not count for much
in this scene or the next. This next scene is a "journeying" scene: it
begins rather vaguely with the murderers awaiting Arden, then shows
him near Rochester, then going on toward Raynum Down, and finally
meeting the murderers there, the company of another traveler pre-
venting them from attacking him.

Act IV has four different scenes, the first and last not far from
Arden's house, the two others near the ferry, in one of which Shakebag, because of a fog, referred to half a dozen times, falls into a
ditch (d., the trapdoor?). The text makes the scenes clear, entrances
of the characters whether through different doors or together are
significant, but which doors are used does not seem of consequence; the
central entrance can, however, be kept as leading more or less immediately to Arden's house, though only the first part of the first
scene is really there. It would not, however, be a bad touch for Mosbie
and Alice to enter fondling each other from Center through the curtains as they go to meet Arden.

In Act V the doors count for a good deal again. Scene i begins rather
vaguely, but by line 111 is definitely at Arden's house; the countinghouse is referred to in line 113, and at line 153 the door to it—shall
we suppose it Right?—is certainly pointed out: the murderers are to
be hidden behind it: "When this doore oppens next, looke for his
death," they say, and go out there, locking the door behind them.
Michael enters from the street door, say Left, and is sent, through
Center, to "fetch in the tables." Certainly by this time if not from the
beginning of the scene, and probably before line 111, the curtains
have been opened. The plan is that as Arden and the rest play at
tables, with Arden sitting on a stool so as to be more easily over-
powered, and Mosbie on a chair as the honored guest, Will and
Shakebag, until then hidden in the countinghouse, shall, at a signal,
rush out and do the long desired murder. Michael is to guard the

counting house door, and as soon as Arden and the rest are in is to lock the street door so that later guests may not intrude. All this is carried out: it is noticeable that Michael says he has locked the doors, line 210, though actually only the single street door is locked. It is not necessary to emphasize, I think, how greatly the dramatic effectiveness of this scene is heightened by keeping the significance of the doors clear and centering the attention on the door Right, where the murderers are hiding. They show themselves to increase the interest, before they attack, and finally enter, a curious detail, between Michael's legs. After the murder is committed, a direction reads: "they lay the body in the Countinghouse," that is, inside door Right. Then Will and Shakebag exeunt Left, or more secretly through the house, Center. Susan announces that guests are at the [street] door, Left, and Mosbie goes out to greet them, while Arden's wife and Susan try unsuccessfully to remove the blood. Mosbie, returning, tells them to cover the blood with rushes. Then the guests enter, and Mosbie takes Arden's seat, while Arden's wife by her nervous behavior seems likely to give the whole situation away. Finally the guests are got rid of; and the wife, almost hysterical, and Susan the maid "open the countinghouse doore and looke vppon Arden" (d). They are bringing out the body when Mosbie and Greene return, only to be warned by Michael that the mayor and the watch are coming. Again the street door is locked and Mosbie and Greene are told to go out "at the back dore, ouer the pyle of woode," but first "they beare the body into the fields" (d). The fields, as I have already said, are surely only a detail from the story as it happened; so, perhaps, are the back door and the pile of wood though neither is mentioned in Holinshed. Certainly they need not appear in the staging. Of course, when the curtains are open, as in this scene, the usually assumed side doors within the rear stage are available for use as well as the two front stage doors, but no assumption of extra doors is necessary here: exeunt Right, through the countinghouse, or better, Center, through the house, fits the text, and keeps the significance of the doors unbroken. The officers are finally let in at the street door, Left, search is made, the blood is found beneath the rushes, and the wife and servants are taken away to view the body.

Scene ii is a quite unlocated soliloquy of Shakebag's, obviously done on the front stage with entrance at one door and exit at the other.

Scene iii is back at Arden's. It begins with the Mayor saying, "See M[istris] Arden, where your husband lyes." This seems, therefore, clearly a discovery, and in Arden's house. The last two scenes are only vaguely located and do not use the doors significantly.

So long a discussion of a play not belonging to the Red Bull repertory is justified here only because it requires less explanation of other points not concerned with the usage of the doors than do the Red Bull plays and because the significance of the doors does appear so clearly. The play, according to Brooke's division, has eighteen scenes, each "journeying" scene being counted as one though the location changes. The following scheme will summarize at a glance what has just been explained:

At Feversham	Other definite locations	Indefinite locations
*I. i, At Arden's house in Feversham, first before it, then within.		
		II. i, Not definite.
	II. ii, Before a shop in London.	
	*III. i, Arden's house in London—inside.	
	* ii, Arden's house in London—outside.	
	* iii, Arden's house in London—inside.	
		III. iv, Not definite.
III. v, In or before Arden's house in Feversham.		
	III. vi, Raynum Down.	
IV. i, In or before Arden's house in Feversham.		
	IV. ii, Near the ferry.	
	iii, Near the ferry.	
IV. iv, On the way to Arden's in Feversham.		
*V. i, Before, then in, Arden's house in Feversham.		
		V. ii, Not definite.
*V. iii, Within Arden's house in Feversham.		
		V. iv, v, Not definite.

The doors count especially in the starred scenes, but have more or less significance in *all* the scenes, except those of the last column, all of which are short; even in these the entrance of the characters separately in III. iv, has meaning, and if, in V. ii, and iv, Shakebag and Will enter at one door and go out at another the action will be clearer. Thus the doors are shown to have, first, real significance in single scenes; second, continued significance in many scenes. The care with which the location is shifted and the significance of the doors changed are added evidence in support of the point in question.

(5)

With this illustration of the significance of the doors in mind, we may turn to the Red Bull plays in which the significance matters. They offer some especially interesting problems in scenes first inside, then outside, gates or doors. Some I have discussed already as taken care of by the exit-enter convention; others are *A Woman Killed with Kindness, I If You Know Not Me, The Golden Age, The Silver Age.* If the succeeding discussion is too full of "probablys" and "perhapses" and seems to admit too many alternatives, the reader may still notice that whatever may be the true explanation, all the scenes do emphasize the significance of the doors.

The simplest of these cases, *The Silver Age*, B, Act II, necessitates the assumption of no unusual conventions. It concerns the familiar story of Jupiter's trick on Amphitrio, and is not particularly difficult if we assume that the door to the house in this series of scenes is one of the side doors. "Thunder and lightning. Iupiter descends in a cloude," 98. He is joined by Ganymede "shapt like Socia," whom he directs to knock at the door. Socia's fellow servants come from the house to welcome him. Then "Enter at one dore Alcmena" and her servants, "at the other Iupiter" like Amphitrio. Since this formula usually indicates use of the side doors, we have the door to the house as one of them, say Left. Alcmena orders elaborate preparations for his reception and a banquet, which is "brought in." After it is over they retire and Ganymede remains, 102, outside the house, "set heere to keepe the gate." To him enters, 102, Right, the real Socia, whom he proceeds to confuse in 125 lines or more, and then drive away. Jupiter and Alcmena re-enter from the house, Left, and Jupiter goes away, Right, taking the false Socia (Ganymede) with him, 107.

The real Amphitrio and the real Socia come (Right), and are greeted by his wife (enter Left), surprised at his quick return. Angered at her story that he has already been at home, "Amphitrio beats in his men" (Left), 114. Jupiter, still in disguise, returns and goes in with Alcmena. Ganymede comes and says, 116, "Iupiter and Alcmena are entered at the backe gate [is that through Center?] whil'st Amphitrio is beating his seruants out at the foregate [that is Left]. Als in vp-rore: I do but watch to see him out in the street, to shut the gates against him." "Enter Amphitrio, beating before him his seruants" (Left), 116. Ganymede exits (Left) saying, 116, "Now for a tricke to shut the gates vpon him." Amphitrio turns to go in (Left) and finds the gate locked; "Knockes, enter Ganimed aboue," 117. After a short conversation, Ganemede says he will come down, but it is the real Socia who enters. Jupiter, Alcmena, and Ganemede now enter (Left), 119, and Jupiter persuades Amphitrio's friends that he is Amphitrio and says, "These gates [Left] that them exclude, Stand open to you." Then, seeing Juno, he withdraws, 120, and Amphitrio and the real Socia lie down to sleep outside the house. "Iuno and Iris descend from the heauens," 121. Juno enters the house (Left). "Thunder and lightning. All the seruants run out of the house [Left] affrighted . . . Iupiter appeares in his glory [above] vnder a Raine-bow, to whom they all kneele," 122, and the act ends.

Thus we never surely see the interior of the house at all unless the banqueting scene with its seats, 101-102, was discovered, and also possibly, 109-115. If these passages were given on the rear stage, the opening and closing of the curtains would signal a change of scene adequately enough, and after the scenes were over, the doors could still keep in succeeding scenes the significance previously given them. If no curtains were employed, the use of the left door consistently as the "foregate" or principal entrance, would still keep the location clear. That, it seems to me, would be a necessary assistance for doing so.

Next in complexity is *I If You Know Not Me*, B. A throne recurs throughout the play (scenes ii, ix, xii, xxiii); Elizabeth "enters in bed" in scene iii. In scene xviii Phillip listens "behind the arras." Keeping these circumstances in mind, we may notice scene vii and those following, 210-215. Scene vii is before the Tower gate; Elizabeth, brought to the Tower by river, steps "too short into the water"; she resists going "vnto a grate of iron," sits on "this cold stone," rain falls: certainly some of these details are only imagined in the actual setting. She finally enters the Tower, and a friend says of the Constable "you need not bolt and lock so fast," the bolting being done, aparently, out of sight behind the door. The Constable re-enters (d) three lines later, and though some of the people who were looking on outside the Tower are still on the stage, the scene is now within the Tower, and soldiers are serving dishes to Elizabeth's chamber. (This being true, it is hardly necessary to object if the throne, used a few scenes before and to be used again in a scene a little further on, is also on the stage in view all the time.) Not too much should be made of this play because of the scrambled condition of the text. But this scene could be staged not too obscurely in Elizabethan custom by having Elizabeth enter, first, say Right; exit with the Constable through Center as the Tower gate, and the Constable re-enter at once as from Elizabeth's prison at Right or Left, thus signaling the change of location. If when the Center door was the Tower gate the curtain was open, and if after Elizabeth had gone in, the curtain was closed to conceal the doors, there would also be a visual change of the stage to show that a change of scene had taken place, but this is not at all necessary, and there is no hint of it in the directions or text.

Another illustration of the change of location by exit and immediate re-entry, but with a difference, occurs at the end of *The Silver*

Age, B, 156-164. At the first of this scene Theseus and his friends are beating at the gates of Hell (d), where Cerberus kills one and wounds another. Then Hercules comes, binds Cerberus in chains, says:

> Keep thou this rauenous hell-hound gyu'd & bound
> Hels bowels I must pierce, and rouze blacke *Dis.*
> Breake (with my fists) these Adamantine gates,
> The Iron percullis teare, and with my club
> Worke my free passage (maugre all the fiends)
> Through these infernals. Lo, I sinke myselfe
> In *Charons* barge, Il'e ferry burning Styx.
> Ransacke the pallace where grim *Pluto* reignes,
> Mount his tribunall, made of sable Iet,
> Despight his blacke guard, stownd him in his chaire,
> And from his arme, snatch beauteous *Proserpine.*

Then (d) "Hercules sinkes himselfe: Flashes of fire; the Diuels appeare at euery corner of the stage with seuerall fire-workes. The Iudges of hell, and the three sisters run ouer the stage, Hercules after them [now, I think through one of the stage doors]; fire-workes all ouer the house. Enter Hercules." After ten more lines, "Enter Pluto with a club of fire, a burning crowne, Proserpine, the Iudges, the Fates, and a guard of Diuels, all with burning weapons." Pluto defies Hercules, but the latter "fels Pluto, beats off the Diuels with all their fire-workes, rescues Proserpine." Hercules appeals for judgment to the Planets, seven of whom enter and "take their place as they are in height" (d). Twice the hearing is referred to as "a sessions." Finally "exeunt three ways . . . Hercules dragging Cerberus one way: Pluto, hels Iudges, the Fates and Furies downe to hell: Iupter, the Gods and Planets ascend to heauen," and Homer, concluding, says "Ioue and his mount, Pluto with his descends." Translated literally this seems to mean that the section began with the Greeks beating on the trapdoor. Cerberus enters through it or at one side. Hercules, after binding Cerberus, goes, if he follows the order of his speech, down the trap, and then re-entering at a side door, drives the officials of Hell before him, so changing the scene, though it is clear that Cerberus bound is still on the stage.

It is tempting to think that the curtains may also have closed for the ten lines after Hercules' last entrance, to allow the putting in place of Pluto's tribunal with seats for Pluto, Proserpine, the Judges, and the Fates—eight in all. This would put the tribunal on the rear stage. But I am skeptical about a literal carrying out of this final direction; for ten people either together or singly to use a trapdoor is bad enough, but for seven to use the lift is worse. As a matter of fact, Pluto and his powers could logically exeunt at the door where Hercules entered, or they could exeunt through Center. Either could consistently lead to "Hell," and if Jupiter and the other Heaven-bound personages went out at another door, all the proprieties and conventions would have been observed.

A Woman Killed with Kindness, B, raising a similar problem to that of *Arden*, is more difficult than the scenes just discussed. The play has three scenes which suggest the use of the curtained space: "Enter in prison," IV. i; a lute is found "flung in a corner," V. ii; and "Enter in bed," V. v. The gate sequence comes in IV. ii-iv. In IV. ii, furnishings for a table and seats for four are ordered fetched. This would suggest that the scene is on the front stage, but if we actually see the servants lock the gate in IV. iii, it will help if the curtains are open so that closing them will show the action has then moved outside. As a matter of fact neither dialogue nor directions require the locked gate to be in sight in IV. iii. The real problem begins in IV. iv. Frankford, returning to trap his wife, enters, shall we say, Right. First, he comments on the keys he is carrying; then says, "Now to my gate," presumably unlocks the left door, though there is no direction, asks for his dark lantern, warns Nicholas to "Tread softly, softly," and then they must exeunt Left, though again there is no direction. According to the convention already mentioned, they should then enter Right, cross to Left, which Frankford now designates as "the last door," the one he had called a little earlier, when talking of the keys, "that door that's bawd unto my shame." He exits there after unlocking it (in pantomime), re-enters again for a passionate speech on what he has found, goes into the room again, drives Wendoll out on the main stage, is followed by Mistress Frankford, and finally exits to his study (t), presumably Center. Since we do not see within the study, apparently the curtains did not open when he entered the house. The change in the significance of the Left door may seem to contradict the point I am making, but that point is not that the doors always remain the same throughout a sequence of scenes, but rather that they keep or change their significance according to customary conventions; in this case it is changed by the exit and immediate entrance at another door, and perhaps the closing of the curtain after the locking of the gate in scene iii.

From the Red Bull plays the series of scenes presenting the most problems occurs in *The Golden Age*, A, 53-71. The unusual difficulty in this sequence is that we see both the inside and the outside of a gate at the same time. A half-open door, by convention supposed locked, is perhaps possible, for convention permits almost anything, but does not seem very likely nor would conversations so held be very effective at best. A half-door, the lower half locked, is also possible, but I know of not even a hint of such an arrangement in any Elizabethan play. Perhaps there was a door at the side of the rear stage, visible through one of the front stage doors or perhaps the rear stage projected (as in the Messallina picture) and had a door in its side wall. Then this rear stage side-door would be the "gate" of the sequence in question.

The sequence concerns Jupiter's affair with Danae. After a short introductory speech by Homer and a dumb show, there is a scene in which Jupiter hears how Danae is held by her father, King Acrisius, in a tower of brass, guarded by four old beldams, and determines to make his way to her.

On page 57 we are at the tower: I assume the curtains to be open and the old women are talking in the curtained space. There is a direction, "The 'larme bell rings," and one of them says: "The larme bell rings, It should be K. Acrisius by the sound of the clapper." Another adds, "Then clap close to the gate and let him in." So they move toward the "gate," that is, the rear stage side door, which we may designate as X. The direction says only, "Enter Acrisius"; he begins, "Ladies well done: I like this prouidence And carefull watch ore Danae." Danae is summoned (she enters Center), is later dismissed (Center) to her chamber, and the scene ends, 60, with one of the old women saying, "Come let vs set our watch, and take our lodgings before the Princesse chamber." That is, they sit at Center.

So far the scene is clearly supposed within the tower. Whether the gate is in sight or not is not clear, but I have assumed that it is.

The next scene begins with the direction, "Enter Iupiter like a Pedler, the Clowne his man, with packs at their backes." They enter, shall we say, at Right. Jupiter tells the clown to ring the bell; the clown says, "Nay do you take the rope in your hand for lucke sake," and there is a direction, "He rings the bell [at X]. Enter the 4 Beldams," one of them saying, "To the gate, to the gate, and know who 'tis ere you open." So they in the tower go to X. There are forty lines in all spoken by Jupiter and the clown outside the tower (X) and twelve by the women within before one of the latter invites Jupiter into the Porter's lodge. A bit later one of them says, "Shut the gate for feare the King come, and if he ring clap the Pedlers into some of yon old rotten corners." Unquestionably we have had to see simultaneously both the inside and the outside of the tower. From now on for a while all the scene is inside the tower.

Next Danae (at Center) "Enters in state with the Beldams," and Jupiter courts her, while the clown shows off their peddler stuffs, and tries to keep the beldams from 'looking back' at Jupiter; presumably the clown and the old women are on the front stage.

Finally Danae says, "Yon [Center] is my doore. Dare not to enter there" and she exits, presumably through Center. The beldams say, "Some attend the Princesse; others see the Pedlers pack't out of the gate." Jupiter replies:

> This castle stands remote, no lodging neere,
> Spare vs but any corner here below,
> Bee't but the Inner porch, or the least staire-case,

and one of the women replies, "For this night take a nap vpon some bench or other." There is no direction, but the beldams withdraw, Jupiter tells the clown to sleep, while he, putting off his disguise, goes to make ready to court Danae "like a King."

I am not sure where he went out, certainly not Center for that was the door to Danae's room; hardly X for that would put him outside the tower; therefore, perhaps to Left. Once I was tempted to think the curtains closed at this point, but as the door at Center remains in sight, that is impossible. There is no exit direction for him, but there is a later entrance direction.

Then, 67, "Enter [Center] the foure old Beldams, drawing out Danae's bed: she in it. They place foure tapers at the foure corners." Her bed now stands on the rear stage or is brought through it to the front stage, changing, presumably, the scene to her chamber. She asks for music and dismisses the women, but there are no directions for music or for their exeunt. "Enter Iupiter crown'd with his Imperiall Robes," 68. Then "He lyes vpon her bed." Strictly he should have entered at Center but his, "Yon is the doore, that in forbidding me She bad me enter," hardly fits a door he had just come in by. "Iupiter puts out the lights and makes vnready." Danae says, "Before you come to bed, the curtaines draw," 69. These are, it would seem, the bed curtains. Six lines later, 70, "The bed is drawne in [at Center], and enter [perhaps he came from Center] the Clowne new wak't." The scene is thus changed back to the room in the tower before her chamber. The clown says, "I would I were out of this tower . . . if we should fall asleepe, and the King come and take vs napping where were we? . . . Fye vpon it, what a snorting forward and backeward these Beldams keep? [They, I suspect, are off stage behind Center, presumably in Danae's chamber.] . . . Well, here must I sit and waite the good howre, till the gate be open, and suffer my eyes to do that,

which I am sure my cloake neuer will, that is, to take nap. . . . Exit.
Enter [Center] Iupiter and Danae in her night-gowne." Jupiter says,
"The day-starre 'gins t' appeare, the Beldams stir, Ready t' vnlocke the
gate, faire Queene adue." Danae "exits" (Center). Jupiter asks the
clown for "Some cloud to couer mee." The clown says, "Cast your old
cloake about you." "Enter the foure Beldams in hast" [Center] saying, "Where be these Pedlers? nay quickly, for heauen sake: the gate
is open, nay when? farewell," and the final direction is, "Exeunt
diuers waies," 71, which, I take it, means that Jupiter and the clown
leave the "tower" at X and the stage at Right, and the old women
through Center, although it is barely possible that the curtain closed
when the bed was drawn in. This gate is not necessarily in sight at the
end of the scene.

I do not press this explanation, especially because it assumes a fourth
door, and requires that the outside of the rear stage be visible. Still,
with this fourth door the other scenes I have cited might be more
easily explained: thus in *Arden* and *A Woman Killed with Kindness*,
X would be the door locked with so much emphasis, and no real problem would remain. But those plays can be explained otherwise: *The
Golden Age* cannot. Granted this explanation, the rest of the sequence
is clear enough. Also this explanation by means of a fourth door of
which both sides are visible is important for our next chapter. It will
be returned to there.

(6)

There is another point to consider concerning the doors. Brought
up on modern ideas of realism of staging, we naturally tend to make
the doors and the balcony above them fit into some sort of consistency.
But it is doubtful whether the Elizabethans shared this feeling. The
most striking inconsistency in the use of the balcony in the Red Bull
plays has been called attention to already: *The Rape of Lucrece*, A,
242, where one part of the balcony is a hill outside the city; another
part the wall of the city; and one of the doors below, a bridgehead
leading to the city. Just about as far from realism is *The Four Prentices*, A, 230. The Persians and their prisoners (at least eleven persons)
appear on the walls of Jerusalem, the Persians flourishing their ver-
milion flag and defying the Christians below. The Sultan finally "sets
vp his standard & Crowne" (d), 233; the Christians attack, are re-
pulsed; then Guy and Eustace "enter at two seuerall dores, Guy and
Eustace climbe vp the wals, beate the Pagans, take away the Crownes
on their heads, and in their stead hang vp the contrary Shields, and
bring away the Ensignes, flourishing them, seuerall wayes." Then

come, 234, eighteen lines by the Persians *within the city*, and, it appears, *not* on the walls since they end the scene by going to defend them. Next, 235-240, we are with the Christians, before the city again, who talk of the shields on the walls as in sight, 237. The Persians, scorning to fight from behind walls, now come out (nothing is said whether through the "gate" or not) "at one doore," the Christians marching forth presumably at another. There is much talk of "the Saviours Sepulchre" in "this vale," the breach, cannon, the gate Antiocha. "Behold our campe." "Suruey ours too." Attacks and counter attacks follow. By page 246, the Persians, it would seem at bay within the city, say that the Christians have taken the pagan standards from the walls and put up a cross instead. Finally, 247, "The foure brethren each of them kill a Pagan King, take off their Crownes, and exeunt: two one way and two another way. Retrait." They immediately re-enter, rejoicing in their victory. I see no reason for this separate exeunt and re-entry except its processional value. How much of all the detail just enumerated was imaginary? A good deal of it, I think, as is also the case with what follows: allusions to Eustace's tent, Christ's tomb, etc. The only way these scenes could be kept intelligible would be by differences in costume of pagans and Christians. Whether one door served throughout as an entrance to the city I cannot be sure. Certainly some of the doors were quite incongruous with the walls above.

City gates occur in conjunction with the walls in *The Brazen Age*, A, 206, 223-225, where probably they are entered only by people fleeing to the city. In *I Iron Age*, B, 298-302, 319-320, use of the gates seems to be avoided (is it because the rear stage is Achilles' tent?). *II Iron Age*, B, 371 ff., with the great horse, raises an interesting problem, but this has already been discussed (see above, sec. 3). In this play the gate to the city seems one of the side doors.

House fronts with balcony raise somewhat different difficulties. *I If You Know Not Me*, 241, is not, however, an example, for the scene is thought of as inside the house. Elizabeth and her friends are looking off across country for messengers. One after another enters. The horse of the first is described as having fallen at the gate (naturally, off stage). Others enter in turn. Either of the side doors would serve for them to come in through, but neither could be very illusive of entrance from a distance.

(7)

The conclusion of all this discussion about the doors is that there could have been little verisimilitude of relation of the doors with the balcony above, but that some at least of the plays do show care to keep the significance of the doors clear, the author going to some pains to give them definite meanings, and by textual allusion or convention to make any change in that significance unmistakable. The purpose of this attention to the doors, is, therefore, not realism but clarity. It is, perhaps, a survival of medieval custom when different mansions stood for different locations; on the Elizabethan stage the doors took the places of most of them, and some assistance had to be given the audience that they might more easily follow the story.

CHAPTER VII

WAS THERE A REAR STAGE? PRINCIPLES OF STAGE MANAGEMENT

(1)

TO QUESTION after all these years of discussion whether the Red Bull or any Elizabethan theater had a rear stage seems absurd or even impertinent. For this reason I have so far assumed, with specific notice, that such a permanently curtained space was always present. But now we are in a better position to consider this question without any assumption, and that is the first purpose of this chapter. The question is, after all, not so absurd as it may appear. The clearest evidence we have for the arrangements of the Elizabethan public theater is the Swan picture, and on it as it stands no permanently hung curtain is practicable. The other contemporary pictures of the theaters are scarcely more in its favor. They have, it is true, hangings at the back, but lack stage doors, and one of the few certainties about the Elizabethan theater is that all its stage doors were not concealed by the curtain. The Messallina does, perhaps, allow for such doors beyond its margins, but not the Roxana and not the so-called Red Bull picture. Yet reconstruction after reconstruction of the Elizabethan stage appears disregarding this fundamental evidence of the Swan picture. Of course all writers on the subject have furnished explanation—I have myself. But the hard fact remains that the Swan picture permits no permanently curtained rear stage at all without drastic structural rearrangement.

At the same time there is no possible doubt that the Red Bull had a curtain, arras, traverse—different names, it would seem, for the same thing—and that this curtain was sometimes used for discoveries. Proof of this will be furnished presently; now I am concerned with this positive disagreement of the evidence.

(2)

A possible reconciliation is suggested by various points already presented in earlier chapters, but not so far brought together in this connection. To state the idea as quickly and briefly as possible, it is this: instead of a permanently placed rear stage, a structural part of the theater, was there perhaps a curtained framework easily removable, and so not used in all plays and, as it happened, not present on the Swan stage at the time of De Witt's visit? Such a framework is at least a possible way to provide a discoverable space on the Swan stage with no fundamental change in construction. If, as has been suggested, the play illustrated in the Swan picture is *Twelfth Night*, it is interesting to notice that *Twelfth Night* does not require, indeed hardly permits, the use of a curtained space—a circumstance which would explain the absence of a curtain in the drawing. There is nothing essentially unusual in the idea of a removable framework, but the possible uses have scarcely been much considered.

Sir Edmund Chambers in *The Elizabethan Stage* (1923), III, 106, admits practicable tents "pitched on the open boards," and suggests, III, 86, that the Swan, if it had no alcove stage, was "probably driven to provide for chamber scenes by means of some curtained structure on the stage itself." He does not elaborate on this idea nor point out its implications, but it is significant that he thinks of it. And we have already seen in chapter IV that separate structures did stand on the Elizabethan stage. Even without that discussion they would be clear from Henslowe's inventory. A rock and a cave—properties listed by Henslowe—could be used for discoveries; and to these may be added the shop and the tent. ("Studies" present a different problem, to be noted presently.) The picture of an arbor on the title-page of *The Spanish Tragedy* is especially applicable evidence, since even though some of the properties just mentioned may have been only rearrangements of an unindividualized curtained space, this arbor is clearly a special structure. It may indeed have been this on which Hieronimo "knock[ed] up the curtain" in the last act—an instance which at least shows that a curtain was sometimes specially put up on the stage. Or this curtain could have been "knocked up" over one of the stage doors, though how the spectators in the gallery would have seen it is not clear. What is clear, however, is that separate structures and a curtain, not always in place, did exist on the public stage.

Also significant is Chambers' suggestion (*op. cit.*, III, 72), that the description from *The English Wagner Book* (1594), of the stage appearing in the sky on a rainbow to the people of Wittenberg in 1540, is really based on contemporary theater practice. I quote from the original as edited by Alfred E. Richards (Berlin, 1907), chapter VIII, pp. 66-75:

They might distinctly perceiue a goodlye Stage to be reard . . . therein was the high Throne wherein the King should sit, and that prowdly placed with two and twenty degrees to the top, and round about curious wrought chaires for diuerse other Potentates, there might you see the ground-worke at the one end of the Stage whereout the personated diuels should enter in their fiery ornaments, made like the broad wide mouth of an huge Dragon. . . . At the other end in opposition was seene the place where in the bloudlesse skirmishes are so often perfourmed on the Stage, the Wals . . . environed with high and stately Turrets . . . and hereat many in-gates and out-gates . . . brieflie nothing was there wanting that might make it a faire Castle. There might you see to be short the Gibbet, the Posts, the Ladder, the tiring house there everything which in the like houses either use or necessity makes common.

Thus this stage had at one time a throne, hell-mouth, a castle, a gibbet, posts, etc., but not even a hint of a rear stage.

Years ago I suggested that separate structures might have been used on the Elizabethan stage, but I did not pursue the argument because it was possible to show the essential medieval quality of the stage without it. In 1917 Miss Charlotte Porter constructed a model with a castle gate, trees, etc., as permanent structural features of the stage, which shows that she found the idea of separate structures necessary. A stage with a separate structure or several structures, of such a form as to allow discoveries of people and properties, is not, therefore, so impossible or unthinkable as may at first appear.

Whether the discoverable space was provided by a permanent rear stage or by a removable structure may not seem an important distinction. Really it shifts the whole emphasis of our inquiry. It is true that proof that the curtained space did not hide all the doors still would remain valid; "clashes" and "split" scenes would still be worth noticing; the idea would still hold that recurring properties in the curtained space or on the front stage would be left undisturbed so long as needed. But if we assume a permanent rear stage, our natural tendency is to look for scenes in which to use it, and to try so far as possible for modern consistency and realism. A removable structure, on the other hand, at once emphasizes the likeness of the Elizabethan to the medieval stage and largely minimizes these tendencies. It also explains without forced interpretations at least some of the "enters" which to the modern reader seem necessarily to mean "discovered," some of the numerous bringings-in of properties, and especially the curious and never satisfactorily accounted for lack of directions for the use of the curtains in many scenes where modern scholars have supposed them. Perhaps there were fewer discoveries because there was not always a curtain on the stage by which to make them. Thus the question whether there was a permanent rear stage or a removable curtained structure is of real significance.

What is the evidence in the matter? Let me say at once that I do not think that it is possible to prove certainly whether there was a permanent rear stage or not at the Red Bull. If the curtained space was used in most of the plays, it seems likely it would sooner rather than later have become a permanent fixture. Whether this had happened by 1625 at the Red Bull I see no way surely to determine. But certainly in view of the Swan picture, it is hardly sound to assume, as practically all students seem to be doing, the existence of such a permanent rear stage at all the public theaters, and, specifically, at the Red Bull.

The other pictures of the stage as a whole, as we have seen, do not help us much. Neither does the cut on the title-page of *Swetnam*, probably the nearest we come to a pictorial representation of the Red Bull stage in our period. This cut gives no hint even of a curtain, nor of doors at the side or in the center, nor of side walls. The play itself has no certainly discovered scene, but G 4—H 1, in which a hearse with a body on it is assumed as present and is not removed at the end of the scene, certainly suggests the use of a curtained space. It is hard, moreover, to imagine the pictured barrier as set up on the front stage. But if there was a curtained space, permanent or removable, should we not see its sides? The space represented in the picture is wide enough to allow five or six Elizabethan ladies to stand skirt to skirt, or perhaps about twenty feet across, certainly the extreme limit of the curtained space. The other title-page pictures (*Dr. Faustus, Friar Bacon and Friar Bungay*) also show no curtains. Thus these pictures in their minor way, and the Swan picture as most informing, are all definitely against a permanent curtain.

There are other arguments for a removable structure. If such a structure provided the curtained space, it must have been exposed on three sides instead of forming an alcove in the wall of the tiring-house. Such a structure would at once explain the gate sequence of *The Golden Age*, which demanded so much explanation in the last chapter, and the other gate sequences as well, because such a structure could easily have a visible entrance in its side walls.

Such a structure might also make more applicable some of the descriptions of the curtained space. These descriptions do not always occur in the scenes played in the curtained space itself; sometimes they come in scenes given in front of it. Of course, usually these descriptions must be taken as dramatic; that is, as arising from the story and the scene as imagined by the dramatist, rather than from the theater and what he knew the audience would be seeing. An instance curiously combining the dramatic and theatric occurs in *A Woman Killed with*

Kindness, B, IV. v, where near the end of the scene Frankford says that he will retire into his "study." I have in chapter VI interpreted "study" as meaning the curtained space, because this was a common term used for it. Here we do not see the interior, and Heywood could have used almost any suitable term as well. He did call the curtained space "study" here because that term fitted his story dramatically and also his habit: the curtains suggest the term "study" even though we see no "study" setting.

But "study" is not the only word for the curtained space. In the Red Bull plays "study" is used only when it is dramatically suitable, other situations calling forth other words. Thus in *II Iron Age*, B, 411, Egisthus hides in "the chamber behind the Bed-curtaines" (d); and "chamber" is naturally used (t) to describe a bedroom scene in *The White Devil*, A, V. iii. 174. It is worth noting, also, that in the first part of this scene, the man later shown in bed is said to withdraw into his "cabinet," when he, presumably, went to the curtained space. "Closet" may also sometimes refer to the curtained space, as perhaps in *Match Me in London*, B, 184-188, which is described as *in* a closet. (More often, where the interior of the closet is not shown and emphasis is put on locking it, as in *The Devil's Law Case*, A, V. iv. 156, 167, "closet" seems only a dramatic designation for one of the doors.)

More significant terms for the curtained space to show what it really looked like are those which do not exactly fit the dramatic situation. Such terms suggest that the playwright as he wrote saw the stage rather than the imagined location. Thus, is it too fanciful to suggest that there seems no dramatic reason for describing the sleeping devil discovered in *If It Be Not Good*, A, I. 1 as "cabind," unless he was in something that looked like a small room? Similarly in *Sir Thomas Wyatt*, B, 100-102, Suffolk describes himself as hiding in "a simple Cabin," where "cabin" seems a curiously precise word for the scene. In *Appius and Virginia* (only a *C* play, but on this point the distinction matters less) IV. ii, a scene in a camp, a soldier asks, "Is our hut swept clean" [why not our "tent"? or did the actual stage influence the dramatist?]. And in *The Fair Maid of the Exchange*, C, 66, a shop is spoken of as a "darke, and obscure cell." So far the words used might fit a small alcove as well as a projecting structure, but notice the following: Perhaps the most interesting descriptive term for the curtained space occurs in *A Match at Midnight*, C, E 2v; in a tavern scene, Tim hides, and others say, "Looke and he have not insconst himselfe in a wooden Castle." Certainly this has no dramatic fitness, but the term is not a bad one for a projecting structure, such as has already been suggested for the removable rear stage. And this "castle" reminds one of the "tower" in which Danae is confined in *The Golden Age*, A, 55 ff.; it is referred to again with curious emphasis at the first of *The Silver Age*, B, 86. Another striking descriptive phrase occurs in *Match Me in London*, B, 150-158, a shop scene. Men in the street point to a woman in the shop, saying, 154, "What thinke you of yonder parrot i'th Cage." "Cage" suggests a projecting structure as we have supposed the shop to be, rather than an alcove. But perhaps all this discussion based on terminology shows how easily one may be led off into fanciful conjectures, and I press it no further.

(3)

Of unquestionable importance in proving or disproving the existence of a permanent rear stage are those plays which require in the same scene or in immediately successive scenes two or more separate spaces permitting discoveries. Two rear stages seem contradictory: one would have had to be a removable structure, and if one why not both? But two structures at once suggest the medieval "mansions" and bring up the question, even more important than that of the existence of a permanent rear stage, of the fundamental principle of the stage and its management.

Approaching this subject from its own historic backgrounds, the only way in which it can properly be approached, we find two basic patterns which the Elizabethans may have had more or less definitely in mind. First, there is the pseudo-classic pattern of Sidney and Jonson, who insisted on observance of the unities and on some adequacy of spectacle. Roughly contemporary illustrations of it are the woodcuts in the Lyons edition of Terence, 1493, the designs of Serlio, 1551, and the theater at Vicenza, 1565-1584. The designs for Terence are basically the same for the different plays but show arrangements various in detail. The common feature is a background of four or more curtained openings, above each of which is inscribed the name of the character whose house it represents. In a few instances the curtain is opened far enough to show an interior—a bed, a window. This is a definitely Renaissance conception of a Terentian stage. How different this background with entrances close together and possible interiors is from the true Roman stage of vast dimensions and no interior scenes needs no emphasis.[1] More elaborate in detail but identical in principle

---

[1] Reproductions of the pictures referred to in this section are to be found in many books on the stage, perhaps as conveniently as any in Prof. Allardyce Nicoll, *The Development of the Theater* (1927): Terence, p. 83; Serlio, p. 87; Vicenza, p. 95; Mahelot, p. 117.

are the designs of Serlio and of the theater at Vicenza. In all three the setting remains in place throughout the play and the imagined locality is also unchanged. In general, the stage represents one locality with no incongruous features.

The other basic pattern was the simultaneous or multiple setting of the medieval plays. In contemporary pictures it is represented by the Valenciennes miniature of the sixteenth century, showing on one stage Paradise at one end and Hell-mouth at the other, with the Sea of Galilee and perhaps half a dozen doors or "mansions" in between, and by Mahelot's designs for the Hotel de Bourgogne in Paris in the mid-seventeenth century, with, in the design reproduced by Nicoll, a boat, the exteriors of a temple and a palace, and a practicable prison. The fundamental idea of the simultaneous stage was that it could represent at one time places really wide apart, or, to state it differently, that it really represented no place at all, but was the stage itself, the properties displayed being supposed present only when they were made use of in the action or explicitly mentioned. This form of staging is now so commonly understood that it does not require as lengthy explanation as when in 1905 I showed that it existed in the Elizabethan as well as in medieval plays; see "Some Principles of Elizabethan Staging," *MP*, I (1905), 581-614; II, 69-97. It has even been used in recent popular productions, as by Jacques Copeau for *As You Like It* in the Boboli Gardens, Florence. The *New York Times*, July 31, 1938, describes its settings, all displayed at once, as made up of "Oliver's house, a conventional pavilion for entries and exits (and hidden orchestra); an approach to Frederick's palace; a cliff of wood and canvas for the forest action." This is multiple staging with a vengeance; one may doubt if the play originally had so disintegrated a presentation. But this shows that a modern director may still be interested in simultaneous sets and modern audiences accept them.

But to return for a moment to Terence. Are the woodcuts really medieval or classical in principle? Just how far apart must the imagined locations be, just how close together must the settings be, to create incongruity? Even on the Roman stage the position of respectable citizens' houses and a brothel on one street might raise some questions. Or—to go to the other extreme—the Valenciennes Sea of Galilee and the Temple at Jerusalem are not very far separated imaginatively on a stage which extends from Hell to Heaven. It is all a question of proportion. The Renaissance Terentian stage and the medieval simultaneous stage seem not so dissimilar, after all. So possibly also with Serlio's settings for comedy and tragedy, and with the "great houses" of the Revels records, and even with the simple staging in some school or nobleman's house using only its usual doors. If a stage manager at court wished to use Serlio's settings for a play requiring one house in Babylon and another in Jerusalem did the imaginary distance deter him? One may doubt it. A theoretical test of simultaneity is the unity of place: if the separate locations could be reached in one day the settings are "classical"; if not they are "medieval." The discovery of interiors also sets the Renaissance Terence apart from ancient classical practice. But it is doubtful if the usual popular dramatist or stage manager, Heywood in *The Rape of Lucrece*, for example, thought of these distinctions. Though the playwrights for the Red Bull must have been familiar enough with performances of the Terentian comedies and their imitations, this knowledge would hardly disturb them in their simultaneous practices. Indeed, the Terentian staging may have rather encouraged them. All this, is, I know, pretty theoretical. All I am trying to do is to keep in mind the various forms of staging known to the Elizabethans, and to consider how they may have influenced the Elizabethan plays. And the Renaissance Terence is, it seems to me, hardly likely to have seemed to the ordinary playwright and stage manager very different from the simultaneous staging they were acquainted with.

Modern explanations of Elizabethan staging have changed as knowledge concerning it has increased. The "naked stage" theory, which saw the stage as devoid of properties and hence untroubled by staging problems, was followed by the alternation theory, which, admitting properties, arranged them all on the curtained space, and held to a strict succession of front and rear stage scenes. Both these views are now discarded. At present the generally accepted opinions are, I suppose, those of Sir Edmund Chambers; the wealth of detail with which they are supported and the thorough fashion in which the drama to 1616 is presented gives them imposing finality; and except for a few minor exceptions to them—by Lawrence, Mr. Granville-Barker's review in *RES*, I (1925), 60-71, questioning the applicability of their logical precision, and William Archer's in the *Quarterly Review*, CCXLI (1924), 399-418, their modernity and anxiety for visual verisimilitude—I have seen few objections to them.

Chambers suggests two different forms of staging, one for the private theater and the court, the other for the public theater. For the private theaters and the court he admits simultaneous, or as he terms them continuous, settings of an extreme form. These he thinks of as transitional or old-fashioned. For the public theater he allows only what he calls a successive staging, in which when different localities were represented "each in its turn had full occupation of the whole field of the stage" not "qualified by the presence in any scene of a [large] property inappropriate to that scene, but retained there because it had been used for some previous, or was to be used for some coming, scene." (*Op. cit.*, III, 88-89.) Such a successive staging is obviously a more realistic form of staging than is the simultaneous and more in conformity with modern ideas. In chapter I, I have questioned the probability of such a difference in practice, since many plays were certainly given at both kinds of theaters, a fact which would imply a likeness of practice. Now we may consider the Red Bull plays to discover if possible whether they support this *a priori* objection or not.

(4)

Some of the Red Bull plays do seem, at least on first examination, to illustrate Chambers' successive staging. Notice, as an example, *The White Devil*, A, given at the Red Bull, 1609-1612, and published 1612. In the following scheme, I am assuming, as Chambers does, the existence of a permanent rear stage, and am staging the play according to Lucas' directions in his notes—*The Complete Works of John Webster* (1927), I, 198 ff.—which follow, apparently, Chambers' ideas. (Scenes which, according to Lucas, used the whole stage are starred; scenes which I agree were discovered are double starred.)

I. i (A street in Rome.)
  *ii (Camillo's.) A carpet and two pillows fetched (d). A door to a "closet" is referred to; a door to a "chamber" is locked; a third entrance for Cornelia is also necessary.
II. i (Francisco's.) Three seats (t).
  ii (Camillo's) Two seats (t). Dumb shows, one with a picture discovered behind a curtain (d; this sounds like a special curtain hiding only the picture), and the other with a "vaulting horse"
*Dumb fetched. (In III. ii. 118, the "horse" is described as two yards
shows high and rushes are spoken of as on the floor.) Dead bodies are removed. Notice, the dumb shows are looked for in different directions (line 34), as if not in the same place.
III. i (Before the hearing concerning Vittoria.) "The Lieger Embassadors [pass] over the Stage severally."
  **ii (The hearing.) The Ambassadors sit with the judge; at least 8 chairs are necessary, and a table.
  iii (Same as III. i.)
IV. *i (Francisco's.) Lucas assumes a table in "the study" for Francisco to write on (line 126), but there is no hint of table or study in the text or directions.
  ii (Before Vittorio's chamber to line 72, then within it.) "She throwes herselfe upon a bed" (d. line 130).

**ii: 72-196 or to end, 246. (In the bedchamber.)

  iii (Outside the Vatican.) The balcony as a "tarass"; a window below. At line 62, "Enter Monticelso [the new Pope] in state" (d). Five lines later, he says, "though this bee the first daie of our seate." Six lines further on he exits only to re-enter after nine lines. That this entrance is for a scene in which he speaks in his private capacity and not as Pope explains his going out and immediate return.

V. *i (Brachiano's palace, Padua, location for the act.) Lucas gives no reason for using the whole stage for this scene.

  ii Vaguely in the palace.

 *iii: 1-80. (Before Brachiano's chamber.) "They fight at Barriers" (d). Brachiano withdraws into his "Cabinet" (line 41).

**iii: 80-180. (In and before the chamber.) "Enter Brachiano, presented in a bed." Three or more are with him. A person already on the stage says, "See heere he comes." The scene is described as "the chamber." The dialogue remains around the bed until after line 180. The scene continues to line 280.

  iv: to line 58.

**iv: 58-line 105. Five discovered (d) behind a "travers" (t), "winding Marcello's Coarse" (d). At line 105, they say, "We may shut up shop," and exeunt. The scene continues to line 143.

  v An unlocated scene of 15 lines.

 *vi Seat for one. Vittoria writes (t). Doors locked and broken in. A man is bound to a pillar (t). Bodies removed (t).

A glance at the outline shows how regularly each starred scene is followed in Lucas' plan by one or more unstarred scenes; and even the double-starred scenes seem to furnish a passable example of successive staging.

There can also be no question that there was a considerable curtained space used for V. iv; and III. i and iii are such obvious front stage scenes, before and after the hearing in scene ii, that this scene seems surely discovered. Moreover, in Act V it is scarcely chance that the last hundred lines of scene iii do not take place beside the bed, and that the first 58 lines of scene iv are definitely before the traverse, so that these 158 lines together permit the removal of the bed and the arrangement of the "coarse" and its attendants.

Yet all is not quite so consistent as it at first looks. A few explainable inconsistencies may be noticed first. The new Pope says in IV. iii, "this bee the first daie of our seate," and he may have been enthroned. If a throne were used it would break up any realistic staging, but its use is very doubtful indeed; "seate" may be only figurative. For some students the three seats of II. i, and the two of II. ii would also be disturbing. But this inconsistency should not be too much emphasized;

seats are negligible properties on the front stage. After all, spectators were customary there, and a stool or two more would hardly be noticed. These points, then, may be disregarded. More important is the circumstance that in I. ii and II. ii properties are "fetched," instead of in place as they would probably have been had the scenes used the rear stage. Certainly not all the action with properties is confined to the rear stage. That stage, as is usually imagined, was hardly an effective place for acting. This may explain why I. ii, II. ii, and the first of V. iii, are on the front stage. In the last scene the remark, "See here he comes," may mean that after Brachiano was discovered in bed on the rear stage, he was brought forward to a more easily observed position. In any case, how does a scene beginning at the barriers and ending in a bedroom illustrate realism? Not realism and consistency but ease and effectiveness determined the staging. III. ii and IV. ii are on the rear stage because that allowed their quick arrangement; V. iv is there to permit adequate explanation beforehand and a dramatic discovery of the corpse.

Thus this at first sight almost perfect example of successive staging is not so convincing as it appears.

(5)

When we turn to other Red Bull plays the case for successive staging, as the only form employed at the public theaters, is definitely contradicted. Notice, for example, *The Rape of Lucrece*. It also is an *A* play. Chambers dates it between 1603 and 1608; the title-page of the 1608 edition says it was given by her Majesty's servants "at the Red Bull neare Clarkenwell." It was presented at court, apparently by the King's and Queen's men together, on January 13, 1612; it was on the Cockpit stage in 1628, and it was published with additions in 1638, but the stage directions of the first edition remain unaltered. Thus the first edition is about as sure evidence as we shall find of conditions in the public theaters.

The play is not divided into acts or scenes. I indicate the scenes, therefore, by pages, but also number them for ease of reference in the later discussion. Scenes in spaces which can be concealed—I cannot for reasons which will soon be apparent describe them as rear stage scenes —are again starred. The general locations of the play are mainly in various places in Rome, especially at Lucrece's house; or in the generals' camp, two hours' journey from Rome. But some other locations also occur, for example, scene v. To show the significance of the play for staging, it is necessary to tell the story in some detail. The play lacks exit directions at the end of many scenes; e.g. iii, iv, etc., but usually the division is unmistakable. In the left-hand margin I have for ease of reference indicated the staging as I conceive it, but I suggest that this be disregarded until the evidence itself is discussed.

i Front stage.

*ii Throne on front stage; benches in the curtained space.

iii, iv Front stage.

*v Oracle discovered.

A scene in Rome not specially located, 165-168, is followed by one, 168-175, in the capitol, in which when at least seven members of the Senate take their places, apparently on benches, 169, Tarquin seats himself on the throne (t), and when the king comes and calls on him to descend, Tarquin kills him.

Scenes in Rome not specially located, 175-177, 177-184, are followed by a scene, 184-186, at Apollo's oracle:

"Apollo's Priests, with Tapers, after them Aruns, Sextus, and Brutus, with their oblations, all kneeling before the Oracle." After the oracle has said he shall rule who first kisses his mother, Brutus falls and kisses the Earth, saying he slipped on the blood of the sacrifice. The scene ends with Sextus's saying,

Lets now returne, treading these holy measures
With which we entred great Apollo's temple;

so, though the oracle was probably discovered, as the "after" of the first stage direction also suggests, the people were not.

vi Front stage.

The next scene, 187-196, is back in Rome; the direction reads, "Senate. [A musical direction apparently; see also 202.] A table and chaires prepared," and in it, while "The Lords fall off on either side and attend" (d), Tullia talks to Tarquin. "On either side" suggests a front, quite as much as a rear, stage position for Tullia. When Tullia's sons, returning from the oracle, rush in to kiss her, she says to Sextus, "Ascend and touch our lips," but as he is kneeling we cannot necessarily conclude she is sitting on a raised seat, i.e. the throne of scene ii. Rather she seems to be occupying one of the chairs by the table. If the table and chairs are on a discoverable space, there is a "clash" with scenes v and vii. The chair of scene vii is fetched and could be on the front stage, but the rest of that scene implies that Lucrece's room is somewhat set off from the rest of the stage. Of course a third discoverable area could be assumed, but that seems unnecessary. This scene therefore is easiest to suppose as a front stage scene.

*vii   Lucrece's; the curtained space.

In the next scene, 196-202, Lucrece enters, calls for a chair, and then has her servants "spie" her husband. He, referred to as entering obviously at a distance, approaches the house, talking to his friends; not until page 199 does he present them to Lucrece.

? *viii   If "this place" is Lucrece's, this scene also is on the curtained space, or at least before it.

Pages 202-204 show a review of troops marching "over the stage," certainly not "above." A curious little passage, quite unexplained, is: "Luc." [which may mean Lucretius or Lucrece —neither is mentioned in the directions] says, "You from this place [the curtained space?] may see The pride of all the Roman Chivalry." Possibly scenes vii and viii should be counted as one. Or viii may be an unlocated scene concerning only the generals.

ix   Front stage, before the tent (to page 205) and then *in it.

The location now changes to the camp to which the soldiers were going on page 204. "Two soldiers meet, 204-205, as in the watch," talk of how the "Chieftaines Rest in the Generalls tent"; and one of the soldiers goes to "attend Vpon their Rouse"; the other remains on watch. Page 205 has "a banquet prepared" and seven are feasting, obviously in the tent. They make a wager as to what their wives are doing in the now "dead of night," and exeunt, 209, to mount their steeds and in two hours reach Rome. Nothing is more certain than that they do not make the whole journey across the stage. Possibly the change of scene was indicated by exit at one door and entrance at another a page later.

*x   At Lucrece's: the curtained space.

Lucrece begins the next scene, 209-214, sitting and reading, while her two maids work; but we are carefully told she is not in her chamber. On page 210 the men enter, telling of how they have found the other wives revelling. "Now Collatine, to yours," and seven lines later, 211, they see Lucrece, who welcomes them. Then they return to camp, while she soliloquizes on the duties of a wife.

xi Front stage.

The next scene, 214-217, begins: "midway to the camp" (t), where Sextus turns back to Rome; at the end, the other soldiers have arrived "to the skirts of the campe," and again it is clear that part but only part of the journey is made *on* the stage. Nothing is said of horses.

*xii At Lucrece's; the curtained space.

Sextus has returned, 217-220, to Lucrece, and they enter together for a banquet: two seats seem required. At the end they say good night and after he has retired, she goes to her own room.

xiii Front stage before Lucrece's chamber.

A scene, 220-221, follows with the Clown. The clown is upbraided for making so much noise that Lucrece cannot sleep: so the scene is clearly set as before her chamber, and all the servants are got out of the way. After they are gone, 221, "Enter Sextus with his Sword drawne and a Taper light." For a full page he soliloquizes, saying nothing that suggests he sees her, until after the direction, "Lu. discovered in her bed." Then he says, "beneath these curtaines lies That bright enchantresse," as if she were still concealed, but if so, by six lines later, he is looking at her. When she screams he threatens to stifle her with "these pillows," and finally "bears her out," 225.

xiv Front stage before Lucrece's chamber for 35 lines,
*   then discovery in bed.

xv Front stage before Lucrece's.

After a short scene, 225-226, in which one of the servants calls another (showing that they enter from different ways), "Enter Sextus and Lucrece unready," 226; "she flings from him and Exit," and he goes also, 227.

xvi The same.

xvii Front stage, before the tent.

The next scene is at the camp, 227-234, with exit to a tent, 229.

xviii Discovered, at Lucrece's.

Again we are at Lucrece's, where there is obviously discovered "A Table and a Chaire couered with blacke," 234. The scene ends, 240, after Lucrece has killed herself, and friends have borne out the body to the Forum.

xix Front stage, before Rome and the tent.

The next pages, 240-243, are filled with warfare outside Rome, culminating in Horatio's defense of the bridge. With the best will in the world for spectacle I cannot join Chambers, III, 107, in imagining anything *on the stage* to represent the bridge. The direction, "A noise of knocking downe the bridge, within," 243, makes this clear, I think. Horatio stood at one door, and

(Scene division by clearance of the stage becomes meaningless in this section.)

"Alarum, and the falling of the Bridge" (off stage) marks the end of the fight as he made his exit through the stage door. To imagine he jumped into some trap seems quite unnecessary. Meanwhile Heywood further taxes the imagination of his audience: "Enter in severall places, Sextus and Valerius above," 243, one supposedly on a hill outside Rome, the other, presumably, on the walls.

*xx (Stage not cleared.) Discovery in the tent.

Porsenna retires to his tent, where the directions call for a table and lights, and, 245, soldiers with torches form a guard, but Scevola succeeds in entering to murder him. Instead, he kills Porsenna's secretary, burns his own hand to punish it for its mistake, and is sent back to Rome by Porsenna, 247.

xxi Front stage.

xxii Front stage.

Pages 247-248 are within Rome, from which the Romans go to fight Porsenna and there is "Alarum, battell within," but almost at once, 248, we are outside the city, with the battle continuing. Tarquin, with "an arrow in his brest" tells Tullia to flee on a "Iennet within my tent," but she refuses. So the battle continues. The Tarquins are all slain, and the Romans, 250, "rear them Against this hill in view of all the camp." Brutus fights Sextus; the direction is characteristically specific: "Fight with single swords, and being deadly wounded and painting for breth, making a stroak at each together with their gantlets they fall." Orders are given for the disposal of the bodies. The play ends with "marching on to Rome," 253.

First, it is worth noticing how easily an outline, such as that in the margin, misleadingly simplifies this staging. Glanced at hurriedly, this play also seems a consistent example of a fairly realistic successive setting. To be sure there are clashes of properted scenes at v, vi; vi, vii; ix, x, but a little ingenuity should be able to remove them. However, even a careless reading of the fuller description shows the simplicity to be only superficial, and a reading of the play itself enforces this conclusion all the more. One reason I have given this play so much space is to make clear, first, how necessary it is to consider every play in detail instead of in a misleadingly simplified outline, and, second, to consider every play as a whole.

For the most striking fact about the staging of this play when it is considered as a whole, is that it clearly demands not one, but two, discoverable spaces: the house of Lucrece in Rome, and a tent, thought of in the first part of the play as belonging to the generals and standing some two hours' journey from Rome, and—surely the same property —in the last scenes as Porsenna's, and standing just outside Rome. That a permanent rear stage was not used alternately first as Lucrece's house, then as the tent, is shown, first, by scenes ix, x, which offer an unremovable "clash," and, second, by the fact that such an arrangement would throw too great a burden of locating the scenes upon the dialogue. With tent and house represented by separate settings, the problem of location is comparatively simple.

Since it is inconceivable that the tent was put up and taken down for each of its scenes, we must suppose that tent and room were on the stage simultaneously. Also if the raised seat, the "throne" of scene ii, is used in scene vi, as is possible but hardly likely, and again in scene xxi for the "hill," for which the evidence is very slight, there would be a third simultaneous setting continuing throughout the play. In Chambers' view of the public theater the idea of even two is intolerable. But Heywood seems to have found it undisturbing. And of course it is quite in accordance with the idea of a simultaneous stage. This view is also suggested by scenes vii, x, in which guests are shown first at a distance and then at Lucrece's house, and by scene xi, which begins away from the camp and then is in it. A further suggestion that this play had no tidy realistic staging, but a very freely imaginative one, occurs in scenes xx to xxii, which begin before Rome, then change before our eyes, without any clearing of the stage, to Porsenna's tent (not, imaginatively, the tent of previous scenes) and then back again, first inside and then outside Rome. In scene xx occurs also the use of the balcony for at the same time the walls of Rome and a hill outside the city.

So many of these unrealistic features in the short space of one play may seem strangely naïve and confusing, but no one of them is really unusual in Elizabethan public theater plays, as I shall show presently. First it must be noted, however, that though it is impossible to adjust *The Rape of Lucrece* to Chambers' successive staging by resort to "split" scenes or trapdoors, the expedients he has suggested, it is quite simple to arrange a simultaneous staging for *The White Devil* with no adjustments at all. Though this may in practice amount to saying scarcely more than that the prompter for *The White Devil* took his time about removing the properties of one scene, not minding if they happened to be on in other scenes as well, it shows that the difference theoretically between the two stagings is as wide as from the seventeenth century to the nineteenth.

It must be noted also that the staging of *The Rape of Lucrece* does not exactly follow the medieval staging pattern. There are at least two differences: First, passage from one imagined location to another is not shown by going on the stage directly from this "station" to that: the journey from the camp to Rome is never made without an exit. Still, the medieval idea remains, as has been pointed out, in scenes in which people gradually approach a destination, and part of the journey is shown on the stage. The clearest example is scene xi, where the soldiers enter "midway" to the camp, and within three pages arrive there.

The other difference I am not so sure was a difference. Perhaps a medieval play could use the same "mansion" to stand for different places—the same house, shall we say, for Nazareth and Bethany, but I know of no such case. Or it is possible that the Elizabethan stage had a larger number of "mansions" than anyone has yet suggested. But the curtained space used for Lucrece's house could also have been used, so far as the plan of the play shows, both for the Senate benches (scene i) and Apollo's oracle (scene v); in other words, one "mansion" could stand for different places, a convenient and necessary arrangement for a restricted space. But no single space could, as has been pointed out, stand for the house of Lucrece and the tent.

(6)

The Rape of Lucrece is not the only Red Bull play to suggest a simultaneous form of staging. Not all of them demand two discoverable spaces, but they are in one way or another definitely simultaneous.

The evidence from the plays for the simultaneous principle is mainly of two kinds: (1) shifts of the imagined scenes before the eyes of the audience without clearing the stage, and (2) incongruous properties and locations on the stage together. There is also (3) such evidence as has been presented in chapter III from *The Two Noble Ladies*, and *The Hector of Germany*, and that to be cited in chapter VIII from *Fortune by Land and Sea*. A stage that represented a drowning by carrying men off through its stage doors, a ship approaching a rock by the entrance of a few men on the front stage, and a fight between two ships at sea mainly by words and noise, scarcely needs to be proved inconsistent from a realistic point of view. Still, some further evidence for unrealistic inconsistency may not be out of place.

Under the evidence for changes of scene before the eyes of the audience without any clearing of the stage, is not included the change from outside to inside a city, house, or room by the drawing of a curtain, for, though it is likely the action supposed to be in the curtained space soon usually spilled over into the main stage, this makes no great breach with realism. Nor is it necessary to include a change of the imagined location produced by bringing out a property like a bed. Such changes hardly fit a strictly realistic stage, but still are not too contradictory to it.

What does show an essentially different idea of the stage is the convention of exit at one door and immediate re-entrance at another. This has already been discussed and illustrated. Also mentioned several times have been the "journeying" scenes in which characters move from one place to another at some distance away, as in the approach to the camp in *The Rape of Lucrece,* scene xi, or a slight variation from this, as in scene x of the same play, which first shows Lucrece sitting at home, then visitors entering at a distance, and finally drawing nearer. Of course the two are essentially the same. Other examples are:

Sir Thomas Wyatt, B, 85-88, "A dead march and passe round the stage," to show a journey to the Tower.

How a Man May Choose, B, IV. i, begins at some distance from a church and ends within it.

I If You Know Not Me, B; the last scene begins in some vague location; finally there comes the direction, "The Queene takes state." Two pages later Elizabeth says, "Now to London, lords, lead on the way," there is a direction, "Sennet about the Stage in order," and presently the Mayor of London meets the procession and begins, "I from this citie London do present This purse and Bible." Clearly the "sennet about the Stage" indicated the journey to London.

II If You Know Not Me, 288-295, shifts from the Mayor's court to Cornhill. (An exeunt direction in the quarto is omitted in the Pearson edition, 288, setting off this scene from a preceding one at Hobson's shop. In the actual staging this omission is of no significance, but I mention it to justify the scene division.)

Match Me In London, B, 138-143, at some distance from, then near Malevento's house.

The Brazen Age, B (discussed above). Page 176 is at court, by 178 the scene is the bank of a river, and by 182 it is on the other bank. (The change is shown by exit and quick re-entry at another door.)

I Iron Age, B, 302, "March two and two, discoursing as being conducted . . . into the Citty." This instance should not, perhaps, be included in this list, since it seems likely the change of scene was marked by opening the curtain.

This is not a complete list of "journeying" scenes, but it is sufficient to show their general characteristics.

Another sign of the simultaneous idea in staging is to be found in the way properties are used in the plays. The important plays may be classified in three ways: (1) Those in which in the same scene incongruous properties are employed; (2) those in which immediately successive scenes use different settings with no possibility of an interval for rearranging the stage, thus causing "clashes"; and (3) those in which properties difficult to move recur in several scenes, suggesting that they were left on the stage in scenes in which they did not belong. In the first group come those plays which not only show changes like "journeying" scenes of the imagined location but also use properties more or less indicative of those locations. The second class may perhaps be questioned; how can we be sure that short intervals were not introduced at any convenient time? Of course we cannot be sure, but the probabilities when a large part of the audience were standing, and the playing time was limited by circumstances and custom to not much more than two hours, are all against such intervals. In this class of evidence also come those plays which suggest the use of more than one discoverable space. Sometimes it is not a question of merely rearranging a rear stage, but of providing something quite different. Recurring properties—the third class—occur in two circumstances. When they were used on the curtained space, they were likely to be left there until they were no longer necessary, even if this forced other settings out on the front stage.[2] Other recurring properties were those which stood on the front stage and which were too cumbersome to move easily: notably the throne and trees. Even if substitutes were used for the trees the principle of simultaneity was still illustrated, and it is this principle, the way in which the stage was regarded, that really matters. I shall not attempt to arrange my illustrations strictly under each of these classifications: one play will sometimes show two types at once.

Of the recurring properties the most common are, of course, seats

---

[2] I have discussed recurring settings in "Another Principle of Elizabethan Staging," *Manly Anniversary Studies* (1923), pp. 70-77. Lawrence's disagreement with my argument in his *Pre-Restoration Stage Studies* (1927), pp. 321-324, shows how curiously Elizabethan stage directions can be differently interpreted. Briefly my argument was that *The Honest Whore*, Part I, definitely illustrates the usage in question. Because a shop occupied the rear stage from I. v to IV. iii, other intervening scenes with properties were forced out on the front stage. One scene of this kind, III. iii, begins, "Enter Bellafront with lute, pen, inke, and paper being placed before her." Lawrence says this is a discovery, and that it interrupts the use of the rear stage as a shop; but *"being* placed" to me suggests quite clearly a front stage position. These arguments in proof of separate structures, of which the curtained space was only one, naturally change in some degree the application of this principle of recurring properties, but it still seems to me generally true.

of one kind or another. But these are so often brought in or so often assumed to be present that it is impossible to say how they were usually managed; moreover, as they would be really no more obtrusive than the spectators on the stage they can scarcely be used as evidence in one way or the other. We may therefore disregard them. Next in frequency of occurrence are the formal seat and "trees." I have already shown (chapter IV) that they usually stood on the front stage, could not easily be moved, and were therefore present even if incongruous in intervening scenes.

As one example of simultaneity arising from recurring properties, notice *A Shoemaker a Gentleman*, B: the recurring properties are capitalized to make the plan visually clear. I. ii, "Enter discover'd in a SHOP [5 persons]," I. iii, "Enter out of a WELL"; II. i, ii, no definite staging; iii, probably a seat; III. i, at the WELL (t); ii, probably at the SHOP: iii, iv, v, no definite staging; IV. i, slight suggestions of being at first in a room, then in the street, and then at the SHOP. The evidence for the shop in IV. i, is too slight to emphasize, but I. ii, iii, and III. i, and perhaps ii are clear enough. If there was a permanent rear stage either the shop was in it and the well outside, or *vice versa;* or, lacking such a rear stage, both must have been in sight at once. Thus, we have illustrated at one time a "clash," recurring settings, and unquestionable simultaneity.

Or examine *The Devil's Law Case*, A. III. ii, begins before a house, but presently shows a man in bed and ends with others working over him. III. iii, begins, "A Table set forth with two Tapers, a Deaths head, a Booke. Jolenta in mourning, Romelio sits by her." No device of a "split" scene is possible, and the only likely solutions are either that there was an unmarked interval—hardly likely—or that two curtained structures permitted these scenes to be discovered successively.

In *The Brazen Age*, A, 172-182, Oeneus "sits crown'd"; we may therefore suppose a throne. Without a clearance of the stage, the scene shifts to a river bank, and then changes to the opposite bank; 184 has an altar with a sacrifice, presumably discovered, and 184-187 alludes in the text to "this violet banke." In the scene, 208-216, a throne is also highly fitting for Oetes when Jason is first brought before him; on 216 the two fiery bulls, the golden fleece, and a dragon are discovered. A "split" scene is possible between these last scenes, but in view of the general staging of the play, seems hardly likely. And the end of the play would drive a realistically minded person quite frantic.[3]

---

[3] For the full description see Chapter VIII.

There are, obviously on the stage at once, an altar and a rock with trees, besides the monuments of Hercules' labors. This suggests that that whole play was presented on a simultaneous set: We may suppose one curtained space used in turn for the altar, 184; for the unremoved "dead" body, 193-194; perhaps for the banquet where nine are seated, 198-203, though this may be on the front stage; for the "two fiery bulls," etc., 216-218; and for the altar of 241-256. Another discoverable space is the cave-arbor. Perhaps it was used for the "violet bank," 184-187; it was certainly employed in 226-231 and 235-239, and perhaps for 241-246. With a throne on the front stage, a trapdoor, the lift, and the stage balcony even this extraordinary play can be staged, if not illusively at least expeditiously.

And as with this so with the other *Ages*. *The Silver Age*, B, can have been given on a very simply furnished stage, with only one discoverable space; and Parts I and II of *The Iron Age* also ask nothing very unusual. But it is, I think, easier and more probable to imagine all the *Ages* staged simultaneously thus:

The Golden Age, A, needs a throne 6-10, ? 11-16, 27-31, 47-48, and "trees" on the front stage, 27-35; the arbor, 32-35; Danae's tower, a structure permitting scenes within it, 57-71. This same structure may also be used as the tower of the Fates, 77-79, and it may even be the arbor. Thus one or two discoverable spaces are indicated as necessary for this play.

The Silver Age, B, may have used words, 126-130, 146 (in the rewriting of this scene in *The Escape of Jupiter* there is also "an arbor discovered"), the throne, 92-96, 159-164. Besides these it may have had some structure for the gate scene of 98-107. Is it fantastic to suggest that this structure was Danae's tower of *The Golden Age*, before which, 86-90, 92-96, and 96-98 of *The Silver Age* are said to occur? In addition to these items all that is needed is the cloud, and the bed of Semele, which is brought in, bursts into flame, and flies up.

I Iron Age requires Achilles' tent, the interior of which is shown in 310-315 and 324-325; a rock and a tree, 300; and should have a large discoverable space perhaps for the banquet, seating 10 or more, which is, however, brought in, 273-285; and more surely for the scene seating 16 or more, 302. This same space would be used for the formal hearing, 334-344, after which, also, there is no one left to remove Ajax's body.

II Iron Age has, besides the walls, the gigantic horse concealed in some manner 371-378, 378-381; the altar, 390-394 (notice the remark about "yon horse," 391, as if it were also in sight), and 425-431; and in 411-414, a bedchamber and a bed. This play could be staged with no great difficulty with a rear stage as ordinarily conceived, used first for the horse, then the altar, then the bedchamber, and then the altar again. But in view of the other plays and of "yon horse," why should this be?

The Honest Lawyer, A, should perhaps be presented at length, but may be sufficiently summarized as follows: The action is variously, without clearing the stage, before Vawter's house, then before an inn now used as a brothel, then by a convent near which is a hollow tree and "a thievish rode," and before Gripe's house. On occasion we are told that the convent and the "thievish rode" are "solitary," B 2; in Act IV, the convent is separated from the inn by a river; but when there comes an opportunity for a jibe at the close proximity of thieves, brothel, and Abbey, it is taken advantage of and the imagined distance forgotten. The river is certainly not represented on the stage: it is alluded to only when the plot requires it. Doors could, if necessary, represent Vawter's house, the inn, and the convent, but the interior of Gripe's house is shown in Act IV. In Act V a jail is in the background; perhaps the door used formerly for Vawter's or for the inn stood for it. Or its interior may be seen. Also in Act V a raised seat for a judge is necessary, a tree is climbed, and bushes are hid behind. There must also have been two or more unindividualized ways of entrance. Passage from one location to another is sometimes made on the stage, as in Act I; sometimes by exit and re-entrance, as in Act V. Yet this is not a simple classical staging—the interior scene, F 4v-G 4, shows that, as does also the presence in Act V of the formal chair in the scene with the tree and bushes. Clearly this stage is not now all this place and now all that. And lest the reader should think this play is exceptional and what one might expect of an obscure author, "S.S.," who probably knew no better, may I call to mind that *The Honest Lawyer* in staging is not essentially different from the work of the practical playwright, Thomas Heywood, in *The Rape of Lucrece?* Both are revealing illustrations of the simultaneous idea and both are public theater plays.

A few less complete illustrations of simultaneity may also be cited:

II If You Know Not Me, B, 256-263, with the shop and with an arras thought of as in a tavern, has already been mentioned in connection with shops. It may also be cited, perhaps, as an example of simultaneity, though no great distance is involved.

The Four Prentices of London, A, has, 175-178, a series of "dumb shows" located by the Presenter successively in "Bulloigne," France, Italy, and Ireland. But this is obviously exceptional. Throughout the play trees and woods are mentioned as present; tents are also spoken of. I doubt the real use of tents and do not feel very sure of the trees. But standards placed on the "walls" of Jerusalem, 233, are replaced, 234, by shields which certainly remain there through the next scene (in Jerusalem), 234-235, because in 235-240 they are still in sight. There is also vague reference to

Christ's sepulchre as present, 230, 241, 254. Its real presence is doubtful. If trees, tent, sepulchre, were really represented, of course, the play would be visually simultaneous in staging as it certainly is in theory. In any case the shields, unless the balcony curtain closed to conceal them,—and of this there is no hint,—are a clear case of simultaneous properties in the scene, 234-235.

The Royal King, B, offers staging of no special interest till the last scene. The scene begins "Enter Clinton [who is plotting against the Marshall, the Earl Chester] to the Earle Chester in his study." But it continues as if in a public place for "a Barre [is] set out" for a trial, seven take seats, the Marshall is brought "to the Barre as out of his bed," and the king calls for "a laurel wreath, a scaffold, and a block," which presumably are brought. There may also be a formal seat for the King because the Marshall in his defense speaks of "the State 'fore which I stand," or this may be only a figurative allusion. The study, bar, scaffold are surely present and are incongruous.

Herod and Antipater, A, has a similar final scene. It has recurring throughout the play "a regal chair" associated with or the same as a tribunal which seats three people. This occurs in I. iii, (t), v (i); II. i (d), ii (d); IV. iii (d). So far the play seems a very consistent successive setting with this formal seat on the rear stage except that IV. ii assumes a rack, and might be interpreted as a "clash." But V. ii (K 3v-L 2v), shows a different idea of the stage. The scene is at once in Antipater's prison, and in the palace of Herod, to which a scaffold is brought. Passage from one to the other is made only by exit and re-entrance. (L 2, L 2v.)

Swetnam, C, (H 4v-K 2) raises the question of the congruity of a banquet and the raised chair pictured on its title-page, with the orchard in which the scene is set by the text.

The Two Noble Ladies, I. ii, has Barebones, fleeing from slaughter, take refuge in his master's study (t); a direction at that point reads, "Ciprian discovered at his booke"; presently Ciprian "hides him vnder the table." I. iv, has textual allusions to a wood and a castle gate: in II. i, a man sits in a camp scene; III. iii, has the extraordinary drowning already referred to several times, with more allusions to woods; in V. ii, Justina is "discovered in a chaire" and later in the scene Ciprian throws his books into the flames. The play ends with allusions to the Gate of Antioch. I doubt the presence of these woods and anything special for the gates, but the study seems thought of as on the stage throughout the play. Thus, perhaps it is used in I. iii, 210, where without any preceding appearance in the scene or any notice taken of him Ciprian makes a short aside.

This, then, is the evidence from the Red Bull *A* and *B* plays for simultaneous settings. It may not seem, as listed, extensive in amount, but it is enough to disprove Chambers' assertion that simultaneous settings were not admitted to the public theater stages. These are not plays by obscure authors nor early in date, nor, may I repeat, were they given at an obscure theater. Moreover, since the staging was simultaneous for some plays is it not likely that it was so, in principle at least, for all of them? The plays that seem most obviously successive could all have been staged more or less simultaneously: while the plays which require simultaneous settings can be staged in no other way. We have no reason to believe that the popular theater was self-conscious about its procedure. Also it may not be out of place to notice that the stage doors—always in sight—the balcony, the pillars, the curtain—according to the ideas of most students always present—are appropriate only in a simultaneous setting. What is the consistency of insisting on the consistency of a stage where these features were conspicuous in every scene? A door or an arras in a forest scene is as incongruous as a bed. To say that the doors in such scenes were conventionally disregarded as always in sight anyway, is to beg the whole question. We, it is true, have conventional features in our own modern, realistic theater, but they are seldom or never allowed to intrude within the picture frame of the proscenium. The Elizabethan stage had no frame, and to look to it for a consistently realistic staging is to show an anachronistic point of view. The stage to the Elizabethans was not now all this, now all that, but only the stage, and if the curtained space did allow some approach to the realistic portrayal of a room, this, everyone admits, was not of enough importance to cause all interiors to be staged there. Thus the answer to one question we have been asking, is clear and positive: the Red Bull, an Elizabethan public theater in the seventeenth century, was not consistently realistic, and it did admit simultaneous settings to its stage. Whether the Globe and Fortune did so is, of course, another matter, but that they did is surely not an improbable suggestion.

(7)

It is now possible with a minimum of repetition to return to our first question: Was there a permanent rear stage, and as having a bearing on that, were there now and again two discoverable spaces on the stage at one time?

The hints that there were may be briefly referred to: There are the tent and Lucrece's chamber in *The Rape of Lucrece* ix, x and *passim;* the irremovable "clash" in *The Devil's Law Case,* III. ii; the suggestion that the two dumb shows in *The White Devil,* II. ii, were in different places (though I doubt if the one with the "horse" was discovered); the young apprentices in *II If You Know Not Me* hiding behind the arras in a tavern while Hobson looks for them in the shop; the two shops of *The Fair Maid of the Exchange;* the two tents of *Richard III;* the hint in *II Iron Age* that the great horse and the altar, both discovered, were on the stage together, and the less certain cases of the other *Ages.* All the plays named except *The Fair Maid* and *Richard III* are *A* or *B* plays.

Sometimes, at least, then, there were surely two discoverable spaces on the stage at once. One may have been the permanent rear stage and one a removable structure at one side of it, but that seems an awkward arrangement. Or both may have been removable structures placed advantageously on the stage for ease of sight for the audience and ease of exit and entrance for the actors. This latter arrangement is quite in line with a simultaneous staging, but a permanent rear stage fits such a staging equally well. Only the advocates of a consistently realistic stage have to prove that there was a structurally permanent rear stage. In the face of the Swan picture that is not so easy to do, and the proof that two discoverable spaces were sometimes necessary makes that proof at least no easier.

(8)

One way to approach the question whether there was a structural rear stage is to determine how useful it would have been. But this is exceedingly difficult to agree about. Should or should not the discoveries in shops, tombs, tents, caves, arbors, etc. be included? These all could have been and sometimes certainly were separate structures. And though in some scenes beds were discovered, in others they were definitely brought out, and readers will not agree which are which. Another cause of uncertainty as to the use of the curtained space is to be found in the various meanings of "enter." In such a direction as "Enter at a table reading," "enter" must, it seems, mean "discovered." There are less certain cases. In *The Wonder of a Kingdom,* B, 237, "Enter sicke in his chaire" accompanied by five other persons, "enter" surely seems to mean "discovered." But, "Enter sicke in a Chayre," *Herod and Antipater,* A, H 2v-I 1, is accompanied in the dialogue by "Now he's comming forth To change the ayre," indicating that the character concerned actually was brought in, and was *not* discovered.

The Silver Age, B, 123, has "Enter Homer one way Iuno another," and Homer definitely says, "Behold where Iuno *comes,*" though she is supposed to have been sitting cross-legged at the gate for three days to prevent the birth of Hercules. Clearly Elizabethan ideas of congruity are not ours. So it is possible that if there was no permanent rear stage, "Enter at a table reading" may sometimes have meant, "Enter and read at a table," and even if there were a rear stage, this might still have been the action performed. It follows that though to a modern reader, "enter" in some scenes seems necessarily to mean "discovered," one cannot safely insist on it in all instances.

There are certain stage settings which seem to demand a discoverable space of some general character, not individualized as are shops, tents, tombs, etc., by their outward appearance. Tables, banquets at which a considerable number of people sit, other scenes using a good many seats, trial scenes, council scenes, and especially "studies," are examples of settings which, it seems likely, were often discovered in a noncommittal structure, whether permanent or removable. But of these doubts also arise. Tables were often assumed as present, banquets were served in. How many seats must there be to require a discovery? Trial scenes and council scenes have already been discussed in chapter IV with no very certain conclusions. Of all these settings, the "study" is perhaps the one which always seems to have been discovered. Certainly if the pictures on the title-pages of *Dr. Faustus* and *Friar Bacon and Friar Bungay* are of theatrical origin, the books, the chair, the table, the astronomical instruments, etc., would require so much time for putting in place, that discovery seems necessary.

Yet definite as the word "study" seems, some stage directions using it are uncertain in meaning. When Frankford in *A Woman Killed with Kindness*, B, at the first of Act II, is said to "enter in *a* study" and nothing further in the scene suggests a study setting, perhaps the word refers only to his attitude, as in our own phrase, "a brown study," and the same may be true of *Greene's Tu Quoque*, B, 191, "Enter as in his study reading." The phraseology is at least peculiar.

Thus all these indications of the use of the discoverable space are open to doubt. In "William Percy and his Plays," *MP*, XII (1914), 118-120, I named some seven signs of the use of the rear stage. Besides those already mentioned, these included the use of three doors, the use of a door emphasized as leading to the balcony, and the use of a door as the gate to a castle or city. In "Another Principle of Elizabethan Staging," *Manly University Studies* (1923), pp. 70-77, a further sign of its use was suggested: recurring properties other than "trees" and the formal seat. The possibility of separate structures for some of these scenes was mentioned in the former article, but the evidence for them now presented gives that possibility more importance, and naturally modifies the application of these tests in some degree. More important still is the chance that the curtained space itself was a removable structure. If it was, it could have stood at different times in different positions on the stage. Usually there had to be some

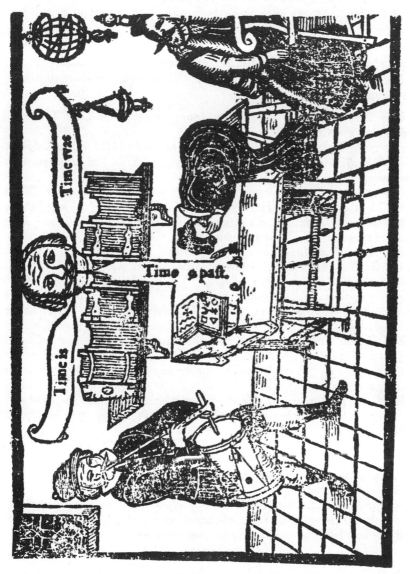

A STUDY SETTING?

From the title-page of *Friar Bacon and Friar Bungay*, 1655.

means of entrance to it from the rear. If no other structure was employed the natural position for it would be before the center door; if two structures, as in *The Rape of Lucrece*, perhaps they stood side by side, both served by the center door. In any case, the use of the center door would no longer *necessarily* be a sign of the opening of the curtains.

Though all tests of the use of a discoverable space are thus open to more or less question, still a list of scenes which seem practically certain to have used such a space, and of those which seem a little more doubtful may be of some use.[4]

B *Sir Thomas Wyatt*, 92, "Enter [four or more]; the Lord Treasurer kneeling at the Counsell Table."

(?) 100, "Enter the Duke of Suffolke": he speaks of "this hard lodging, a simple Cabin." In the next scene, thought of as in the same place, a man buries gold.

(?) 124-130. In the Tower. Winchester orders a Lieutenant to "fetch forth" his other prisoners: "Here lyes young Guilford, here the Lady Jane"; "Conduct them forth." "Enter Young Guilford and the Lady Jane." Five lines are spoken by Guilford and Jane before they notice the others.

B *How a Man May Choose*, Act IV begins away from, then is before, and finally is within a church. A woman discovered in a tomb (d).

B *A Woman Killed with Kindness*, (?) V. ii, a lute assumed; (?) V. v, away from, then before a house, and then in it; enter in bed (d). If a discoverable space is used at all, it may also have been used in II. i, "Enter in a study," in IV. i; "Enter in a prison," and in IV. iii, for a gate scene.

B *I If You Know Not Me*, (?) 198-201, before, then in, a bedroom.

(?) 210-214, the center door as the Tower gate.

(Notice in 234-238 the listening from behind an arras, which shows that hangings were present.)

B *II If You Know Not Me*, two shop scenes and in one of them (?) 256-263 an arras hid behind. In 288-295 bricks are assumed as present (?).

B *The Travails of Three English Brothers*, (?) 75-82, a jailer says to Sir Thomas in prison, "Where are you here? ha!" "Enter Sir Thomas." "Exit Iayler leauing Sir Thomas in the stocks." A rack assumed. See: chapter IV.

A *The Rape of Lucrece*, seven pretty certain scenes in a curtained space, besides the scenes in the tent. See discussion above.

B *Fortune by Land and Sea*, no necessary discoveries.

---

[4] In this list (?) means a doubtful case. Discoveries in ships, tents, etc., are noted but not counted as rear stage scenes. All *C* plays are omitted: they could have little weight in determining whether the Red Bull had a rear stage or not, and examination shows that if they were listed they would not furnish any distinctive information or materially change the conclusions arrived at.

B *A Shoemaker a Gentleman,* at least one shop scene, possibly more. See discussion above.

A *The White Devil,* four or five scenes in a curtained space: ? a picture with a curtain, a trial; two scenes before, then in, a bedchamber; five persons discovered behind a traverse. See discussion above.

B *Match Me in London,* a shop, and (?) 212-214, in a dumb show, "Enter two Fryers setting out an Altar."

B *Greene's Tu Quoque,* 181, a shop discovered; also (??) 191-194, enter "as in his study reading"; (?) 257-262, the prison "hole."

A *If It Be Not Good,* (?) 267-271, a sleeping devil perhaps discovered.

[295-303, "A Table is set out by young fellowes like Merchants men, Books of Accounts vpon it, small Deskes to write vpon, they set downe to write Tickets." There are seats for three or four. But this scarcely seems a discovery because of "set out" and "they sit downe."]

331-334, "A table is set with a candle burning, a deaths head, a cloke and a crossee; Subprior sits reading."

338-342, (?) Before, then, in a bedchamber.

348, "Enter leaping in great ioy [3 devils] discouering behind a curten [4] standing in their torments."

A *The Golden Age,* "Enter in bed;" an arbor; Danae's tower; and a bed drawn out, then in. No sure use of a concealed space except the arbor.

B *The Silver Age,* (?) 98-107, before, and then, 101-102, perhaps in a house.

(?) 141-146, seats for eleven at a banquet.

[152-155, "a bed drawne out," later it "flyes vp"; therefore *not* a rear stage scene.]

(?) 156-164, perhaps the central door as the gate to hell. (See chapter VI, section 5.)

A *The Brazen Age,* 183, a dumb show with an altar.

(?) 184-187, "this violet banke."

194, a "dead" body not removed.

(?) 198-203, a banquet; seats for nine.

217, "Two fiery Buls are discouered, the Fleece hanging ouer them, and the Dragon sleeping beneath them; Medea with strange fiery-workes, hangs aboue in the Aire, in the strange habite of a Coniuresse."

247, "Enter to the sacrifice two Priests to the Altar."

Also a cave-arbor.

B *I Iron Age,* besides Achilles' tent (used 310-315, 324-325):

(?) 302-309, a banquet with at least sixteen seated.

(?) 334-344, the body of Ajax, "dead," left with no one to remove it.

B *II Iron Age,* 372, "The Horse is discouered."

390-394, "Priam discouered kneeling at the Altar," four with him.

411, Egisthus "hideth himselfe in the chamber behind the Bed-curtaines."

425-431, "An Altar set foorth."

A *The Hector of Germany,* (?) B 4-C 2, "Enter in the Garden [2]. They sit on a banke."

(?) G 2v-G 3v, one man left to remove three "dead" bodies; he says, "I must cast you all into the Riuer," but how could he?

A *The Four Prentices of London,* no discovery.

A *The Honest Lawyer,* (?) F 4v-G 4, begins in a room and changes to a road.

B *The Royal King,* 74-83, Enter "to the Earle Chester in his study."

A *Swetnam,* G 4-H 1; a hearse, no one to remove it.

(?) H 4v-K 2, the trial scene, pictured on the title-page. See discussion above.

A *The Devil's Law Case,* III. ii, before, then in, a bedchamber; the scene ends in a situation.

III. iii, "A Table set forth with two Tapers, a Death's head, a Booke. Jolenta in mourning, Romelio sits by her."

B *Edward II,* (?), V. iii, a possible discovery of Edward in a dungeon.

B *The Two Merry Milkmaids,* I. i; B 1-B 3, "Enter Bernard in his Studie, Candle and Bookes about him."

III. ii; I. 1v-I 2v, "Enter . . . in his study."

(?) III. iii; I 2v-K 3, "Enter [6 or more], the forme of a Court." The first 14 lines of this scene are unplaced, permitting a "split" scene.

[IV. iii, M 1v-N 4, "A Bed thrust out." A bystander says, "Z foote he shifts his Rome"; so the bed really was thrust out on the front stage, and not discovered.]

A *The Heir,* no discovered scenes.

A *Herod and Antipater,* no surely discovered scenes.

[H 2v-I 1 is *before* a study (t).]

(?) I 1-I 4v assumes the presence of a rack.

B *The Welsh Ambassador,* 774-892, has a tableau of two persons discovered *above.*

1184-1313: at 1156 "bee redy Carintha at a Table" (d). 1183, "Enter Carintha at a Table readinge."

1962-2068: at 1934, "sett out a Table"; at 1962, "Enter Clowne in his study writinge."

A *The Two Noble Ladies,* 82, "Ciprian discovered at his booke."

(?) 110-220, an aside possibly spoken in the study. See discussion above.

1712-1910: at 1752, "Iustina is discovered in a chaire asleep, in her hands a prayer book, divells about her."

B *The Wonder of a Kingdom,* the only discovered scene is 257-262, "A Bed discouered, Fyametta upon it." Enter at least ten "ut antea Fyametta."

This list shows thirty-three scenes almost certainly using a discoverable space below but not connected with structures of definite significance; and thirty-four scenes not quite so certain. Few students will, I think, reject any considerable number of the scenes listed without a question mark, and many would include a good many more: Lucas, for example, finds five more in *The White Devil* than I do; Lawrence would add most of the throne scenes. This list is therefore probably a minimum; I find it impossible even to guess what a maximum number might be. But taking this list as a minimum, it is still not possible to dogmatize. The *A* and *B* plays have some 600 or more scenes: do these sixty-seven uses of a discoverable space justify or not the assumption that this space was structurally provided? And even though plays were not written to illustrate the staging—it is sometimes difficult to remember this—is it likely that six plays would make no use of a discoverable space if it was always there ready to be used?

To be considered, also, are the large number of properties which were, according to precise directions, brought in or thrust out or set out. Sometimes, it is true, this seems to mean thrust out or set out in the discoverable space. I have taken this interpretation for "A table is set out" in *If It Be Not Good*, 331, because the direction continues, "Subprior sits reading"; and in *The Welsh Ambassador*, 1934, because it is clearly a direction to prepare for a discovery. But in *The Virgin Martyr* there are directions for thrusting properties out with no such hints. The first scene with, 6, its "Enter a Priest with the image" suggests a discovery, but, 48, "Enter Priest with the Image . . . followed by [two] leading Dorothea," shows it is not. Later in the play a bed is thrust out, 59; a pillar set up "in the middle of the stage," 68; a scaffold "thrust forth," 71; and a rack ordered, 89. It seems as if a rear stage was definitely being avoided. But "Enter Theophilus in his study. Books about him," 77, shows clearly that the play used a discoverable space. Perhaps the rack was on the front stage because the setting of the study could not be removed in time, and 59 and 68 may be similarly explained. Or perhaps the study was too small for these scenes or it was too obscure a place to stage them. At least it surely was not employed. Other plays furnish similar instances; the total impression is again that for some reason the discoverable space, which certainly existed, was not used as much as one would expect.

The size of the curtained space has been mentioned. An inspection of the list of discovered scenes shows that in the majority of instances only a small space is required. The largest scenes definitely described as discovered are those of the five persons winding Marcello's body in *The White Devil*, A, V. iv; the gigantic horse of *II Iron Age*, B, 372; the five persons discovered kneeling at an altar in *II Iron Age*, B, 390-394; the fiery bulls, fleece, and dragon of *The Brazen Age*, A, 217 (perhaps the last was a painted curtain). Then there are also the eight persons sitting as judges in *The White Devil*, III. ii, and the sixteen or more at table in *I Iron Age*, B, 302-309. When a bed was discovered, as in *The Wonder of a Kingdom*, III, ii, with ten or more beside it, a considerable space was required. The last two scenes are pretty large, though not impossible for a removable structure, but they are also difficult to imagine on any permanent rear stage which will fit into other demands of these plays.

(9)

What does this all amount to? Does it warrant the conclusion that the discoverable space was not a permanent feature of the stage? Perhaps because the rear stage has for so long been a part of our thinking, I find it hard to picture the Elizabethan stage without it. On the other hand, a removable curtained enclosure would solve some difficulties, as was pointed out at the beginning of this discussion. Perhaps most important of all, it explains the absence of a curtain in the Swan picture and the absence of directions for curtains and for discoveries in these plays. Notice how few such definite directions there are in the above list: one discovery above; four below—exclusive of those in beds or in shops and other structures; one mention of a curtain before a picture, two of an arras used for concealment, one of a traverse, only one of a discovery precisely by a curtain. If the number of discovered scenes showed a distinct increase in later plays, we might guess that the curtained space had become a structural feature; that would be a natural development. But no such change appears. The only safe conclusions seem to be: (1) a curtained space was available on the Red Bull stage; (2) there is enough evidence to raise a doubt whether it was a permanent feature of the stage, but not enough to allow a positive assertion; (3) there were sometimes two discoverable spaces in use in the same play; and to sum up the whole chapter, (4) some plays in this public theater were certainly staged in the simultaneous manner, and it is doubtful if the Elizabethan stage manager thought of the other plays as essentially different.

It does not follow that we are to picture the Red Bull as resembling the Valenciennes miniature or Mahelot's designs. The greatest demands are of *The Brazen Age* with an indefinite structure or rear stage to conceal the altar, the bank, a banquet, the "fiery bulls," and then the altar again; the cave-arbor; and possibly a throne and woods. *The Rape of Lucrece* is perhaps next with a tent and a discoverable space successively used for the senate, a temple, and Lucrece's house; also perhaps a throne. Many of the plays require a setting no more elaborate than that shown in the Swan picture. But the simultaneous principle of the Red Bull stage is, it seems to me, as definitely established as anything can be with the evidence at our disposal.

(10)

Was the discoverable space elevated at all? Even if not structural it could have been. The formal seat had a dais; perhaps the dais was used in other circumstances as well. This would provide for some descents for which so little time is allowed as to make the use of the balcony doubtful, such as *The Heir*, V. ii, where only one line intervenes. But *II Iron Age*, 319-320 has only "Alarums" to cover a descent definitely from the walls, so that this explanation is hardly convincing. The principal argument for a slightly raised rear stage or curtained space is, I think, its greater effectiveness, and this would be denied by many, and the applicability of the argument doubted by many more. It is interesting to notice that Jocza Savits in his plan for a modern Shakespearean theater, *Shakespeare und die Bühne des Dramas* (1917), provides for a rear stage raised two steps. The principal argument against a raised curtained space is advanced by Lawrence in *The Physical Conditions of the Elizabethan Public Playhouse* (1927), p. 58; heavy properties, he says, such as beds and scaffolds, were often thrust out from the rear stage; how could this have been done down steps? But it is hardly proved that beds, etc., were always thrust out from the curtained space; perhaps they came through a door. Only when discovered must they have stood in the curtained space. I do not see how we can prove whether the curtained space below—we must not forget that the balcony had its own curtain above—was slightly elevated or not.

CHAPTER VIII

ELIZABETHAN STAGE EFFECTS

(1)

THE Elizabethan theater is often, perhaps usually, represented as a theater in which the spoken word was the principal means for the creation of dramatic illusion. *The Cambridge History of English Literature* (1910), is scarcely yet so out of date as to make citation from it (VI, 305) inappropriate: "The creation of the atmosphere for the play . . . was left to the descriptive words of the poet, the voice of the actor and the imagination of the audience." Material stage effects are in this opinion entirely ignored. Since on the one hand we read mostly Shakespeare's plays, and on the other imagine if no longer a naked stage at least one of small visual resources, such an opinion is natural enough. On Shakespeare's stage his poetry had indeed an incomparable magic, and other methods of exciting the imagination seem feeble beside it. But may we not be justified in doubting whether Heywood's and Dekker's verse, not to mention that of weaker poets, was the main imaginative inspiration for the groundlings at the Red Bull? It was not distinctively a literary theater, and it would be surprising indeed if its audience was really moved more by poetry than by other theatrical appeals.

Yet it would be as mistaken an idea in the other direction to think that the spoken word did not count for much even at the Red Bull. The Prologue to one of its plays, *If It Be Not Good*, A, cites not the stage manager nor the actor but the poet as the person who is to

> call the Banishd Auditor home, And tye
> His Eare (with golden chaines) to his Melody;

it is the poet who is to make

> creatures
> Forg'de out of th' Hammer, on tiptoe, to *Reach* vp,
> And (from *Rare silence*) clap their *Brawny hands*,
> T'Applaud, what their *charmd* soule scarce vnderstands.

To be sure this is the point of view of Dekker, a poet, but no scenario writer would make that claim today. In all Elizabethan drama, no matter how unliterary, we find an attempt to use the appeal of words, which does sharply distinguish it from our inarticulate movies. Our

heroes resort to swift punches or kisses using yards of film, where the
Elizabethans delivered twenty or more good set lines of oratorical in-
vective or passionate eloquence and, as Jonson sneered, paraded "foot-
and-half-foot" words.

That the Red Bull playwrights were not wizards with speech did
not deter them from doing what they could with it. I do not remember
that Heywood in all his six volumes of plays wrote a single magic
line of dialogue, but he has pages of verse obviously planned to stir
the emotions. Sometimes it is oratorical: look for example at *The Four
Prentices of London*, A, 230-231, when the Christians are about to
assault Jerusalem. After nearly forty lines of exclamatory enumera-
tion of the sacred associations of the place, and after the Soldan from
the walls has scorned the Christians, saying:

> Looke (forreiners) do not the lofty Spires,
> And these cloud-kissing Turrets that you see,
> Strike deadly terrour in your wounded soules?

Godfrey defies him thus:

> *Soldan* and *Sophy*, ye damn'd hel-hounds both,
> So quakes the Eagle to behold a gnat,
> The Lyon to behold a Marmosat.
> I'le beard and braue you in your own beliefe,
> As when the heathen God, whom you call *Ioue*,
> Warr'd with Gyant, great *Enceladus*,
> And flung him from Olympus two-topt Mount
> The swaynes stood trembling to behold his fall,
> That with his weight did make the earth to groane.
> So, *Soldan*, looke, when I haue skal'd these wals,
> And won the place where now thou stand'st secure,
> To be hurl'd head-long from the proudest Tower,
> In scorne of thee, thy false gods, and their power.

So the oratory goes on for pages interspersed with alarms, attacks,
parleys, and the classic crackle of much stychomythic dialogue. This is
a fairly obvious example of the faith of the Red Bull dramatists in
the power of words to lift very prosaic fact to impressive levels. The
fact was only the open stage of the Red Bull and its associated gallery
with, quoting Ben Jonson again, half a dozen rusty swords to stand
for the hosts of Turks and Christians. Even some property like Henslowe's "city of Rome" could have added little. The dream is of
"lofty spheres and cloud-kissing turrets."

Yet for all their faith in words the Elizabethans did not often in-
dulge in direct description of scenery supposed to be before the audience. A remark like that in MacCracken, Pierce, and Durham's *An*

Introduction to Shakespeare (1919), p. 47, if not actually false is at least misleading:

The absence of pictorial scenery forced the dramatist to use verbal description far more than is customary today. To this fact we owe some passages of poetry which are among the most beautiful in all dramatic literature.

It was not so much the need for pictorial scenery that set a stiff task to the dramatist in the creation of the proper atmosphere: the lack of any illusive lightning was surely as important a difficulty. There was, for instance, the problem of suggesting darkness. Some fifteen of the *A* and *B* plays have important night scenes.[1] The problem was solved by the use of pantomime, the bringing in of lights, and of course words; examples are *A Woman Killed with Kindness*, B, IV. iv and *II Iron Age*, B, 378-381, both to be discussed later in this chapter.

Still more troublesome was their desire to represent on the stage actions which even the cinema with all its facilities for illusion would scarcely attempt. Even then, the dramatist did not usually solve these problems by using passages of extended description. Instead, he resorted to pantomime, noises, and other stage effects, and so far as he did use words, trusted to the violent expressions of feeling as above, or to only scattered descriptive phrases. To show this by citing Red Bull plays would require considerable space. May I refer rather to more commonly known plays? How much good set description of the scene before us occurs in the balcony scene in *Romeo and Juliet*, the wood scenes in *As You Like It*, the garden scene in *The Merchant of Venice*, the heath scene in *King Lear?* To let one serve for all, note specifically the last. There are several lines in the preceeding scene describing Lear's contention with the elements, but in the scene itself scarcely any; instead, we have Lear's apostrophe to the storm and Kent's speech full of allusions to the noises of the night but with few details of sight:

> Things that love night
> Love not such nights as these; the wrathful skies
> Gallow the very wanderers of the dark,
> And make them keep their caves. Since I was man
> Such sheets of fire, such bursts of horrid thunder,
> Such groans of roaring wind and rain, I never
> Remember to have heard.

This is a speech certainly not inserted to take the place of scenery but rather to supply a lack which our realistic stage must also admit. But

---

[1] In this chapter discussion of the *C* plays is usually omitted as adding little of additional interest.

while in a realistic performance such a speech unaccompanied by these noises comes discordantly (and if the noises are adequately supplied, they only distract), on the Elizabethan stage where so much was imagined, the speech itself even with only suggestive noises off stage, might serve admirably.

When extensive description does occur it often concerns what is really thought of as out of sight of the audience. This is notably the case, of course, with Shakespeare's two most famous descriptions: those of the high cliff in *King Lear* and of Cleopatra in her barge. Heywood does this too. His horrific sea-monster which comes to devour Hesoine in *The Brazen Age*, A, 206 does its violent deeds before its entrance. More daring is *The Rape of Lucrece*, where not five minutes after the audience saw Tullia prosaically step on her father's body, there comes the gory description, cited in chapter III, of how she had her chariot drive across it. And sometimes the Red Bull dramatists do definitely assert with vigor the most astonishing things which the audience was expected to accept in defiance of what it really saw. Outstanding examples of such descriptions—some of them have already been cited in detail and need only a reference here—occur in *The Two Noble Ladies*, A, where explicit directions show that soldiers who are supposed to be drowning in the Euphrates are really carried out by supers through a rear door; the death of the mad Hercules in *The Brazen Age*, A; the sea fight between two ships in *Fortune by Land and Sea*, B; the rescue in *The Hector of Germany*, B, of a man from a rocky cliff (the balcony) by a ship which draws up in the open sea (the front stage). Examples of scenes described in detail in which one may doubt if any reality corresponded to the description are the numerous portraits in the Dean's gallery in *II If You Know Not Me*, B, 275-282, the beauties of Gresham's Exchange in the same play, 295-297, 316-319; the turrets of Jerusalem, just referred to, in *The Four Prentices*, A; the room in *The Wonder of a Kingdom*, B, I. iv; and—again to choose a well-known illustration—the martins playing about Macbeth's castle. Perhaps we are inclined to condemn with Jonson and Sidney the taste which permitted such eking out of spectacle with words; it may seem childishly naïve. Yet Chinese drama and its modern imitations show how easily audiences, even those accustomed only to realistic presentation, accept and enjoy the sketchiest of stage suggestions.

To state truly, then, the importance of words as substitutes for stage effects in the Elizabethan theater demands care, especially in emphasis, and an avoidance of blanket generalizations. For there were other effects commonly employed, both visual and auditory. Among the audible effects[2] are songs, instrumental music, off-stage noises as well as a good many on the stage; among visual effects are costumes, properties, processions, business, pantomime. Appealing to both sight and hearing are the numerous fireworks. Evidence for these various means of appeal follows:

(2)

Songs are not an especially emphasized part of the Red Bull plays, but some are to be noted. Nearly a score of "sundry songs," with little connection to the play, are printed in later editions of *The Rape of Lucrece*, A, among them the lovely "Pack clouds away, and welcome day," a song in Dutch, and a merry catch for three voices. In *The White Devil*, A, V. iv, while Marcello's corpse is being wound, Webster's dirge, "Call for the robin red-breast and the wren," is sung; there is a song and dance by an Italian zany and five courtezans in *If It Be Not Good*, A, 331; satyrs sing to Diana in *The Golden Age*, A, 27; there is a song for Ceres and Proserpine in *The Silver Age*, B, 133; a song in parts in *Swetnam*, A, G 2-G 2v, furnishes an emotional setting for an execution off stage; a mountebank sings his wares in *Herod and Antipater*, A, C 4-D iv, F 4v-H 2v, and *The Two Noble Ladies*, A, V. ii, has a song while a lady sleeps.

That the Elizabethans employed instrumental music to create suitable emotional backgrounds scarcely needs illustration. The instruments specified as used at the Red Bull are drums, trumpets, horns, cornets, "hoboyes," recorders, a fife, a lute. Bells heightened situations in *I If You Know Not Me*, B, 222, *If It Be Not Good*, A, 280-287; in *The Golden Age*, A, IV, *passim;* and in *The Devil's Law Case*, A, II. iii. Either a bell or a clock struck twelve for the beginning of *Match Me in London*, B.[3] Some of these instruments were used conventionally; the horns to suggest hunting scenes in numerous plays,

---

[2] For a justifiable emphasis on the audible effects in Shakespeare's plays, but somewhat personally imaginative and possibly over-subtle, see G. Wilson Knight's *Principles of Shakespearean Production* (1936), pp. 67-78, *et passim*. The neglect or slurring of off-stage sound effects is, he says, "probably the most outstanding defect in modern Shakespearean production." I attempt only a simple statement of representative factual material, and not such a detailed consideration of the sound effects at the Red Bull, doubting if their artistic quality warrants it.—On the use of music in the theaters and some of the other subjects of this chapter, see J. Isaacs' "Production and Stage-Management at the Blackfriars Theatre," The Shakespeare Association (1933).

[3] On bells in the theater see Lawrence, *Those Nut-Cracking Elizabethans* (1935), pp. 84-96. I must confess, however, that I see no evidence that, as he suggests, the bell in *The Golden Age* hung in the hut above the stage; would not the long rope dangling from above have been an excessively awkward arrangement?

for instance, *The Golden Age*, A, 32, and *The Royal King*, B, 11-13; drums for battle scenes, trumpets or cornets for flourishes to announce the entrance of kings and other important personages (these are too numerous to require citation), to heighten the excitement of combats, for instance in *The Devil's Law Case*, A, V. iv; and to render proclamations more impressive. An interesting illustration of this last occurs at the abortive announcement of Lady Jane Grey as Queen in *Sir Thomas Wyatt*, B, 97; "A Trumpet sounds, and no answere. The Herald sounds a parlee, and none answers. . . . A trumpet soundes a parley, the Herald proclaimes [Queen Mary]." There is no hint of music regularly between the acts in the Red Bull plays. A few specific directions for music may be cited: *Sir Thomas Wyatt*, B, 87, "A dead march and passe round the stage"; *The Rape of Lucrece*, A, 184, "Sound musicke" for the scene at Apollo's oracle. In *A Shoemaker a Gentleman*, B, C 2v-C 4, "musicke" encourages Winifred in her piety, and Pluto's entrance in *If It Be Not Good*, A, 265, is accompanied by "the sound of hellish music." "A pirhicke straine" is called for in *I Iron Age*, B, 306, to accompany "a lofty dance"; "loude musicke" heightens Agamemnon's return in *II Iron Age*, B, 405, and his body is borne off "with a sad and funerall march," 414.

These references suggest the uses made of off-stage noises. Directions for these are pretty numerous and varied; thus, to show pursuits, off-stage slaughters, and the like, the following occur: *Sir Thomas Wyatt*, B, 113, "Within crie arme"; 119, "A great Noise, follow. Enter Wyat with his sword drawne, being wounded"; *A Shoemaker a Gentleman*, B, B 1-B 4, "Within a cry follow, follow," for pursuit after a battle; I 3-K 2v, "A cry within, arme, arme, arme; then enter a sort of Country people at severall doores"; *The Two Noble Ladies*, A, I. ii, "Alarm still. Cry within, Kill Kill Kill"; iv, "Crie within follow, follow this way." "A confused noyse to come pressing in" in *If It Be Not Good*, A, 358, is caused by the Puritans, with whom Hell is full, trying to get to Pluto. In *The White Devil*, A, V. iii, "Charges and shoutes" accompany a fight at the barriers, and in the later quartos of *II If You Know Not Me*, B, 347, "a noise within crying A Furbisher" shows the victory over the Armada. In *The Hector of Germany*, B, E 4-F 2, trumpets within and "a great shoute" suggest a tournament. "A noyse of tumult within" in *The Golden Age*, A, 7, represents Tytan's revolt; in *The Silver Age*, B, 126-130, shouts accompany Hercules' exploits; in *The Brazen Age*, A, shouts, 190, "hornes" and "a cry within," 192, suggest the fight against the boar; "a strange confused fray," 196, furnishes the background for the quarrel among the hunters; "a great showt within," 205, signals the approach of a ship; "a cry within," 206, the approach of the sea-monster; and 210, "a shoote" the coming of the Argonauts to Troy. Similarly in *I Iron Age*, B, 332, "A great crye within" shows the wounding of Achilles, and, 338, "A loud shout within crying Aiax, Aiax," and 340, "a shout within Vlisses, Vlisses" are supposed to show the sympathies of the army in the disposal of Achilles' armor. *II Iron Age*, B, has, 394, "shreiks and clamours" within at the fall of Troy, "healthing within" after the return of Agamemnon, 409, and 413, "A noyse of vproare within" at his death. But the most interesting use of off-stage noises occurs in *The Rape of Lucrece*, A, 243-245, to suggest Horatio's defense of the bridge. As Horatio stands defending presumably one of the stage doors, there is "A noise of knocking downe the bridge, within"; then "Alarum, Alarum," and, after a page of high talk "Alarum, and the falling of the Bridge," and finally "Shout and flourish" to welcome Horatio when he lands from swimming the Tiber, off stage.

A common stage noise is thunder. It sounds at an interrupted wedding in *Match Me in London*, B, 212; it is called for with "rayne" and lightning in *If It Be Not Good*, A, 326; it accompanies the allotment of the sea to Neptune in the fateful lottery of *The Golden Age*, A, 78; the descent of Jupiter "in a cloud," 98, and with "his Thunderbolt burning," 154, in *The Silver Age*, B; the death of Agamemnon, *II Iron Age*, B, 412 ("a greate thunder crack"); and the entrance of a spirit and the approach of the Tritons to rescue Justina in *The Two Noble Ladies*, A, III. iv.

The mention of "rayne" suggests the "shower of rain" which falls in a dumb show in *The Brazen Age*, A, 183, and the textual mention of rain, *I If You Know Not Me*, B, 213, as falling on Elizabeth as she comes to the Tower. In *II If You Know Not Me*, B, 268, a marginal note, "A storme," accompanies a line in the dialogue, "And we stay long, we shall be wet to the skin." Lawrence, *Pre-Restoration Stage Studies* (1927), pp. 229-234, discusses such scenes and suggests that "a copious shower of dried peas from the tiring-house garret . . . on the tiled shadow covering the stage would have created a sufficient illusion." In support of this idea he cites eighteenth century practice. This is not very convincing, but is better than the obvious alternative, a hireling with a sprinkler in the hut above. On the whole I am disposed to think the rain imaginary in all these cases except perhaps *If It Be Not Good*, where it is specified in the direction.

Then there are the "chambers" and guns shot off. *II If You Know Not Me*, B, 338, suggests the fight with the Armada by "a peal of shot within"; in *The Travails of Three English Brothers*, B, 40, "a Chamber is shot off" to announce Sir Thomas's arrival at Ieo, and it goes off again, 42. Similarly in *Fortune by Land and Sea*, B, 416, "a peece goes off" to heighten the effect of the sea-battle.

This does not make many examples after all of artillery; Heywood must have regretted its enforced absence from the *Ages*, for he could scarcely have shared Jonson's distaste for the "roll'd bullet heard To say, it thunders" and the "tempestuous drum" that "rumbles, to tell you when the storm doth come." Carew's scornful reference in 1630 to the Red Bull as a place where "noise prevails" refers to a later period in the theater's history than I am concerned with, but in 1620 the prologue to *The Two Merry Milkmaids*, B, cited in chapter II, shows the liking of the audience for clamor. To extend, however, this reputation for noise to Elizabethan theaters and drama in general as Lee Simonson does in saying "Most Elizabethan plays were filled with enough sissing and booming to make them excellent substitutes for Fourth of July celebrations"—*The Stage is Set* (1932), p. 219—is certainly to be too much impressed by these rather unusual bits of evidence.

(3)

There are more uses of fireworks than one would expect in a theater lighted by daylight and made of wood; I list them in approximately chronological order: *II If You Know Not Me*, B, 292, "A blazing star" as an omen; *If It Be Not Good*, A, 294, "Fire-workes on Lines" to astonish the king; 329, "Fireworkes" to scare a man out of a tree; 346, friars "Sinck downe, aboue flames," a somewhat cryptic direction implying, I think, that the friars sink to hell while there was an effect of flames in the gallery which represented their abbey walls; 350, showing the torments of the condemned in Hell, has a scene with directions calling for "a burning torch," "Hand burn't off," and "Fires the barrell-tops," followed by a considerable explosion. All this makes less unusual the fireworks in the *Ages*. In *The Silver Age*, B, 154-155, occurs the following: "Semele drawne out in her bed" . . . "Thunder, lightnings, Iupiter descends in his maiesty, his Thunderbolt burning" . . . "As he toucheth the bed it fires, and all flyes vp, Iupiter from thence takes an abortiue infant." Then, 159-160, when Hercules overcomes the hellish powers, we have:

Hercules sinkes himselfe; Flashes of fire; the Diuels appeare at euery corner of the stage with seuerall fire-workes. The Iudges of Hell, and the three sisters run ouer the stage, Hercules after them: fire-workes all ouer the house. . . . Enter Pluto with a club of fire, a burning crowne, Proserpine, the Iudges, the Fates, and a guard of Diuels, all with burning weapons. . . . Hercules fels Pluto, beats off the Diuels with all their fire-workes, rescues Proserpine.

Even more spectacular is *The Brazen Age,* A. When Hercules has driven in a dragon, 175, "Enter a Fury all fire-workes," only of course to be beaten in by Hercules, who exclaims, "Fright vs with fire? our Club shall quench thy flame." Then after the presentation of the death of Meleager and the fatal brand, 199-200, which may or may not have been spectacularly presented, there is the capture of the golden fleece, which occasions these directions: 217, "Two fiery Buls are discouered, the Fleece hanging ouer them, and the Dragon sleeping beneath them: Medea with strange fiery-workes, hangs aboue in the Aire in the strange habite of a Coniuresse." But the grand fiery climax came at the death of Hercules after he had been maddened by the poisoned shirt, 252-254:

Enter Hercules from a rocke aboue, tearing downe trees. . . . All the Princes breake downe the trees, and make a fire, in which Hercules placeth himselfe. . . . Iupiter aboue strikes him with a thunder-bolt, his body sinkes, and from the heauens discends a hand in a cloud that from the place where Hercules was burnt, brings vp a starre, and fixeth it in the firmament.

After that anything else must seem an anticlimax. In *I Iron Age,* B, 314, four enter "with burning staues and fire-bals"; the flames of burning Troy in *II Iron Age,* B, are only talked of. *The Honest Lawyer,* A, I 2v, has a direction, "Rob. flashes powder" to simulate a ghost. *The Virgin Martyr,* A, 81, when a devil enters, has "fire flashing out of the study," and *The Two Noble Ladies,* A, V. ii, when devils sink, says "a flame of fier riseth after them." That all this fiery spectacle was not confined to the Red Bull is shown by a passage from John Melton's *Astrologaster* (1620), quoted by Lawrence, *Elizabethan Playhouse and Other Studies,* Second Series, (1913), p. 18, how at the Fortune Theater one might

behold shagge-hayr'd deuills runne roaring over the stage with squibs in their mouths, while drummers made thunder in the tyring-house, and the twelve penny hirelings made artificial lightning in their heavens.

(4)

With this consideration of fireworks we have passed from audible to visible effects. Among these costume certainly played a very important part. Charles J. Sisson in *Le Goût Public et le Théatre Elisabéthain* (1923), pp. 93-94, effectively points out how much more money Henslowe spent for costumes than for properties, and how the Henslowe inventory shows "la pouvreté remarquable des décors en comparaison des costumes." Evidence for special costumes follows, together with instances where ordinary costumes are used for special purposes, as to suggest time or place; disguises are also listed and hints at make-up:

Sir Thomas Wyatt: B, 88, "Enter Queene Mary with a Prayer Booke in her hand like a nun."

A Woman Killed with Kindness: B, IV. ii. "Enter Sir Charles in prison, with irons, his feet bare, his garments all ragged and torn."

I If You Know Not Me: B, 209, "Enter three white-cote Souldiers." 228, Friars and angels.

II If You Know Not Me: B, 297, "The Waits in Sergeants gowns." Note also the probably large number of official costumes for the Lord Mayor, Sheriff, Swordbearer, etc.

The Travails of Three English Brothers: B, 5, "Prologue attired like fame." Also presumably distinctive costumes for Turks, Persians, the Pope, his cardinals; notice, 47, "Enter a Christian in Turkes habit as a Prisoner"; 90, hermit.

The Rape of Lucrece: A, 249, "Alarum, Brutus all bloody."

Fortune by Land and Sea: B, II. i, the text, 382, shows Philip and Susan changed to clothes from the clown's wardrobe, "like a scarecrow"; 413, "Mr. Forrest like a Captain of a ship."

A Shoemaker a Gentleman: B, an angel, hermit, Goths, Vandals, Romans, "a sort of country people," "Enter with a Kercher on," shoemakers' aprons and caps.

The White Devil: A, IV. i, Isabella's ghost; V. i, the Duke of Florence disguised as a Moor; V. iii, two disguised as Capuchins; V. iv, Brachiano's ghost "in his leather Cassock & breeches, bootes, a coule."

Match Me in London: B, 212, friars.

Greene's Tu Quoque: B, 262, "Enter . . . like an Italian."

If It Be Not Good: A, 280, "in a Friers weede"; 285, "2 Pilgrimes"; 306, "a golden Head ascends" and speaks; 331, "Enter . . . like a Turke"; 331, "Enter . . . leading in an Italian zany"; 333, "Enter . . . some spirit in a frightfull shape"; 358, "Enter a Ghoast, cole-blacke." Also other friars, devils, etc.

The Golden Age: A, 27, nymphs, satyrs; 68, Jupiter in "his Imperiall Robes"; 70, Danae in her nightgown; 78, presumably special costumes for the three Fates and the four Winds and Neptune"; "burning Roabe" for Pluto.

The Silver Age: B, 133, "Enter Ceres and Proserpine, attired, like the Moone, with a company of Swaines, and country Wenches"; 135, "Enter Pluto, his Chariot drawne in by Diuels (also 156, 159); 138, "Tryton with his Trumpe, as from the sea"; 141, centaurs described as "doubly shap't"; 146, "Semele like a huntresse, with her traine, Iupiter like a woodman in greene;" 157, Cerberus.

The Brazen Age: A, 173, water-nymphs, the river Achelous; 175, a dragon, "a Fury all fire-workes"; 184, "Venus like a Huntresse"; 187, "Enter . . . in greene" eleven to hunt; 206, the sea- monster; 217, "Medea with strange fiery-workes, hangs aboue in the Aire in the strange habite of a coniuresse"; 228, Aurora attended by Seasons, Days, and Hours; 231, "Vulcan with two Ciclops"; 254, Hercules "burnes his Club and Lyons skin."

I Iron Age: B, 269, "Enter Cassandra with her haire about her eares."

II Iron Age: B, 381, "Enter a Troian in his night-gowne all vnready. . . . Enter his wife as from bed"; 383, Hector's ghost; 385, "Priam in his night-gowne and slippers"; 389, "Enter Prince Chorebus with other Troians in Greekish habits"; 390, Chorebus is killed by Aeneas "by reason of his habite" (this item shows that the Greeks and Trojans wore distinctive costumes); 413, at the death of Agamemnon, "Enter all the Kings with other Seruants halfe vnready, as newly started from their Beds"; 416, "Enter [3] disguised"; 423, the ghost of Agamemnon.

The Hector of Germany: B, B 1-B 2v, "Enter Peter the Hermit, King of Spaine in a disguise"; D 4-E 2, "A taffata Cloake"; E 2v, "2 Saylors canuas Suits"; H 3-I 1v, several in a masque wear masks; "Enter [2] armed and in theyr shyrts" (d).

The Four Prentices of London: A, 176, "Enter Godfrey as newly landed & halfe naked"; 177, "To them, Guy all wet. . . . Enter Charles all wet with his sword"; 181, "Enter Charles like an Out-law, with Bandettoes and Theeues and with the Clowne."

The Honest Lawyer: A, has several disguises including some as fairies; also an Abbott's habit.

The Royal King: B, 13, "Enter Corporall and Cocke ragged"; 14, "Enter Captaine extreame ragged"; 77, the Marshall brought to the bar "as out of his bed."

Swetnam the Woman-Hater: A, E 1, "Lorenzo disguised like an Amazon"; K 3v, shepherds, a nymph, and allegorical figures, Ignorance, Suspicion, etc., in a masque.

Edward II: B, IV. i, young Mortimer, disguised; IV. vi, three disguised.

The Devil's Law Case: A, II. i, Crispiano disguised as a merchant; II. iii, "two Belmen and a Capouchin"; III. ii, "Enter Romelio in the habit of a Jew"; III. iii, "Jolenta in mourning"; IV. ii, "to them Ercole muffled"; Contarino disguised as a Dane; "Leonora with a blacke veile"; V. i, "Angiolella great-bellied"; V. ii, "Enter Ercole with a letter, and Contarino comming in Friers habits as having bin at the Bathanites, a Ceremony used afore these Combates"; V. v, "Enter Angiolella vail'd, and Jolenta, her face colour'd like a Moore, the two Surgeons, one of them like a Jew." Miss Bradbrook in *Themes and Conventions of Elizabethan Tragedy* (1935) p. 16, cites this scene as a striking example of the use of black and white symbolically.

The Two Merry Milkmaids: B, I. i, "Enter Lardosse . . . like a Spirit"; IV. i [Bernard] "Puls of his disguisd Haire"; IV. i, V. i, invisible actors; V. i, "Enuy and pleasure passe o're the stage"; a spirit enters.

The Virgin Martyr: A, 48, a priest of Jupiter; 51, "Spungius and

Hircius ragged"; 74, Angelo "in the Angels habit" which, the text shows, makes him invisible except to Dorothea; 81, Harpax, a devil, "in a fearful shape"; 90, "Enter Dorothea in a white Robe, Crowns upon her Robe, a Crown upon her head, lead in by an Angel, [3] following all in white, but lesse glorious, the Angel with a Crown for [Theophilus]."

The Heir: A, V. ii, Francisco disguised as a parson marries Luce, supposed with child; Franklin pulls a pillow from her clothes and "flings the Cushion at [Shallow]."

Herod and Antipater: A, B 1-B iv, "Enter at one dore Alexandra in her petticoate, at another Aristobulus the high Priest in his wastcoate or shirt, both amazedly"; C 3, a sleeveless shirt; K 3v-L 2v, visions of two appear "like ghosts" followed by seven others; L 3v, "Enter Salumith betweene two Furies wauing a Torch."

The Welsh Ambassador: B, Disguise of three nobles as soldiers, then as Welsh ambassador, Irishman, Welsh serving-man; one as friar; 2220, Prince like Cupid; 2298, Clown like Vulcan.

The Two Noble Ladies: A, I. iv, and III. i, Miranda disguised as a man; II. ii, Cantharides is a spirit invisible except to Barebones; III. iii, "Enter a Spirit Like a souldier in armour on his breast a sable sheild written on with Golden letters"; III. iv, "Enter an Angell shaped like a patriarch vpon his breast a (red) blew table full of silver letters, in his right hand a red crossierstaffe, on his shoulders large wings"; "Enter 2 Tritons with silver trumpets"; V. ii, a lady asleep "diuells about her "; V. iii, Miranda "in her Owne Amazonian attire, an helmet on and the beavor down."

The Wonder of a Kingdom: B, 242, "Angelo like a Doctor"; 249, Torrenti "gorgeously attyred"; 251, his brother "Bare and ragged"; 263, Torrenti "very brave," "women in strang habitts"; 265, "Servants in blew-coats"; 278, Angelo "as a Fryar."

This list of costumes, make-up, and disguise suggests a few observations. There seems to have been a considerable number of conventional costumes, which must have lightened the expository task of the playwright: for Jews; for Turks, Italians, and other nationalities; for Amazons; for huntsmen; perhaps for doctors, merchants, etc.; for ghosts (but all ghosts were not similarly costumed—compare *The White Devil* and *If It Be Not Good*). The "invisible" actors of *The Virgin Martyr, The Two Noble Ladies,* and *The Two Merry Milkmaids,* also the ghosts in *Herod and Antipater,* invisible except to their murderers, remind one of Henslowe's robe "to go invisible in," and, perhaps, "Prospero on the top invisible" in *The Tempest*. But these invisible characters in the Red Bull plays could scarcely have been dressed alike, since they represent variously an angel, men, and a devil. The device of dressing warring parties differently, as the Greeks and Trojans in the *Ages,* the Christians and the Turks in *The Four Prentices,* the pirates and their attackers in *Fortune by Land and Sea,* is a very useful one and was almost inevitable. Finally, Aristobulus's "wastcoate" in *Herod and Antipater*, A, B 1, is a significant reminder that historical accuracy was the least of worries to the Elizabethan costumer.

These costumes must have furnished a good deal of the interest of the processions, ceremonials, dances, dumb shows and extended pantomimes which occur so frequently in these plays. The open projecting stage lent itself particularly well to this sort of thing. To list the directions for all of these would require a great deal of space and serve no particular purpose except to emphasize the number and importance of these appeals. It is also difficult to distinguish them sharply, but by my count in these thirty-two *A* and *B* plays, there are twenty-seven elaborate processionals and ceremonials, eight dances, and seventy-five dumb shows and prolonged pantomimes. A few directions of special interest may be cited:

I If You Know Not Me: B, 244, "A Sonnet. Enter foure Trumpeters; after them Sergeant Trumpeter, with a mace; after him Purse-bearer, Sussex with the Crowne; Howard the scepter; Constable, with the Cap of Maintenance; Shandoyse, with the Sword; Tame, with the Collar and a George. Foure Gentlemen bearing the Canopy ouer the Queene [Elizabeth]; two Gentlewomen bearing vp her traine; six Gentlemen Petitioners. The Queene takes state." On p. 246 this procession is directed, "Sonnet about the Stage in order. The Maior of London meets them."

The Travails of Three English Brothers: B, 90, "Enter three seuerall waies the three Brothers; Robert with the state of Persia as before; Sir Anthonie with the King of Spaine and others where he receiues the Order of Saint Iago, and other Officers; Sir Thomas in England with his Father and others. Fame giues to each a prospective glasse, they seeme to see one another, and offer to embrace, at which Fame parts them, and so: Exeunt."

The Rape of Lucrece: A, 184, "Sound Musicke. Apollo's Priests, with Tapers, after them [3] with their oblations, all kneeling before the Oracle"; 240, "A great shout and a flourish with drums and Trumpets . . . Alarum, Enter in the fight Tarquin and Tullia flying, pursude by Brutus, and the Romans march with Drum and Colors, [4] and Tullia meets and joynes with them; to them Brutus and the Romans with Drum and souldiers; they make a stand."

Fortune by Land and Sea: B, 427, "Enter the Sheriffe, the silver Oare, Purser and Clinton going to execution."

The *Ages* have an especially large number of dumb shows and pantomimes, some of which have already been cited and others are to be brought up in another connection. Here I quote only the following:

I Iron Age: B, 302, "A flourish. Enter all the Greekes on one side, all the Troians on the other: Euery Troian Prince intertaines a Greeke, and so march two and two, discoursing as being conducted by them into the

Citty. . . . Lowd muscicke. A long table, and a banquet in state, they are seated a Troian and Greeke, Hecuba, Polixeua, Cresida, and other Ladies waite, Calchas is present whispering to his Daughter Cresida"; 306, "A lofty dance of sixteene Princes, halfe Troians, halfe Grecians."

II Iron Age: B, The fall of Troy offers a considerable amount of panto-mime: 378-381, "Enter [Greeks to Troy] with souldiers in a soft march, without noise . . . Enter Synon with a torch aboue [to give the signal] . . . [The Greeks] march softly in at one doore; and presently in at another . . . Pyrhus, Diomed and the rest, leape from out the Horse. And as if groping in the darke, meete with Agamemnon and the rest: who after knowledge imbrace. . . . A loude Alarum. Enter a Troian in his night-gowne all vnready . . . Enter his wife as from bed. . . . A great cry within. Alarum. Enter Pyrhus with the rest their weapons drawn and torches."

The Royal King: B, 65, "Sound, Enter with two Gentleman-ushers be-fore them, the Queen crown'd, her sister to attend her as her waiting-maid, with a traine."

The Wonder of a Kingdom: B, 254, "Trumpets sound. Enter an arm'd sewer, after him a company with covered dishes: Coronets on their heads. Two with pistolls to guard it . . . Musicke, drinck, breake the glasse, they pledge it in plate. Which offering, both servitours refuse to take"; "Trumpets sounding. Enter Torrenti very brave, between the two Dukes, attended by all the Courtiers, wondring at his costly habitts. Dance. Exit. He gives jewells, and ropes of pearle to the Duke, and a chaine of gold to every Courtier."

To these may be added a few directions, not so elaborate, but showing an emphasis on "business" in one way or another:

Sir Thomas Wyatt: B, 103, "Enter Homes with a Halter about his necke . . . He strangles himself."

The Rape of Lucrece: A, 168, "Enter [5] one way: Brutus meeting them the other way very humourously"; 173, "Sennat. As they march, Tullia treads on her Father & staies."

The Brazen Age: A, 237, "All the Gods appeare aboue and laugh" at Mars and Venus trapped by Vulcan.

The Royal King: B, 51, "The Clowne goes learing away and shaking his head."

Edward II: B, V. iii, "[The murderers of Edward] wash him with puddle-water and shave his beard away."

The Devil's Law Case: A, V. v, "The Combate continued to a good length."

The Virgin Martyr: A, 23, "Enter Angelo with a book and Taper lighted: they seeing him counterfeit devotion"; 49, "They both spit at the Image [of Jupiter], throw it down, and spurn it"; 61, "Enter Sapritius, dragging Dorothea by the hair"; 69, "Enter Harpax sneaking . . . [Theo-philus] Beats them . . . Beats t'other, he roares"; 76, "[Dorothea's] head struck off . . . Antoninus sinks [i.e. dies]."

Herod and Antipater: A, L 4, "Here the Executioner strikes [Antipater, who dies], and Herod dies."

The Two Noble Ladies: A, 100, [Barebones] "Hides him [self] vnder the table"; 1752-1910, "Iustina is discovered in a chaire asleep, in her hands a prayer book, divills about her" . . . "[Cyprian] offers to Kisse and she starts, wakes, and falls on her knees," . . . "She looks in her booke, and the Spirits fly from her." . . . "Hee kneels to her." . . . "The feinds roare and fly back," etc.

Of course many more directions for business might be cited. But these surely are enough to show that the Elizabethans wanted to see things as well as hear about them. Not that we do not share this desire, but the idea that the Elizabethans were different from us dies hard. They wanted to see the luxury of the rich man in *The Wonder of a Kingdom* as a contrast to his later poverty; they wanted to see the Greeks and Trojans pretending to be friends in a showy manner in *I Iron Age* while Thersites at one side commented, "They all imbrace and hugge, yet deadly hate." And of course only the actual surprise of the city would satisfy them in the fall of Troy. This desire to see everything also goes far to account for the large number of single deaths by violence on the stage. These are so numerous that they could hardly have been sensational unless in special circumstances, like the strangling in *Sir Thomas Wyatt*, B, or the beheadings cited above from *The Virgin Martyr*, A, and *Herod and Antipater*, A. Of course these they would want to see, as also the torturings on the rack in *The Travails of Three English Brothers*, B, 75-82; where the text reads "hoist him vp," "wrinch him againe"; in *The Virgin Martyr*, A, IV. iii, where the text speaks of irons cooling, whips, burning pincers; and *Herod and Antipater*, A, I 1-4v, where the directions say, "They racke Adda," and Herod orders, "So, pull home," "Higher yet," "Take her downe." All this not only gratified the desire for spectacle but added a sadistic attraction. Deaths in great numbers may or may not have appealed in the same way. Take the situation at the end of *II Iron Age*, B. Pyrhus is about to marry Hermione, when Orestes surprises them at the altar. I quote the directions: "A confused scuffle, in which Orestes kils Pyrhus: Pyrhus, Orestes: Cethus wounds Pillades, Diomed, Menelaus, Vlisses, Thersites, &c. All fall dead saue Vlisses, who beareth thence Hermione. Which done, Cethus riseth vp from the dead bodies and speakes." He taunts the dead until, "Synon who had before counterfeited death, riseth vp, and answereth" . . . "They fight and kill one another" . . . "Enter Hellena, Electra, and Hermione" . . . Helen asks Hermione to fetch her looking-glass, who having done so is dismissed. Nothing is said about Electra, but obviously Helen is left alone. She soliloquizes upon the effects of her beauty, now decayed ("See fayre ones, what a little Time can doe,") and then strangles herself. Finally Ulysses, as he freely points out, "the man soly reseru'd," speaks the epilogue. As one reads, the first impression of all this slaughter is distinctly ludicrous; one feigned dead body may be tragic, but a whole stage full, with two conveniently coming to life only to die again seems a little too much. Yet since there is no hint that such scenes seemed in the least amusing to the Elizabethans, these successive deaths not only at the Red Bull but also at the Globe and the Blackfriars were, I suspect, high spots of tragical effectiveness.

Other spectacular effects might be listed. The directions for costumes include a good many for spirits, ghosts, angels, devils. There are also the effects secured through properties. But already it must be clear that the descriptive words of the poets and the voices of the actors were far from being the only sources of theatric effectiveness.

(5)

To try to make any accurate summary of the relative use of the various means of appeal is obviously futile. Much depended on the kind of stories to be told. The nearest I can come to showing their relative importance is to summarize two or three plays or parts of plays of characteristically different levels.

Fortune by Land and Sea, a Heywood-Rowley play, dated by Chambers about 1607 but not published till 1655, offers an example in its naval battle of the presentation of an almost impossible scene with apparently a minimum of scenic equipment. The earlier part of the play requires little; I. ii is set in a tavern and suggests the scene by various small suitable properties; II. iii speaks of the balcony as a hen's roost, from which in III. i the hero leaps down, but neither scene seems to employ any special settings. It is in Act IV that the playwright and the stage manager had a real job, that of presenting a fight between two ships at sea.[4] The means they used were simple enough: Scene i begins, "A great Alarum and shot; enter Purser and Clinton [the pirates] with store of Mariners, bringing in the Merchant bound prisoner with others." They speak, 1.3, of "the spoyl of this

---

[4] Dr. Louis B. Wright discusses this scene and others in an informing article, "Elizabethan Sea Drama and Its Staging," *Anglia*, LI (1927), 104-118. The Red Bull plays offer no positive support of his conjecture that in all probability in a few plays, simple rigging, rope ladders, etc., "ran from the lower to the upper stage." Such properties are possible, of course, but would present troublesome complications.

rich ship," "this our prize"; so the scene, played, of course, on the open stage, is supposed on board the vessel. They order the Merchant placed below the hatches as prisoner; Clinton says, "Come first drink round, my merry mates"; and then they exeunt to divide the spoils.

Then, scene ii, "Enter young Mr. Forrest, like a Captain of a ship, with Sailors and Mariners entering with a flourish." Now the scene is on another boat, described as "a gallant vessel stoutly man'd," and they narrate their past successes. To look for the pirates Forrest sends the boy to "climb to the main-top,"—the balcony—and after five lines he speaks, supposedly from there, describing a vessel as seen first at a distance and then closer by. Meanwhile Forrest gives orders to prepare to meet the enemy:

> You Master Gunner load your ordnance wel,
> . . . Stearsman part the Helm. . . . Master you
> Heed wel your compass, Boatswain with your whistle
> Command the Saylors to the upper deck
> To know their quarters, etc.

The boy tells of the activities on the other ship, presently a direction says, "A peece goes off," and Forrest orders the boy, "Come descend"; and says to the crew:

> Now valiant friends and soldiers man the deck . . .
> Quarter your selves in order, some abaft,
> Some in the Ships waste, all in martial order,
> Our Spright-sayl, Top-sayl, and Top-gallant,
> our Main-sayl, Boar-spright, and our Mizen too
> are hung with waving pendants, and the colours
> of *England* and *St. George* ply in the Stern.
> We fight against the foe we all desire;
> Alarum Trumpets, Gunner straight give fire.

And with no further stage directions, they exeunt. Probably the trumpets did sound—that would be stirring and easy; perhaps the guns did go off again, but there is no explicit direction; but one suspects that the technical terms took the place of wheel, compass, and any visible sails and pendants. Noise and gunfire with appropriate business and costumes are the principal supplements to the words, which still remain nevertheless the main form of appeal.

A short scene follows on the first boat; it begins: "Alarm. Purser and Clinton with their Mariners, all furnisht with Sea devices fitting for a fight." We are told their ship is leaking and they cannot fly; there is much stirring about; but there is again mainly dependence for effect on nautical terms. The pirates exeunt, and an "Alarum" accompanies the entrance of Forrest and his men, and more vigorous language heightens the scene:

> the Seas mouth
> Seems to spit fire and all the billows burn . . .
> Hoyst up more sails . . .
> I spy the pirates in the very prow
> And forehead of their Ship, both wafting us
> With their bright swords . . .
> Boatswain with your baser trumpets sound
> Mingle your whistles shril, oh 'tis a Musick
> The Maremaids love . . .
> It blows a stiffe gale, it makes all for us.

And Forrest cheers on his men with appropriate declamation. They exeunt. "A great Alarum and Flourish. Enter young Forrest and his Mates with Purser and Clinton with their Mariners prisoners." They are now on the pirates' boat; the captive merchant is brought up and released, and the scene ends with no specially noteworthy details.

What has Heywood depended on to create his illusion? First, on his words; we can hardly call them poetry, perhaps not even oratory, but still they are not ineffective; then on noises, "alarums," flourishes, shooting-off of guns: then, though there were no sails, no pumps, perhaps even no wheel, on some properties and suitable costumes; and finally, and surely the most effective of all, on the pantomime and business—watching, rushing about, gesticulating generally. The changes of scene from one ship to another were till the last scene clear from the characters involved; in that scene the change to the pirates' ship was shown to the Elizabethan audience in accordance with the established convention of an exeunt at one door by Forrest and his men and an immediate re-entry at another.

Of course one is reminded of the similar ship scenes in *The Tempest*. Shakespeare uses these same means of effect: nautical language, "a tempestuous noise of thunder and lightning," "cries within," "Enter Mariners wet," "a confused noise within," and, of course, pantomime. One might say that a great difference between Heywood and Shakespeare is that Shakespeare never taxes our imagination quite so much, never has so great a distance between the theatrical fact and the imagined situation. But after all it is not much more difficult to imagine the front stage as first one ship and then another than to imagine it a ship at all. Really, Shakespeare asks quite as much of us as Heywood but helps us more to conceive it. What makes *The Tempest* storm scene memorable is its convincing humanity: the voluble boatswain with his "What cares these roarers for the name of king," and his impatience; the quiet humor of Gonzalo; the hysterical anger of Antonio and Sebastian; and above all the vivid phrasing. Lacking the gift of this last, Heywood could only resort to more rhetoric, more noise, more rushing about.

This is especially illustrated, along with more extravagant demands for material assistance, in such a play as *The Brazen Age*. This play, written about 1610-12 and published in 1613, suggests so astonishing a spectacle that some have denied that it could have been given in the published form. But since its stage directions are definitely theatrical rather than literary, and what they describe is not duplicated in the dialogue and is necessary to the story, its evidence cannot be dismissed as merely that of a closet drama.

Presenting the labors and death of Hercules, the poet and the stage-hands had their work cut out for them, and they must have employed all the resources of the theater. From the costume room came presumably special dresses for the water nymphs; for Aurora attended by the Seasons, Days, and Hours; for the Cyclops; for the hunters all "in greene"; for Medea "in the strange habite of a Conuiresse"; for a Dragon; for "a Fury all fire-workes"; perhaps also for "the sea-monster." Noises were made a great deal of: horns wind within to suggest a hunt; shouts announced the fall of the boar, the approach of a ship, and the Greeks' approach to Troy; "a cry within" signaled the coming of the sea-monster. Special properties required in the directions are a bull's head, the head of a boar, two fiery bulls, the golden fleece, a dragon, a crowing cock, Vulcan's net of wire, an altar, even a shower of rain. There were three or four dumb shows and elaborate processions.

But everything culminated in the death of Hercules. The sequence of scenes presenting it begins with Omphale glorying in the control she has had over Hercules. Then she says:

> Now the Priests and Princes are prepar'd
> For the great sacrifice, which we will grace
> With our high presence.

and a direction follows: "Enter to the sacrifice two Priests to the Altar, sixe Princes with sixe of his labours, in the midst Hercules bearing his two brazen pillars, six other princes with the other six labours. Hercules staies them," and comments on his labors, "slaughtered Lyons, Hydraes, Whales, Boares, Buls, grim Tyrants, Helhounds, Monsters, Furies." Perhaps these are the trophies. He also mentions the pillars, "Two brazen pillars . . . That haue eas'd Atlas and supported heauen." Directions read "set on," and then, "As they

march ouer the Stage, enter Lychas with the [poisoned] shirt."
Hercules puts on the shirt. "All the Princes kneel to the Altar,"
Hercules making appropriate but not especially descriptive speeches.
Then he begins to describe his torments, rushes out, returns, sees
Lychas, "swings [him] about his head and kils him." Going out again,
he is heard crying within. Then, "Enter Hercules from a rocke aboue,
tearing downe trees." Presently he "kils Omphale with a peece of a
rocke." Grandiloquent speeches accompany these actions but can scarcely replace them. The next direction reads, "All the Princes breake
downe the trees, and make a fire, in which Hercules placeth himselfe." "He burnes his Club and Lyons Skin." "Iupiter aboue strikes
him with a thunder-bolt, his body sinkes, and from the heauens
discends a hand in a cloud, that from the place where Hercules was
burnt, brings vp a starre and fixeth it in the firmament." This last
direction is not repeated in the text; something must actually have happened on the stage to represent it. Note also as proof of the actual performance, the purely practical detail, "his body sinks" and also the
technical term, "heavens." Perhaps the total effect of all this as carried
out would have seemed to us very naïve; the trees may have been
unconvincing artificialities, the fire no more than a little smoke, but
something there must have been to symbolize and suggest this action.
In these scenes properties, business, visual effects were depended on
certainly as much as the words to get over the author's idea.

Perhaps a fairer comparison of Elizabethan stage effects with our
own is to be found in the quieter domestic scenes of *A Woman Killed
with Kindness*. This play, first given in 1603 and published in 1607,
was revived at the Red Bull by the Queen's men as stated on the title-
page of the third edition. It begins with the off-stage sounds of music
and dancing at Frankford's wedding; the second scene brings in the
musicians and peasants dancing "here in the yard"; the third, opening
with the winding of horns, shows hunters watching their falcons and
commenting on their achievements off-stage. It ends in a quarrel, the
murder of two men, and the arrest of Sir Charles. All these scenes are
full of color and action, but show almost no phrases descriptive of the
surroundings. Act II begins with a direction for the actor of Frankford:
"Enter in a study," "a" suggesting mood, perhaps rather than a setting; the actor's attitude was as important then as now. Scene iii shows
Heywood's recognition of the fact that seeing something is more effective than being told about it. When Wendoll is thinking of how sinful
it would be to disturb Frankford's ideal home life, Heywood shows
us this happy domesticity in pantomime. At least no other reason is
apparent for the direction, "Enter over the stage Frankford, his Wife,

and Nicholas," while Wendoll comments:

> There goest thou, the most perfect'st man
> That ever England bred a gentleman.

In Act III, scene i, Sir Charles, reduced to penury, speaks of "this poor house," and Shafton, coming to get possession of it, describes it as "a pretty House," but neither phrase implies any special setting, nor can be said to create much of an effect. Scene ii illustrates how business and conversation show the place and time: servants of Frankford's bear in furnishings as if clearing a table and go to arrange other rooms while more lights are called for, and Master Frankford, according to a stage direction, enters "as it were brushing the crumbs from his clothes with a napkin as newly risen from supper." But nothing in the way of properties on the stage itself is implied until later in the scene when a table, tablecloth, lights and cards are fetched in.

In Act IV, costume sets the first scene: "Enter Sir Charles in prison," says the direction, "with irons, his feet bare, his garments all ragged and torn." Sir Charles talks of "this hellish dungeon," "this grave" but there is no other hint of a special stage setting. Scene ii begins a series of scenes in which scattered phrases, business, a careful use of the doors make the location clear, and oratory with few actually descriptive lines creates the emotional atmosphere. The time is set by the remark:

> 'Tis six o'clock already struck;
> Go bid them spread the cloth and serve in supper

and the direction follows: "Enter Butler and Jenkin with a tablecloth, bread, trenchers, and salt." In the next scene in the servant's quarters we are told this supper was in their master's chamber; and we hear the servants ordered to lock the gates. Next in a series of scenes, already discussed in detail in chapter VI, we see Frankford return to his home and make his way to his wife's chamber. The darkness is suggested by Frankford's carrying a dark lantern. There are phrases to indicate the imagined staging—thus, "this is the last door"—but the more powerful indication of location is, as usual, not by description but by business.

How the Elizabethans did depend on words appears in a very different way: after Frankford has entered his wife's bedroom and found Wendoll there, Heywood instead of having the quick physical struggle which a modern scenarist would delight in, has Frankford return to the front stage and deliver an impassioned monologue of fourteen lines:

> Stay, let me pause awhile!—
> O, God! O, God! That it were possible
> To undo things done; to call back yesterday;
> That Time could turn up his swift sandy glass,
> To untell the days, and to redeem these hours!
> Or that the sun
> Could, rising from the west, draw his coach backward;
> Take from th' account of time so many minutes,
> Till he had all these seasons called again,
> Those minutes, and those actions done in them,
> Even from her first offence; that I might take her
> As spotless as an angel in my arms!
> But, O! I talk of things impossible,
> And cast beyond the moon. God give me patience;
> For I will in, and wake them.

Only after this oratory has raised the emotional key of the scene does the action proceed: then "Enter Wendoll, running over the stage in a nightgown, [Frankford] after him with a sword drawn; the maid in her smock"; a little later "Mistress Frankford in her smock, night-gown and night-attire"; and toward the end of the scene the servants "as newly come out of bed." What took the place of settings, then, and created the atmosphere was costumes and business and impassioned verse, but verse concerned with description of the supposed setting scarcely at all.

The last act does not change this conclusion. Wendoll does say he is hiding in "these shadowy woods Afraid of every leaf or murm'ring blast," but this is too slight to count for much. More interesting is the evidence of Elizabethan love of sharp contrast: after the emotional scene in which Mistress Frankford has sent her lute away to be broken and has dismissed Wendoll, the carters, we are told, exeunt "whistling." The scene at Mistress Frankford's death-bed gets its effect from the situation itself rather than from settings or descriptive phrases. This play, in brief, has few more actually descriptive phrases than any similar modern play, *The Second Mrs. Tanqueray*, for example. And it has no descriptive passages of any length.

We must conclude, then, that the Elizabethan theater, in general, had a variety of means for creating dramatic illusion. The plays of that theater anticipated radio drama in the very considerable use to create atmosphere of music and of suggestive noises. But to compare it further with radio is misleading for it also continually emphasized what could be seen. Thus it was, taken as a whole, more spectacular than our usual legitimate theater today, in which many plays, conceived of as happening within the narrow confines of a room or two, are cut off from such appeals. In many ways the Elizabethan stage more resembled the cinema than the radio, notably in this appeal to sight with at the same time the use of very short and very numerous scenes uninterrupted by intermissions or breaks in interest. This allowed, as in the movies, everything to be acted; little had to be related; it also allowed striking contrasts, and smashing climaxes built up not in one dramatic section but a series of them. But in two ways the Elizabethan stage differed profoundly from moving pictures: First, there was direct and immediate response between audience and actor. Personality, limited in radio to the voice and in cinema to talking shadows on a screen, was on the Elizabethan stage unhindered even by an invisible fourth wall. There were no curtain, no proscenium arch, no footlights, scarcely any distance. Second, it used speech intimately, personally, sometimes beautifully, with effects a loud speaker can scarcely achieve. Depending upon this means, the dramatists dared almost anything, sometimes even trying to get over in speech what their stage actually contradicted. They did this not often by direct extended description, but rather by repeated hints and suggestions. When they did resort to formal descriptions we may be almost sure that what they described was not there at all or was only sketchily represented. This naturally enough provoked the scorn of such commonsense persons as Jonson, troubled (as in the choruses to *Henry V*) a poetically minded artist like Shakespeare, but did not apparently disturb the Red Bull dramatists or the audiences they wrote for.

CHAPTER IX

CONCLUSION

THIS study is so clogged with conflicting details and alternative possibilities that a brief summary of the conclusions which seem fairly sure may be desirable, together with some comments on their bearing on the actual work of the dramatists and our appreciation of their technical skill. The order here does not attempt to follow the order of the foregoing presentation.

One fundamental conclusion concerns the evidence itself. Stage directions as well as textual allusions are shown sometimes to be dramatically instead of literally and accurately expressed. Their nomenclature is various, inexact, even imaginative. They must be handled, therefore, with unusual caution. Failure to recognize especially their dramatic quality renders doubtful a good many plausible theories about the Elizabethan stage.

The fact, moreover, that the Elizabethans could be persuaded to accept what they were told in the text even in defiance of what they saw on the stage allowed a wide latitude in carrying out the specifications of the directions. Though settings and properties actually necessary to the action could scarcely be omitted, substitutes could be used for many of them. If a tree was climbed something obviously had to be provided, but it did not necessarily look like a tree.

This easy adaptability of the directions explains in part at least the lack of definiteness in some of our conclusions. The same version, so far as stage directions go, may have been presented in several different ways. In the London theater there may have been real properties which on the road were only imagined; at court "great houses made of canvas," to quote a Revels office item, may have replaced the simple stage doors of the theater. As the years passed the same stage directions may have been carried out more realistically and fully.

On the other hand, no such changes may have taken place; I find no proof or even hint of such a development, nor of any desire for it. Thus our classification of the plays into the A, B, and C lists finally comes to less than one would expect. No significant differences appear between plays given surely and only at the Red Bull and those given elsewhere, nor between plays of early and of late date. Nor can the Red Bull be shown to have differed in any very important particular of structure or staging from the other public theaters. This may, of course, accurately represent the fact, or may only be due to the generalized nature of the evidence itself.

Even such fluid evidence, however, allows a few dependable conclusions though some are only negative. Examination of all the plays given in a definite period at a single theater shows—not what one might expect, a series of customary stagings for similar scenes, but rather the opposite—that similar scenes were often staged differently. After all, why not? We like variety ourselves. "Studies" were, it appears, usually discovered, but prison and temple scenes and various interiors, banqueting scenes for instance, permit no sure generalization as to their staging. Unsatisfactory as such a conclusion is for guidance, it at least guards one against dogmatism.

An affirmative conclusion of considerable importance is that the Red Bull plays, in spite of their use of spectacle, could be given on a stage structurally like that of the Swan, with the single important addition of a third stage door. Clear evidence, even if on some points from only a single play, shows that the Red Bull had a front stage, a railing to protect it, three doors to the stage, an upper stage, a "heavens" or shadow over the stage, and an ascending-descending device, operated, we may guess, from the huts. There were windows below—the *Swetnam* picture shows two—and at least two trapdoors, perhaps more, with some means as well of getting up on the stage at the corners. Some posts and pillars must have been structural and permanent, but some were certainly brought in. There was a curtain for the balcony and also some space below which could be concealed by a curtain. Various plays need two such spaces. Perhaps one structurally permanent rear stage was made use of along with a removable structure like a tent, a shop, an arbor, or the like. Or perhaps the "rear stage" was not a real and permanent structural part of the stage but itself only a removable structure, more non-committal in its outward appearance than shop or tent, but just as easily brought in and removed. Which it was, does not greatly matter in the theories of staging suggested in this study, but does matter considerably to students intent on finding realism and modern congruity in the old performances. The evidence available does not allow a positive answer as to whether there was a structural curtained space or not; in view of the common assumption that such a rear stage existed even this doubt is one important result of this study. There may have been other details of the stage—obliquely placed doors, balconies above them, a third story opening in the tiring-house, etc., etc.—but for all of them positive evidence is lacking in the Red Bull plays.

The Red Bull had a considerable number of larger settings and properties: formal seats, trees, a tent, at least two shops, a tomb, a bank, an altar, a scaffold, barriers, lists, a bar for trial scenes; perhaps there was also a well, a hell-mouth, a large rock, a cave. But we cannot always be sure when these were used, and when they were only talked about or substitutes took their places. The conclusions stated in chapter IV as to their usual positions on the stage need not be repeated. Even if the curtained space was provided for by a removable structure, these conclusions require only slight reinterpretation. Even more surely than with a permanent rear stage the trees and throne would be placed outside such a structure; a removable structure would also account for the use without special directions of some of the other properties on the uncurtained stage. The list of smaller or once used properties at the end of chapter IV need only be called attention to here, as showing that the Elizabethan theater depended to a considerable degree upon visual effects, and not merely on words.

Words on the Elizabethan stage counted a great deal, but were not as unsupported by other appeals as has been often supposed. Music, off- and on-stage noises, the spectacle of fireworks, special costumes, processions, dumb shows, dances, and business were all made use of to an important degree.

The principles of staging were, phrasing them not too exactly, those of the medieval stage. Whether we describe this as incongruity, as a simultaneous or multiple or continuous setting, or as the stage thought of only as the stage and not as some imagined location, it quite clearly appears in the Red Bull plays in the "journeying" scenes, the change of scene by exit and immediate re-entrance at another door, and the presence on the stage of incongruous properties. One of the clearest conclusions of this study is that these were features of Red Bull performances. Although many realistic *details* were emphasized in the presentation, the basic principles were scarcely realism at all, but ease and speed and clarity.

The successful theatrical technique of an Elizabethan playwright did not much appear, therefore, in such points as most concern modern dramatists. He could use direct exposition; asides and soliloquies were suited to his theater. He did not need to tell his story in a small number of scenes placed in half a dozen or fewer plausible backgrounds. He could use as many scenes as he pleased and locate them imaginatively anywhere he liked. What he did have to look out for was to make his story perfectly clear to a not too intelligent or attentive audience, to keep this audience always looking forward to the next scene, to provide vivid contrasts, and by keen expectation unbroken by frequent pauses in the action to build up effective climaxes. This did not mean on his stage the use of long scenes necessarily; it might be managed by a succession of short ones.

The assistance rendered to the dramatist by his stage and the difficulties it created are, I think, imperfectly understood. They can scarcely be detected by only thinking about them. Performances of well-known plays in an attempt at the Elizabethan manner hardly exhibit them either. What is necessary is experimental productions of plays quite unknown to the audience. Of course this audience should ideally be made up as the crowd was at the Red Bull and the Globe—of the apprentices, the honest citizens, the showy young men, the gentlemen with a taste for verse—and all these in the right proportion. And of course we should have Elizabethan actors. That such an experiment is impossible makes its significance no less important. We can never achieve a real restoration of an Elizabethan performance without restoring its most important features—the audience and the actors. Admitting both the necessity and the impossibility of re-creating these features, still we may learn a good deal by trying out little-known plays in the nearest we can come to the Elizabethan manner.

If we did try such productions, we should, I think, find that the most important assistance offered to the Elizabethan dramatist by his stage was the immediate contact of the actors with the audience and the opportunity for the steady onward flow of the play without interruption by a falling curtain and the resulting even momentary pauses.[1] But the often emphasized advantage of the three-fold stage had very little to do with securing this swift movement of the play. The balcony was never used to fill in pauses in the action on the front stage, and though the curtained space could be reset while the front stage was in use, the frequent bringing in of properties on the front stage shows that resort to the rear stage was not a necessary procedure. What really did speed up the action were the various conventional ways of showing

---

[1] These characteristics of Elizabethan performances have been so admirably presented by Granville-Barker in his "The Stagecraft of Shakespeare," *Fortnightly Review*, CXXVI (1926), 1-17, in his various *Prefaces* to Shakespeare and in U.M. Ellis-Fermor's chapter XIV, *The Jacobean Drama* (1936), that they need only be mentioned here. A demurrer must be entered against Miss Bradbrook's comment in *Elizabethan Stage Conditions* (1932), p. 33: "When an important group of characters or when all the characters leave the stage there is a sense of pause, and the prompter drew a line across his copy, while the groundlings probably shifted from one foot to the other." There may have been sometimes a slight relief from tension with a change of characters, though this was often certainly not the case (note, for instance, *Hamlet*, I. iv. v), but a sense of pause, such as is caused by a falling curtain, was precisely what the Elizabethan stage could and did escape.

and changing the imagined location—the "journeying" scenes, exit and immediate re-entrance, skilful hints in dialogue, costume, and business. A dramatist's success with these is some measure of his technical skill. The real assistance offered by the balcony is that it provided a second level for the action, an advantage made admirable use of by many playwrights. The curtained space allowed effective discoveries; it could also have been used for final tableaux, but almost never was so used except in the concealment of "dead" bodies. That it was not more used for "curtains" is perhaps due to the fact that the action tended to flow out on the open stage, and to have forced it back again into the curtained space would have been awkward indeed.

Instead of effective discoveries and tableaux an Elizabethan playwright tried rather for effective exits. Even "dead" bodies could with care be got off with some dramatic gain, and processions and business often furnished significant climaxes.[2]

Another matter concerning exits and entrances was the necessity of providing in most instances for a few lines at least between a character's going out and his coming in again when the location was supposed to have changed to a considerable distance away.[3] These lines represented a lapse of time to cover the time of the journey, so that this convention did not at all conflict with the other of immediate re-entrance to show a change to a nearby locality.

The chief difficulty arising from the stage was that it gave scarcely any assistance in the creation of atmosphere. It provided little of realistic background and less of emotional stimulation. Especially it could offer almost no effective lighting. Of course it could suggest darkness by bringing in a lighted torch or candle, but these are after all only informative and not imaginatively stimulating. It was in the creation of atmosphere by speech, by business, by music, by noises off stage and on that the Elizabethan dramatist solved one of his greatest problems, and offered especial evidence of his skill.

Finally, there was the necessity for clearness. His complicated stories and his swiftly changing locations increased the difficulty. If the suggestions of chapter VI are warranted, one of the principal points an Elizabethan playwright attended to was the significance of

---

[2] Allan Gilbert in "Scenes of Discovery in *Othello*," *PQ*, V (1926), 119-130, uses this pretext to explain Shakespeare's technic at the end of *Othello*. His following statement, however, seems scarcely proved: "The practice of the theater made necessary that at the conclusion of the play all the important characters should crowd the stage or in some way be represented."

[3] See Thomas M. Raysor's interesting discussion of such passages in *SP*, XXXII (1935), 197-209, and *JEGP*, XXXVII (1938), 21-47.

his doors. Keeping that significance clear to his audience was only part of the larger problem, not especially concerned with the stage, of always making sure that the audience had in its mind at each succeeding point in the play just the information it needed to understand the story. This problem the Elizabethan playwright, confronted by his restless and self-assertive auditory, *had* to solve, whatever else he did. His audience was scarcely prepared for a skilful use of "dramatic reminders," that is, those objects made in the progress of a play so significant that in later scenes without explanation they remind the audience of what it needs to know.[4] But the problem was solved by the best dramatists with effectiveness and economy.

In all this, realism counted for very little. Elizabethan realistic effects, such as the use of blood, fireworks, etc., stand out conspicuously as we imagine them in performance, but must not mislead us into exaggerating their significance. On the Elizabethan stage realism was rather a means of superficial appeal than a fundamental factor in dramatic structure.

What is the modern attitude to this procedure? Two opposed opinions are expressed. The first is represented by Lascelles Abercrombie:

In many ways the Elizabethan theater seems to have been the finest instrument which dramatic art has ever devised for itself, and Shakespeare's technique is so exactly adapted to this instrument and shows such complete mastery of it, that one is tempted to call it waste of time to produce him on any stage that does not pretty closely correspond with the stage he wrote for.— "A Plea for the Liberty of Interpreting" in *Aspects of Shakespeare* (1933), pp. 250-251.

The opposite view is expressed by Mr. T. S. Eliot in *Elizabethan Essays* (1934), pp. 12, 17:

The weakness of the Elizabethan drama is not its defect of realism but its attempt at realism; not its conventions but its lack of conventions. . . . The aim of the Elizabethans was to attain complete realism without surrendering any of the advantages which as artists they observed in unrealistic conventions.

Neither critic is, I think, sound in his opinion. One may agree in general with Abercrombie's as it concerns Shakespeare and the presentation of his plays, without subscribing to the idea that the Elizabethan stage is the finest instrument ever devised for dramatic art. That, especially in view of the Elizabethan theater's lack of effective

---

[4] See my "Dramatic Reminders," *Shakespeare Association Bulletin*, IX (1934), 145-149.

lighting, is surely extravagant. And Eliot is not very fortunate in the terms of his criticism. The Elizabethans did not aim at complete realism; they tried for it only at certain definite points. They had many conventions, certainly more agreed upon departures from reality than our theaters today. Their difficulty was that having accepted a certain distance from reality they did not stick to it. Whenever a sensational effect could be secured by realistic business, or a plot required a situation no matter how unsuited to the theatrical conditions, the playwrights, at least most of those at the Red Bull, let no considerations of artistic consistency or of taste deter them from attempting it.

INDEX

I. Plays Referred to

The *Ages* by Heywood: 37, 88
Alahan: 27
Albere Galles: 18
Albumazar: 8
All's Lost by Lust: 22, 67, 69, 96, 113
Andriae: 31
Antonio and Mellida: 62
Antonio and Vallia: 24
Antonio's Revenge: 62
Antony and Cleopatra: 167
Appius and Virginia: 18, 56, 61, 77, 135
Arden of Feversham: 79, 115-121, 128
As You Like It: 35, 137, 166
Bartholomew Fair: 80
The Battle of Alcazar: 40
The Bellman of Paris: 13, 25
The Birth of Merlin: 19, 59, 75, 89, 92, 99, 101, 103, 105, 106
The Brazen Age: 20, 36, 59, 60, 67, 70, 71, 73, 75, 76, 77, 81, 85, 86, 90, 92, 96, 99, 101, 102, 103, 104, 105, 106, 107, 108, 114, 118, 129, 148, 150-51, 159, 162, 167, 169, 170, 172, 173, 177, 182-183
Cambises: 40, 64
The Captives: 23, 24, 28
The City Night-Cap: 28
The Comedy of Errors: 35
Coriolanus: 18
The Coronation: 62
The Costly Whore: 24, 54
The Cra-Marchant: 25
Cromwell: 28
A Cure for a Cuckold: 28
Cymbeline: 46, 62, 107
Dead Man's Fortune: 95
The Death of Robert, Earl of Hunting-ton: 62
The Devil's Charter: 63, 77
The Devil's Law Case: 21, 36, 37, 61, 67, 69, 81, 83, 85, 86, 96, 100, 102, 103, 114, 135, 150, 154, 160, 168, 169, 174, 177
Dick of Devonshire: 28
Doctor Faustus: 41, 53, 98, 156
The Downfall of Robert, Earl of Hunt-ington: 63
The Dumb Knight: 28, 62

The Duche Painter and the French Branke: 13, 29
Edmond Ironside: 23, 28-29
Edward II: 4, 21, 36, 37, 58, 67, 69, 85, 86, 90, 91, 114, 160, 174, 177
The Empress of Morocco: 98
The English Traveller: 28, 41, 104
The Escape of Jupiter: 151
Every Man in His Humor: 38, 53, 165, 171
The Fair Foul One: 26
The Fair Maid of the Exchange: 16, 78, 80, 135, 155
The Fair Maid of the West: 28, 39
A Fair Quarrel: 21
The Fairy Knight: 27
The Fatal Contract: 28
A Fault in Friendship: 26
Fortune by Land and Sea: 18, 19, 36, 72, 86, 96, 97, 100, 103, 105, 147, 154, 158, 167, 171, 173, 175, 176, 179-181
The Four Prentices of London: 20, 36, 42, 72, 76, 77, 84, 85, 86, 90, 92, 96, 102, 103, 105, 106, 109, 112, 128, 152, 160, 165, 167, 174, 175
The Four Sons of Aymon: 26
Frair Bacon and Friar Bungay: 42, 71, 98, 134, 157
George-a-Greene: 48
Godfrey of Bulloigne: 20
The Golden Age: 9, 10, 11, 20, 36, 57, 59, 62, 65, 66, 69, 73, 75, 76, 85, 86, 87, 90, 91, 106, 107, 114, 115-118, 134, 136, 151, 159, 168, 169, 170, 173
Gramarcie Wit: 22-23
Greene's Tu Quoque: 7, 19, 36, 47, 68, 79, 86, 89, 91, 93, 100, 101, 103, 106, 118, 156, 159, 173
Hamlet: 35, 73, 112, 190
The Hector of Germany: 20, 35, 36, 45, 60, 62, 67, 69, 72, 73, 75, 76, 77, 81, 86, 88, 99, 102, 103, 114, 159-160, 167, 169, 174
The Heir: 22, 36, 61, 72, 83, 98, 100, 103, 105, 106, 160, 163
Henry V: 62, 186

I Henry VI: 97
Herod and Antipater: 23, 36, 54, 60, 82,
  83, 85, 86, 103, 109, 153, 155, 160,
  168, 175, 176, 178
The Honest Lawyer: 20, 36, 59, 60, 61,
  70, 71, 72, 83, 152, 160, 172, 174
I Honest Whore: 28, 149
How a Man May Choose a Good Wife
  from a Bad: 17, 36, 82, 84, 89, 91,
  92, 98, 148, 158
How to Learn of a Woman to Woo: 17
Huon of Bordeau: 27
If It Be Not Good the Devil Is in It:
  11, 20, 35, 36, 37, 54, 59, 61, 65, 66,
  70, 71, 72, 76, 84, 86, 89, 91, 92, 96,
  100, 101, 103, 105, 106, 135, 159,
  161, 164, 168, 169, 170
I If You Know Not Me You Know Nobody: 4, 17-18, 33-34, 36, 54, 59, 66,
  69, 75, 76, 85, 86, 100, 103, 123, 129,
  148, 158, 168, 170, 171, 173, 175,
  176
II If You Know Not Me You Know Nobody: 17-18, 36, 42, 54, 59, 60, 61,
  72, 78, 80, 86, 114, 148, 152, 154,
  158, 167, 169, 170, 171, 173
The Inner Temple Masque: 28
I Iron Age: 5, 10, 11, 20, 36, 37, 56,
  70, 71, 75, 77, 100, 102, 103, 129,
  148, 151, 159, 161, 170, 172, 174,
  176, 178
II Iron Age: 5, 10, 11, 36, 65, 67, 69,
  77, 81, 86, 95, 102, 103, 113-114,
  129, 135, 155, 159, 161, 162, 166,
  170, 172, 174, 177, 178
The Jew of Malta: 28
Jugurth: 26
Julius Caesar: 56, 95, 112
Keep the Widow Waking: 27
King John: 62
King John and Matilda: 28, 62
King Lear: 38, 166, 167
The Knight of the Burning Pestle: 6,
  18, 28, 39
Lady Jane: 15
Look about You: 62
Love's Labor's Lost: 35
Love's Mistress: 28, 75
Lust's Dominion: 28
Macbeth: 5, 42, 46, 62, 112, 167
The Madcap: 26
A Maidenhead Well Lost: 28
The Maid's Tragedy: 40
The Man in the Moon Drinks Claret: 29
Marshall Osric: 21
A Match at Midnight: 25, 68, 93, 135

Match Me in London: 19, 36, 72, 79,
  80, 88, 92-93, 109, 112, 114, 135,
  136, 148, 159, 168, 170, 173
The Merchant of Venice: 166
Messallina: 28 (See the Subject Index
  for references to the picture on the
  title-page.)
A Midsummer Night's Dream: 39
Nero: 26, 71, 72, 103
A New Wonder, a Woman Never Vexed:
  19, 98, 101, 103
Nobody and Somebody: 18, 60, 109
The Parliament of Love: 23, 24
The Parricide: 27
The Peaceable King: 25
Philenzo and Hypollyta: 24
Phormio: 31
The Plantation of Virginia: 25
The Prophetess: 63
The Rape of Lucrece: 6, 36, 43, 56, 57,
  60, 61, 65, 66, 69, 78, 80, 86, 87,
  92, 94, 100, 103-104, 128, 138, 141-
  147, 148, 152, 154, 158, 162, 167,
  168, 169, 170, 173, 176, 177
The Rebellion of Naples: 40
Revenge for Honor: 27, 68, 77
Richard II: 23 (see also Thomas of
  Woodstock)
Richard III: 21, 54, 77, 78, 103, 106,
  155
The Roaring Girl: 80
Romeo and Juliet: 95, 106, 118, 166
Roxana: (see Subject Index for references
  to the picture on the title-page.)
The Royal King and the Loyal Subject:
  10, 20, 36, 54, 60, 61, 62, 82, 86, 87,
  114, 153, 160, 169, 174, 177
The Second Mrs. Tanqueray: 185
The Scholars: 53
Sejanus: 35
The Seven Champions of Christendom:
  11, 28, 39
The Seven Deadly Sins: 78, 94
A Shoemaker a Gentleman: 19, 36, 77,
  79, 85, 86, 89, 91, 92, 101, 103, 104,
  106, 107, 150, 159, 169, 173
The Silver Age: 10, 11, 20, 36, 61, 67,
  69, 72, 84, 85, 86, 90, 91, 92, 99,
  101, 103, 105, 106, 107, 109, 122-125,
  136, 151, 155, 159, 168, 169, 170,
  171, 173
The Spanish Tragedy: 73, 74, 76, 104,
  132
Stuckley: 28
Swetnam the Woman Hater: 21, 36, 45,
  60, 61, 70, 71, 83, 85, 93, 106, 108,

153, 160, 168, 174. (For the title-page picture see Subject Index.)
Il Tamburlaine: 47
The Tempest: 34, 97, 107, 175, 181-182
Thomas of Woodstock: 23, 28
The Thracian Wonder: 28
Titus Andronicus: 95
The Torchbearers: 39
The Travails of Three English Brothers: 6, 18, 36, 59, 61, 75, 83, 84, 85, 86, 88, 158, 170, 173, 176, 178
Twelfth Night: 35, 112, 131
Two Lamentable Tragedies: 80
The Two Merry Milkmaids: 12, 22, 36, 61, 67, 69, 83, 85, 160, 171, 174, 175
The Two Noble Ladies: 11, 23-24, 28, 37, 42-43, 72, 84, 86, 91, 92, 153, 160, 167, 168, 169, 170, 172, 175, 178
The Valiant Welshman: 64
The Virgin Martyr: 14, 22, 36, 60, 67, 69, 81, 82, 83, 84, 85, 86, 91, 92, 102-103, 104, 161, 172, 174, 175, 177, 178
A Vow and a Good One: 29
The Vow Breaker: 65

A Warning for Fair Women: 71
The Welsh Ambassador: 23-24, 36, 37, 60, 103, 104, 160, 161
The White Devil: 7, 14, 19, 37, 41, 55, 61, 65, 69, 81, 82, 86, 93, 98, 99, 101, 103, 114, 135, 139-141, 146, 154, 159, 160, 161, 168, 169, 173, 175
The Widow's Prize: 20
The Winter's Tale: 46
The Wise Woman of Hogsdon: 17, 78, 80, 86, 109
The Witch of Edmonton: 28
A Woman Killed with Kindness: 17, 36, 42, 66, 69, 72, 84, 86, 87, 112, 113, 125, 128, 134-135, 158, 166, 173, 183-185
The Wonder of a Kingdom: 25-26, 36, 68, 69, 95, 98, 103, 106, 114, 155, 160, 162, 167, 177, 178
The World Tost at Tennis: 22, 54, 96, 102, 104, 106, 107, 109
Sir Thomas Wyatt: 15, 36, 55, 56, 60, 61, 82, 85, 87, 89, 91, 98, 100, 103, 109, 112, 135, 148, 158, 169, 173, 177, 178
The Younger Brother: 11, 21

II. BIBLIOGRAPHY; OTHER SOURCES AND REFERENCES

(For material appearing before 1923 see Chambers, *The Elizabethan Stage.* It is not listed here unless specifically mentioned in the text. For the contemporary pictures of the stage see the Subject Index.)

Abercrombie, Lascelles: "A Plea for the Liberty of Interpreting," *Aspects of Shakespeare* (1933), 192

Adams, John C.: "Shakespeare's Stage" (*Theater Art's Monthly,* XX [1936], 812-818), 95, and, *ibid.,* "Romeo and Juliet" (896-904), 95; *LTLS* (Feb. 15, May 23, 1936), 95; "The Staging of *The Tempest*" (*RES,* XIV [1938], 404-419), 97, 107

Adams, Joseph Quincy: *Shakespearean Playhouses* (1917), 6, 7, 11, 12, 13, 33, 97; "The Four Pictorial Representations of the Elizabethan Stage" (*JEGP,* X [1911], 329-333), 9, 31, 37; *The Dramatic Records of Sir Henry Herbert* (1917), 19-29; *The Life of William Shakespeare* (1923), 32; "Elizabethan Playhouse Manuscripts" (*The Johns Hopkins Alumni Magazine,* XXI [1932], 21-52), 33; *Macbeth* (1931), 47

Albright, Victor: *The Shakesperean Stage* (1909), 30, 31, 32, 68, 99

Alleyn, Edward: *Diary,* 11, 21

Archer, William: "Elizabethan Stage and Restoration Drama" (*Quarterly Review,* CCXLI [1924], 399-418), 40, 110, 138

Baldwin, T. W.: "Posting Henslowe's Accounts" (*JEGP,* XXVI [1927], 42-90), 9

Baskervill, C. R.: *The Elizabethan Jig* (1929), 8

Bentley, Gerald: 12, 23

Biesterfeldt, P. W.: "Die Oberbühne bei Marlowe" (*Archiv,* CLX [1931], 51-59), 106

Boas, F. S.: *Shakespeare & the Universities* (1923), 23

Bowers, F. T.: "Date of *Revenge for Honour*" (*MLN,* LII [1937], 192-196), 27

Bradbrook, M. C.: *Elizabethan Stage Conditions* (1932), 73, 95, 190; *Themes and Conventions of Eliza-*

bethan Tragedy (1935), 174
Brodmeier, Cecil: 97
Bullen, A. H.: 24
The Cambridge History of English Literature: (1910), 164
Campbell, L. B.: *Scenes and Machines on the English Stage* (1923), 69, 71, 111
Carew, Thomas: 171
Chamber, E. K.: *The Elizabethan Stage* (1923), 1, 4, 6, 7, 8, 10, 15, 16, 17, 18, 19, 20, 21, 22, 25, 28, 30, 31, 32, 39, 40, 47, 49, 54, 57, 71, 80, 91, 92, 99, 111, 118, 132, 138-139, 146, 153; *William Shakespeare* (1930), 14, 26, 33, 34, 37, 38
Cheney, Sheldon: *Stage Decoration* (1928), 63
Clark, Arthur M.: *Thomas Heywood* (1931), 20
Copeau, Jacques: 137
Dekker, Thomas: *Raven's Almanack* (1608), 7; *Work for Armourers* (1609), 7; *The Guls Horn Booke* (1609), 32, 64
Doran, Madelaine: introduction to *II If You Know Not Me You Know Nobody* (1935), 34
Eliot, T. S.: *Elizabethan Essays* (1934), 192
Ellis-Fermor, U. M.: *The Jacobean Drama* (1936), 190
Elson, J. J.: *The Wits* (1932), 30
The English Wagner Book: (1594) 54, 132
Fleay, F. G.: *A Biographical Chronicle of the English Drama* (1891), 10, 17, 27; *A Chronicle History of the London Stage* (1890), 24
Forman, Simon: 46-47, 73
Gayton, Edmund: *Festivous Notes upon Don Quixote* (1654), 10, 14
Gaw, Allison: "The Use of the Turret in the First Part of Henry VI" (*Shakespeare Jahrbuch* (LXIV [1928], 182-184), 97
Gilbert, Allen: "Scenes of Discovery in *Othello*" (*PQ*, V [1926], 119-130), 191
Giordano-Orsini, G. N.: (*LTLS*, Dec. 4, 1930, 1037), 34
Granville-Barker, H.: *Preface to Hamlet* (1937), 35, 50; other *Prefaces*, 190; "A Note on chapters XX and XXI of *The Elizabethan Stage*" (*RES*, I [1925] 60-71), 49, 138; Review of

W. J. Lawrence's *The Physical Conditions of the Elizabethan Public Playhouse*, (*RES*, IV [1928], 229-237), 40; "The Stagecraft of Shakespeare" (*Fortnightly Review*, CXXVI [1926], 1-17), 190
Greg, W. W.: *Henslowe's Diary* (1904-1908), 18; *Henslowe Papers* (1907), 41; *Elizabethan Dramatic Documents* (1931), 23, 33, 37, 40, 94, 111-112; (*RES*, VIII [1932], 457-458), 23
Harbage, Alfred: *LTLS* (June 20, 1936), 26
Hart, Alfred: "The Number of Lines in Shakespeare's Plays" (*RES*, VIII [1932], 19-28; "The Length of Elizabethan and Jacobean Plays" (*ibid.*, 139-154); "The Time Allotted for Representation of Elizabethan and Jacobean Plays (*ibid.*, 395-413); Acting Versions of Elizabethan Plays" (*RES*, X [1934], 1-28)
Henslowe, Phillip: 9, 172; *Diary* (ed. Greg, 1904-1907), 15, 17, 18, 26, 53; *Papers* (ed. Greg, 1907), 41, 65, 70, 75, 76, 80, 84, 132, 165, 175
Herbert, Sir Henry: *The Dramatic Records of* (ed. Adams, *Cornell Studies in English*, 1917), 23, 24, 25, 26, 27, 28
Herrman, Max: *Forschungen zur deutschen theater-geschichte* (1914), 31
Heywood, Thomas: *An Apology for Actors* (1612), 26
Hille, Gertrude: "Londoner Theaterbauten zur Zeit Shakespeares" (Shakespeare *Jahrbuch*, LXVI [1930], 25-78), 31
Hillebrand, Harold N.: "William Percy, An Elizabethan Amateur" (*Huntington Library Quarterly*, I, iv [July, 1934], 391-416), 111
Historia Histrionica (1699): 15, 88
Hotson, Leslie: *The Commonwealth-Restoration Stage* (1928), 6, 8, 14
Hunt, M. L.: *Thomas Dekker, a Study* (1911), 19
Illustrated London News (April 15, Sept. 9, 1911), 32; (Oct. 8, 1932), 55
Isaacs, J.: *Production and Stage-Management at the Blackfriars Theatre* (The Shakespeare Association [1933]), 168
Kirschbaum, Leo: "A Census of Bad Quartos" (*RES*, XIV [1938], 20-43), 15

Klein, David: "The Case of Forman's Booke of Plaies" (*PQ*, XI [1932], 385-395), 47

Knight, G. Wilson: *The Principles of Shakespearean Production* (1936), 168

Lawrence, W. J.: Review of W. W. Greg's *Elizabethan Dramatic Documents* (*RES*, VIII [1932], 219-228), 9, 12, 23; "New Light on the Elizabethan Theater" (*Fortnightly Review*, CV [1916], 820-829), 13; *The Physical Conditions of the Elizabethan Public Playhouse* (1927), 14, 104, 110, 117, 163; *Speeding up Shakespeare* (1937), 15, 50, 85; *The Elizabethan Playhouse*, I (1912), 30, 111; II (1913), 99, 172; *Those Nut-Cracking Elizabethans* (1935), 32, 69, 168; *Pre-Restoration Stage Studies* (1927), 33, 34, 40, 53, 62, 68, 69, 87, 92, 149, 160-161; *Texas Review* (Jan., 1918), 64; 138

Lucas, F.: *The Complete Works of John Webster* (1927), 18, 20, 139-140, 160

Maas, H.: *Der Englischen Theater-Truppen* (1907), 6, 26

MacCracken, Pierce, and Durham; *An Introduction to Shakespeare* (1919), 165

Malone Society: introductions to *The Welsh Ambassador*, *The Two Noble Ladies*, *Richard II* (*Thomas of Woodstock*), *Edmund Ironside*, 23-24, 28, 34; to *II If You Know Not Me*, 34

Melton, John: *Astrologaster* (1620), 172

Middleton, Thomas: *Black Book* (1604), 88

Moseley, H.: 35

Murray, J. T.: *English Dramatic Companies* (1910), 6, 13, 22

Nicoll, Allardyce: *The Development of the Theatre* (1927), 98, 136

Parrott, T.: *Chapman* (1910-1914), 27

Poel, William: 115

Porter, Charlotte: 32, 133

Prynne, William: *Histriomastix* (1633), 13

Raysor, Thomas M.: "Aesthetic Significance of Shakespeare's Handling of Time" (*SP*, XXXII [1935], 197-209) and "Intervals of Time and Their Effect on Dramatic Values in Shakespeare's Tragedies" (*JEGP*, XXXVII [1938], 21-47), 191

Reynolds, George F.: "Some Principles of Elizabethan Staging" (*MP*, I [1905], 581-614, II, 69-97), 32; "'Trees' on the Stage of Shakespeare" (*MP*, V [1907], 153-168), 46; "Two Conventions of the Elizabethan Stage" (*MP*, XVII [1919], 35-43), 113, 114; "William Percy and his Plays" (*MP*, XII [1914], 109-128), 116, 156; "Another Principle of Elizabethan Staging" (*Manly Anniversary Studies* [1923], 70-77), 149, 156; "Dramatic Reminders" (*Shakespeare Association Bulletin*, IX [1934], 145-149), 192; 40

Revels accounts: *Documents Relating to the Office of the Revels in the Time of Elizabeth* (ed. Feuillerat, 1908), 10, 70, 73, 75, 76, 84, 137, 187

R. M.: *Micrologia* (1629), 98

Savits, Jocza: *Shakespeare und die Bühne des Dramas* (1927), 163

Schelling, Felix: *Elizabethan Drama* (1908), 17, 18, 21, 22, 23, 25

Shaver, C. L.: "Date of *Revenge for Honour* (*MLN*, LIII [1938], 96-98), 27

Sibley, Gertrude M.: *Lost Plays and Masques, 1500-1642* (1933), 26, 51

Simonson, Lee: *The Stage Is Set* (1932), 39, 171

Sisson, C. J.: *Lost Plays of Shakespeare's Age* (1936), 27; *Le Goût Public et le Théâtre Elisabéthain* (1923), 72

Skemp, A.: *Messallina* (1910), 30

Sprague, A. C.: *Shakespeare and the Audience* (1935), 113

Stevens, T. W.: 32, 40, 50

Stork, Charles W.: *William Rowley* (1910), 18, 19, 21, 22, 25

Summers, Montague: *The Restoration Theatre* (1934), 40

Tannenbaum, Samuel: *Shakespeare Forgeries* (1918), 17, 18, 20; *Shakespearean Scraps* (1933), 47

Thorndike, Ashley: 68

Vox Gracvli or Jack Dawes' Entertainment: (1622) 12

Wallace, C. W.: "Three London Theatres" (*University of Nebraska Studies*, IX [1909], 287-342), 6, 9

Wiggin, P. G.: *An Inquiry into the Authorship of the Middleton-Rowley Plays* (1897), 25

Wilson, J. D.: *Life in Shakespeare's England* (ca. 1913), 55

Wither, George: *Abuses Stript and Whipt* (1615), 9

Wright, Louis: *Middle-Class Culture in Elizabethan England* (1935), 8;

"Elizabethan Sea Drama and Its Staging" (*Anglia*, LI [1927], 104-108), 179

III. Subjects

(The list of modern reproductions of the Elizabethan stage, p. 32, the list of plays, pp. 15-29, and the list of small properties, pp. 85-87, are, except for a few items, omitted from this index.)

A, B, C lists in this book: 5, 187

Act divisions: 50, 169

Altar: 80-81

Alternation theory: see Staging, systems of

Arbor: 57, 73, 74

Arras: see Curtain

Artillery: 170-171

Bank: 73, 76

Balcony, second story level: in the contemporary pictures, 31, 94; how designated, 47, 94-99; trapdoor in (?), 99; obliquely placed windows (?), 99; height, 99-100; uses, 100, 103 (see also 28, 29, 50, 76, 111); curtain in, 104; maskings for (?), 104; how reached, 105, 116, 159; furniture, 106; how far consistent, 128-130 (see also 93); not concealed by a front curtain, 154; advantage of, 191; third floor level: 93, 94, 97-98, 107

Bar: 45, 46, 81, 82-83

Barriers: 81

Bed: 65-70

Beeston, Christopher: 8, 12

Bells: 168

Blackfriars theater: 2, 3, 14, 15, 97, 179

Blood: 40-41, 85

Boar's Head inn: 17

Business, pantomime, etc.: 29, 176-178, 181, 183, 189

Canopy for throne: 55, 56, 65

Cave: 47, 64, 75, 76, 99, 132

Clash: 57, 133, 149, 150

Cockpit theater: see Phoenix

Conclusion of a play, appearance of all characters (?), 191

Continuous staging: see Staging, systems of

Conventions: 192-193 (see also Curtain, Exit-Reenter, Door locking, Journeying scenes)

Costume: 17, 29, 172-176, 182

Crane: (?), 107

Court: see Staging, systems of

Cunningham forgeries: 17

Curtain: in the pictures, 31, 134: use of ends for entrances, 109, 110; use for suggesting change of scene, 117-118; certainty of, 131; some times removed, 132; none at the Swan, 152; none in the description in *The English Wagner Book*, 132-133; precise demands for, 162; no front curtain, 49, 104; possible curtain for throne, 62; bed curtains, 65, 127 (see also Discoverable space)

Curtain theater: 6, 7, 8, 9, 10, 12, 16, 17, 25, 88

Dance: 176-178

Darkness: 166, 184, 191

Deaths on the stage: 178-179

Dekker, Thomas: 164

Description: see Words

Devil: 133, 172

De Witt: frontispiece, 88

Discoverable space: provided (?) by a removable curtained frame work, 131-132, and by large separate structures, 132, 188; importance of, instead of permanent rear stage, 133; suggestions of a projecting structure, 134-136, 156; sometimes two discoverable spaces, 136, 146, 150, 154-155, 162; uses of the discoverable space, 72, 155-162, 191; size, 161-162; elevated (?), 163; why not more used, 141, 161, 191

Disguises: 29, 173-175

Dr. Faustus: picture, 134

Doors: number, 109-110, 125-128, 156; size, 110; placed obliquely (?), 94, 110-111; significance, 111-128; convention of locking, 114; door to rear stage (?), 118; relation to balcony, 128-129; summary, 129-130; side doors always in sight, 154; central door leading to balcony (?), 156; replaced by "houses" at court (?), 187

Dragon: 41, 63, 86, 133
Dramatic reminders: 192
"Drawn out": on front stage, 69
Dumb show: 176, 182
Elizabethan stage: contemporary pictures of, see frontispiece, and *Dr. Faustus, Friar Bacon and Friar Bungay, Messallina, Roxana,* Swan, and *Swetnam the Woman Hater* in this index; restorations of, 32; quality of its illusion, 38, 49; merits and deficiencies of, 38, 39, 190, 192-193; its delight in realism, 40-42; its lack of consistency, 40, 49, 95, 129-130, 155, 193; trust to the imagination, 42-47; substitutions permitted in the staging, 50; compared to movies, 164-166, 186; to radio, 185-186; principles of: clarity, 130; ease and effectiveness, 141; not "all this, then all that," 154; shows everything, 183; contrast, 185; few customary stagings, 188; roughly speaking, medieval, 189
Elizabethan theaters: pictures of exterior, 32
Ellisworth: 22
"Enter and knock": 47, 118
"Enter": meaning of, 48, 68, 69, 133, 155-156
"Exit-Reenter": 94-95, 115, 118, 148, 181
Experimental productions: 190
Fire: 183
Fireworks: 98, 171-172
Formal seats: 45, 49, 53-65, 132, 149, 150
Fortune theater: 6, 7, 8, 13, 14, 15, 26, 88
Friar Bacon and Friar Bungay: picture, 157; discussed, 42, 98
Front stage: spectators on, 8, 10, 13, 64, 141; used in bed scenes, 69; principal uses, 85; railing, 88; trapdoors, 92; posts, 92-93; rushes on the stage (in *Arden of Feversham*), 120; and the lift, 107; useful for processions, 176
Garden scenes: 72-77
Gates: 117-118, 122-128, 129
Gatherers: 9
Gibbet: 133
Ghosts 175
Globe theater: 2, 3, 7, 8, 15, 31, 47, 88, 154, 179
Grass: 39
Grate: see Window

Greene, Thomas: 6, 7, 8
Hangings: 104
Heavens: 97, 98, 172, 183
Hell mouth: 84, 134
Heminge, John: 27
Heywood, Thomas: 3, 7, 11, 17, 21, 33, 39, 164, 165, 171, 181-182
Hill: 47, 57, 146
Holland, Aaron: 6
Hope theater: 88
Horse: 87, 151
House: 50, 137, 187
Hut: 53, 65, 97, 107, 110, 168, 188
Interval: see Pause
Jigs: 8
Jonson, Ben: 34, 65, 136, 167, 186
Journeying scenes: 112, 113, 119, 146, 147, 148, 149
Ladder: 104, 133
Lift (ascending-descending device): 53, 54, 63, 87, 99, 106-108, 188
Lighting: 166 (see also Darkness)
Lightning: 53, 172
Lists: 81
Locality boards: 111-112
Mahelot: 137, 162
Make-up: 173-175
Medieval staging: see Staging, systems of
Messallina picture: frontispiece, 30-31, 88, 94, 126, 131
Methods of study of the Elizabethan stage: 1-5, 32, 48, 50, 52, 62, 65, 93, 95-96, 97, 145, 187
Multiple staging: see Staging, systems of
Music: 104, 167, 189
Noise: 166-167, 169-171, 182, 189
"Over the stage": 94
Parliament, senate scenes: 59, 60, 61, 95
Pause: 149, 150, 190
Percy, William: 111
Phoenix theater (the Cockpit in Drury Lane): 9, 10, 12, 14, 15, 18, 19, 22, 24, 25, 28, 88
Pictures: test of theatrical origin, 40, 46
Pillar, Post: 14, 45, 46, 71, 92-95, 133, 154
Prince's Arms inn: 22
Problems of an Elizabethan dramatist: 112, 115, 189-192
Processions: 129, 176-178, 189
Properties: 52-87; large properties, how got on stage, 110; recurring properties, 133, 149-153, 156; substitutes for properties, 46, 50, 57, 65, 71, 72, 76, 149, 187, 189; Henslowe's small expenditures for, 172

Pseudo-classic staging: see Staging, systems of
Pulpit: 56; see Formal seat
Rack: 83-84
Railing: 88
Rain: 170
Rear stage: see Discoverable space
Red Bull theater: why its plays chosen for this study, 2-3, 35; its site, 6; building and opening, 6-7; occupied by the Queen's men, *ca.* 1605-1619; their plays, 9-11, 15-21; rivalry with other companies, 7; value of a share in, 7; disorders at, 7, 13; profits of, 8; occupied by the Prince's men (?), 1617-1618, 11-12; their plays, 21-22; occupied by the Red Bull and Revels company, 1619-1623; 12-13; their plays, 22-25; occupied by the Prince's men, 1623-1625, 13; their plays, 25-28; the theater rebuilt, 13-14; a strange company there, 13; an amateur company there, 20; fencing contests there, 27; its company forbidden to play Shakespeare, 27
Description of the theater, 7, 15, 88; its reputation, 7-8, 14-15, 171; its audiences, 7, 8, 10, 11, 12, 15, 190; jigs at, 7; gatherers at, 9; food, etc., sold at, 9; seats on the stage, 8, 13; rain in the yard, 13; actors at, 14, 15; length of plays at, 36
A possible picture of part of its stage, 31, 44, 46, 134. For its parts, furnishings, etc., see separate topics; for a summary, 188-189. See also 47, 134, 153-154, 162, 164-165, 179, 186, 193
Red Bull theater picture, so called: 30, 94, 131
River: 39, 43, 92
Rock: 75-77, 132
Rolling stage: 69-70
Roman stage: see Staging, systems of
Rose theater: 10, 17, 24
Roxana picture: frontispiece, 30, 31, 88, 94, 131
Salisbury Court theater: 15, 24, 31
Scaffold: 82
Scene division: 50
Scenery: 41, 104, 166
Serlio: 136-137, 138
"Set out": 68
Shakespeare: 3, 164, 166, 168, 186
Ship scenes: 45, 179-182
Shop: 78-80, 115, 118, 135, 150

Sidney, Sir Phillip: 111, 136, 167
Songs: 168
Sound effects: 168-171
Split scenes: 36, 58, 59, 133, 150
Stage directions: 1, 33-48; literary, 9-10; often omitted, 34, 133; anticipatory, 38; often dramatic, 47, 93, 100, rather than theatric, 100; their words mean different things in different places, 76; variously carried out, 187; interpretation of, 187
Staging, systems of: multiple, medieval, or simultaneous staging, 1, 32, 50, 52, 57, 63, 77, 105, 115, 130, 133, 137, 141-154, 155, 162, 189; the alternation theory, 33, 49, 59, 138-141; the Roman stage, 136, 137; pseudo-classic staging, 136-138; the "naked stage," 138; Chambers' "continuous" staging and "successive" staging, 138-139; the latter illustrated, 139-141; plays contradicting it, 141-154. (See also Elizabethan stage.) The court staging: 1, 4, 5, 138, 187; (see also Revels records, Index II)
State: see Formal seat
Stocks: 83
Structures, separate: 76, 85, 133, 149, 155-156, 189
Study: 135, 156, 183; picture, 157.
Successive staging: see Staging, systems of
Swan picture: 1, 8, 30, 31, 88, 93, 94, 97, 131, 132, 134, 155, 162
Swetnam the Woman Hater: picture, 31, 44, 45-46, 55, 93, 94, 98, 109, 134, 188
Swynnerton, Thomas: 6
Tables: 156
Tent: 77-78, 132, 146
Terence: 31, 136-138
Terrace: 99
Textual allusions: 1, 38, 40, 48, 95
Throne: see Formal seat
"Thrust out": 68, 69
Thunder: 170-172
Tomb: 84-85
Torture scenes: 29, 178
Trapdoor: 71, 76, 88-92, 110, 115
Traveling companies, plays for: 23, 24
Traverse: see Curtain
Trees: 42, 45, 46, 47, 49, 70-72, 149-150
Trial scenes: 82-83
Turret: 96-97
Valenciennes picture: 51, 137, 162

Vicenza, theater at: 136-137
Walls: 28-29, 47, 103, 133
Webster, John: 7
Well: 84, 150
Window: 98-99, 188
Woodford-Holland lawsuit: 8

Woods: see Trees
Words: specially full descriptions prob-
    ably not carried out, 49, 98; words
    as a means of effect, 164-168, 181,
    184-185, 186, 189